BYRON THE SATIRIST

FREDERICK L. BEATY

NORTHERN ILLINOIS UNIVERSITY PRESS

DEKALB · ILLINOIS

Library of Congress Cataloging in Publication Data

Beaty, Frederick L., 1926–
  Byron the satirist.

  Bibliography: p.
  Includes index.
    1. Byron, George Gordon Byron, Baron, 1788–1824—
Humor, Satire, etc.   2. Satire, English—History and
criticism.   I. Title.
PR4392.H62B9   1985   821'.7   85-2943
ISBN 0-87580-109-9

Copyright © 1985 by Northern Illinois University Press
Published by the Northern Illinois University Press,
DeKalb, Illinois 60115
Manufactured in the United States of America
All Rights Reserved

Design by Joan Westerdale

TO MARTHA, MARGARET, & EMILY

ॐ CONTENTS ॐ

BYRON THE SATIRIST

❧ CHAPTER 1 ❧

THE DEVELOPMENT OF
BYRON'S SATIRIC IDENTITY

A NALYZING the growth of Byron's satiric identity is comparable to exploring the intricate paths of a maze, for the process through which Byron became an accomplished satirist is a complexity of many facets and an intertwining of many strands. One must consider his native ability, his motivation, his temperament, and the raw material—such as the state of society and the traditions of literature—with which he had to work. One must also consider the problems he encountered in his artistic development. To succeed as a satirist Byron needed to resolve the conflict between romanticism and realism, create an interesting and convincing persona, establish his own ethical norm, find a poetical medium compatible with his mobile nature, and strike a balance between personal involvement with and detachment from the targets of his satire. By constant experimentation with diverse forms and subjects, upon which he impressed his own distinct personality, he was increasingly able to resolve these problems and ultimately to achieve that fortunate coalescence of flexible form, rhetorically effective persona, and psychological balance that characterizes his masterpieces. It is the purpose of this study to investigate the numerous ingredients of personality and external circumstance that went into his poetry and to follow the strands as they mix in varying combinations (and with varying success) throughout his satires.[1]

From the beginning Byron possessed the essential attributes that distinguish the satirist—a strong sense of the comic and a refusal to tolerate wrongs. He often delighted in laughter for its own sake, without any malice, tendentiousness, or the wish to

humble someone else. The unalloyed pleasure he derived from
verbal wit, the incongruities of everyday life, and humorous anecdotes concerning people he had never known is recorded in
many of his letters and in surviving anecdotes about him. Moreover, some of his poetical comedy, such as the riotously funny
episode in Donna Julia's bedroom, shows him to be a master of
the purely ludicrous. But the satirist, unlike the less complicated
comic writer, is obliged, if he strives to rise above the level of
mere denunciation, to put his comic talents in the service of
splenetic tendencies, for he must debase some target so that it
becomes absurd in the eyes of the world. He cannot, like the
writer of comedy, suspend his moral judgment and observe with
detached amusement the follies of humanity.[2]

If a reluctance to ignore personal injuries to himself triggers
the satirist into striking back at his enemies, that very unwillingness to "turn the other cheek" makes him seem vengeful. Try
though Byron might to laugh off some of the calumniation
heaped upon him, he still, on many occasions, did not feel obliged
to forgive or forget. Apparently he had a strong inclination, as
every satirist has, to alleviate those sufferings deemed unmerited
by projecting them onto whomever he thought responsible for
their infliction. To realize that Byron's nature was never averse to
justifiable vengeance one has only to recall Minerva's curse upon
the ravagers of Greece, Childe Harold's address to Nemesis the
avenger in the Roman Coliseum, Byron's epistolary endorsement
of Dante's "pretty eulogy on revenge,"[3] and his lifelong determination to see God as the arbiter of divine retribution. In an
effort to palliate that tendency, Lady Blessington attributed it to
"violence of temper," which "might induce people to believe him
vindictive and rancorous."[4] In her view, Byron exaggerated his
true feelings for rhetorical effect and imagination gave them "a
stronger shade" than they actually possessed in him. Apparently
these forceful, often mordant, verbalizations were in her opinion not to be taken as literal rendering of his sentiments since a
"habit of censuring" had through long practice become "his ruling passion."[5]

In the writing of satire, Byron seems to have been impelled
primarily by two motives—the desire to wreak vengeance for a
real or imagined wrong done him and the desire to improve society by exposing to public shame its follies and vices. When one

or the other incentive predominated, his satire tended to be only partially successful. When his sole intention was to squelch an enemy, as in attacks on Mrs. Clermont or the Prince Regent, the poetic product was often banal. Or when he was moved altruistically by the wish to rid European societies of their instruments of oppression, as in *The Age of Bronze*, his didactic aim without emotional involvement became flat, devoid of wit and sparkle. His most successful satires judiciously mixed these two strains in his nature. His earliest satiric experiments were prompted mainly by the self-oriented, defensive strain. "British Bards," the antecedent of *English Bards and Scotch Reviewers*, apparently arose from the unselfish desire to improve his country's literature, but the poem that evolved was elevated to a feverish intensity by the indignation he felt at having his *Hours of Idleness* unjustly condemned. As he matured, he exerted a more disciplined control over his animosities or at least pretended that they did not upset his equilibrium. In *Beppo* the poet has artistically directed his animus toward William Sotheby and Henry Gally Knight so that they become exemplars of obnoxious literary types plaguing all men rather than just the poet. In *Don Juan* and *The Vision of Judgment* the poet's ridicule of Lady Byron and Robert Southey usually rises above the level of private vendetta because they are personifications of traits detrimental to all mankind. Byronic satire is indeed at its very best when personal and social motives bolster each other in blended equipoise.

In the progressive development of Byron's satire one can also identify a dialectic reflecting a cleavage in his own personality. The determination to be truthful and realistic is opposed to an apparently natural inclination to be fantastic and romantic. As the rational urge restrains the self-indulgent, the spirit of satire arises to assume its obligations: it must purge man and his society of romantic illusions obscuring truth. This straightforward approach was important in Byron's molding of sensible personae whose pragmatic opinions would be acceptable as satiric norms even when those personae themselves were clearly flawed. From his juvenile excursions into satire onward, Byron protested his determination to overcome the useless, deluding romantic vision with one that was useful and true to life. Nevertheless, these two seemingly antithetical principles remained in unstable balance throughout his career, permitting satire and sentiment to exist side by side. *Childe Harold's Pilgrimage I & II*, especially in the manuscript stage, demonstrated early that sentiment might be tempered, even alleviated, by touches of satire. By the time of *Beppo* and *Don Juan*, satire and sentiment were so subtly blended that it is sometimes difficult to extricate one from the other. It was primarily the ottava rima stanza, allowing a comfortable alternation of mood between sestet and couplet, that enabled Byron to sustain this dual perspective in the unresolved tension we now call "Byronic irony."

Exactly what caused Byron to become a satirist is uncertain. Some of his acquaintances, following the traditional belief that any physical deformity sours the disposition, attributed his caustic wit to lameness and the difficulties it imposed on him. His congenital misfortune no doubt heightened his awareness of nature's inequities and accentuated a desire to redress wrongs that were more likely amendable. Unfortunately the society he wished to improve showed itself stubbornly resistant to change, and compatriots whom he wished to better mistook his indignation for petty rancor. He was also aware that, in a Christian ethos extolling forgiveness, the retaliatory motive of satire could not always be condoned. In half-jesting ridicule of his satiric mentors, as well as himself, he asserted in the manuscript version of *Hints from Horace* that "Satiric rhyme first sprang from selfish spleen" and cited John Dryden, Alexander Pope, and Jonathan Swift as evidence of the satirist's irascible ego.[6] To substantiate that contention, Byron in a footnote offered *MacFlecknoe, The Dunciad,* and Swift's lampooning ballads as examples, claiming that the acrimonious retorts of those works detracted "from the personal character of the writers" (*Complete Poetical Works*, I, 432; hereafter *CPW*). With ironic humor he later had Mazeppa imply that satire might be simply the product of pique, for at the Polish court the one unpensioned poet became a satirist, boasting "that he could not flatter" (ll. 148–50). Whatever the cause, satire as Byron conceived it presupposed that some injustice had been committed and that the wronged individual felt strongly enough to launch a militant counterattack. In many instances, therefore, satire became a means of achieving retributive justice.

Evidently Byron believed that his own inclination toward satire had been abetted by a predisposition in his family to deride, for when he described the qualities in Teresa Guiccioli that he thought would ingratiate her with his half-sister Augusta, he added: "She has a good deal of *us* too—I mean that turn for ridicule like Aunt Sophy and you and I & all the B's."[7] Apart from the familial propensity to ridicule, Byron attributed his conversion into a satirist to the scathing critiques of his *Hours of Idleness*. In his unpublished 1811 Preface to *Hints from Horace* he credited Francis Jeffrey, whom he mistakenly thought responsible for the *Edinburgh Review's* attack, and Hewson Clarke with provoking him to demonstrate "how very easy it is to say ill-natured things" and even make money by doing so (*CPW*, I, 428). Thus in time a desire to *right* wrongs was transformed into a pleasure in *writing* about them, and he deduced that "A Satire if not very bad indeed will generally meet with temporary success because it administers to the malignant or ? propensities of our Nature" (*CPW*, I, 428).

Yet it was the hypersensitivity of certain temperaments (his own in particular) that he considered the prime requisite for creation of a satirist. In that 1811 manuscript Preface he remarked on the extreme vulnerability of what he termed the "Genius Irritabile." Similarly in 1823 he conceded to the Countess of Blessington that it was primarily his sensitivity that predisposed him to suffer more acutely and nurse his wounds longer than ordinary men would. As he told her, "The events in life that have most pained me—that have turned the milk of my nature into gall—have not depended on the persons who tortured me,—as I admit that the causes were inadequate to the effects:—it was my own nature, prompt to receive painful impressions, and to retain them with a painful tenacity, that supplied the arms against my peace."[8] That Lady Blessington nevertheless saw her friend as a militant champion of justice is clear from her editorial comment: "Knowing Byron as I do, I could forgive the most cutting satire his pen ever traced, because I know the bitter feelings and violent reaction which led to it; and that, in thus avenging some real or imagined injury on individuals, he looks on them as a part of the great whole, of which that world which he has waged war with, and that he fancies has waged war with him, is composed."[9]

In many instances satire served Byron therapeutically as catharsis. Anger tended to come quickly, as with a lightning flash, and to depart with equal celerity. As he himself asserted: "When any one attacks me, on the spur of the moment I sit down and write all the *méchanceté* that comes into my head; and, as some of these sallies have merit, they amuse me, and are too good to be torn or burned, and so are kept, and see the light long after the feeling that dictated them has subsided. All my malice evaporates in the effusions of my pen."[10] Though the purgation of venom was often less thorough than he insisted, even in the composition of biting epigrams, it certainly diminished his wrath. Apparently he showed similar tendencies in conversation. Lady Blessington recorded that "the force of his language" was such as to convince one that its underlying feeling "must be fixed in his mind."[11] Yet if one saw him only a few hours later, the "angry excitement" that had given rise to exaggerations we might term satiric fictions could well have passed without leaving a trace behind. Satiric outbursts—in conversation, as well as in letters and poetry—served to vent splenetic irritation.

Like many other satirists, Byron felt that social corruption in his day was so pervasive that it virtually cried out for someone to expose the discrepancy between what was cantingly professed and what was actually practiced. Though perhaps every age tends to think itself more degenerate than its predecessors, there may have been some validity to the belief that dissipation and depravity had never before so permeated the governing classes of England. George III, the monarch who reigned during most of Byron's lifetime, asserted two years after his accession to the throne that his epoch was "the wickedest age that ever was seen" and lamented that "ingratitude, avarice and ambition" seemed to govern his contemporaries.[12] Nor did two decades of debilitating European wars, in addition to American and Asian conflicts, improve the moral fiber of the nation. Moreover, the standards of aristocratic behavior set by the Prince of Wales, his brothers, and their consorts made the Regency era synonymous with debauchery. Byron told Thomas Medwin in Pisa that he had seen much of Italian society but that "nothing could equal the profligacy of high life in England."[13] And later, in Greece, Byron defended his public-spirited mission to Dr. James Kennedy on the grounds that it was his duty "to remove the cloke, which the manners and maxims of society . . . throw over their secret sins, and shew them to the world as they really are."[14] Byron knew that Kennedy had not "been so much in high and noble life" as he himself had been but assured him that had he "fully entered into it, and seen what was going on," he would have been "convinced that it was time to unmask the specious hypocrisy." In times such as those Byron might have asserted, as Juvenal had, that it was difficult *not* to write satire.

Yet when Byron began to write verse, satire was not in vogue among the best practitioners of poetry. In fact, the whole tradition of English satire was under attack from the new school of Romantic poets. Although Thomas Moore wrote some early poems employing both raillery and biting satire, they apparently left no impression on the youthful Byron. In the first decade of the nineteenth century there did appear some ephemeral satires ridiculing contemporary literature, politics, politicians, and socialites. However, while it can be shown that Byron was acquainted with some of those now-forgotten productions (which are resurrected later in this study), they would not have served as models and could not have taught him much. Strangely enough, before the publication of *English Bards and Scotch Reviewers* in 1809 there had been no formal satires of significance in England since the 1790s, and those that appeared did little more than keep a faint afterglow of satire alive in the twilight of a once distinguished tradition. From that last decade of the eighteenth century, the poetry of William Gifford and the collection entitled *Poetry of the Anti-Jacobin* (1799) deserve special consideration because they had a noticeable impact on Byron's poetry.

The influence Gifford exerted in his day is difficult to correlate with his slender satires and his translations of Juvenal and Persius. Yet as editor of the *Anti-Jacobin* and later of the *Quarterly Review*, in addition to being editorial adviser to John Murray's publishing firm, he commanded enormous respect in conservative literary circles. His *Baviad* (1791), in imitation of Persius's first satire, demolished the Della Cruscan school, led by Robert Merry, whose sentimental and revolutionary effusions had enjoyed a coterie popularity. Gifford continued his attack on the Della Cruscans in his *Maeviad* (1795), in imitation of Horace's Satire I.10, and proceeded therein to ridicule the affectations of the contemporary stage. Gifford's championing of the English satiric tradition, resting as it did on the Roman, against the assaults of literary faddists won Byron's lifelong respect and personal friendship. When Byron wrote *English Bards*, he clearly announced his affiliation with that tradition by asserting that he

ventured "o'er / The path, which Pope and Gifford trod before"
(ll. 93–94). The fledgling poet subsequently invoked Gifford to
expose the heinous vices of the day and "Make bad men better,
or at least ashamed" (ll. 829–30). In his "Reply to *Blackwood's*"
(1820) Byron called Gifford "the last of the wholesome satirists," [15] and as late as 1824 Byron wrote from Missolonghi that he
had always considered Gifford his "*literary* father" (*Byron's Letters
and Journals*, XI, 117; hereafter *BLJ*).

   Poetry of the Anti-Jacobin, on the other hand, had none of
Gifford's pretensions to literary distinction. Even so, this compila-
tion, which Byron owned and certainly read, contained many
short poems exemplifying a wide variety of satiric forms and
technical devices. Many of them reflected the kinds of poetic re-
duction that English schoolboys were encouraged to perform in
their assimilation of the classics and would therefore have had a
special appeal to the youthful Byron. In addition to satiric epigrams, pseudo-translations, and mock-heroic addresses, the collection contained imitations of Horace and Catullus that preserved the spirit and style of their models but modernized them
through contemporary substance and context. From this one
volume Byron might have learned the basic techniques of satiric
writing: certainly a number of these poems, of which the following are illustrations, could have served as prototypes for his earliest experiments. "The Soldier's Friend," a travesty, showed how
the use of inappropriate language and style could render revolutionary philosophies absurd. "Ode to Lord Moira" caricatured
through wild exaggeration the distinguishing features of Whig
politicians. "The Friend of Humanity and the Knife-Grinder"
parodied the sapphics of Southey by retaining the metrical form
while substituting ludicrous content. "The Progress of Man" and
"The Loves of the Triangles" burlesqued the social philosophy of
Richard Payne Knight and the botanical love poetry of Erasmus
Darwin through frivolous treatment of serious subjects. Perhaps
the most sophisticated satire in the collection was a poem in
Popean couplets entitled "New Morality," which forthrightly
assailed innovative French philosophies that, with the aid of
English Jacobins, were allegedly subverting English virtue and
taste.

   Although Byron ultimately acquainted himself with the major writers of English satire from Samuel Butler onward, his

literary model throughout life was Alexander Pope, whom he regarded not only as the greatest satirist but also as the greatest English poet.[16] Until he discovered, while living in Italy, a poetical medium more compatible with his nature than the heroic couplet, he attempted (with varying degrees of success) to emulate his master's wit, conciseness of phrase, metrical variety, precision in language, and axiomatic polish. Though Byron never achieved the control over his art that was necessary to reach those goals, his continued study of Pope gave his couplets a sharpness, as well as a sense of antithesis and balance, that they would not otherwise have attained. Furthermore, it was as the outstanding champion of the classical tradition in English poetry that Pope laid claim to Byron's reverence. The whole generation of nineteenth-century poets and critics who depreciated Pope were in Byron's estimation "not worth a Canto of the Rape of the Lock—or the Essay on Man—or the Dunciad—or 'anything that is his'" (*BLJ*, VI, 31). From *English Bards* to the first of poetical commandments in *Don Juan*, it is clear that in Byron's view the English classical tradition rested on three pillars—Milton, Dryden, and Pope.[17] Pope had done the most to keep that hallowed tradition alive by employing several of its vital genres and, moreover, had codified its major precepts for English usage in the *Essay on Criticism*. Hence Byron, rather diffidently in *English Bards* and more confidently in *Hints from Horace*, tried to establish himself as the Alexander Pope of his day, priestly keeper of the sacred flame, and satirical critic watching over his country's literature. Byron admired Pope not only for being a sincere moralist, as his first reply to William Lisle Bowles in 1821 attests (*The Works of Lord Byron: Letters and Journals*, V, 560; hereafter *LJ*), but also as a satirist with an ethical mission—to effect reforms that other men were powerless to achieve.

We might know much more about Byron's concept of the English tradition and his defense, both moral and artistic, of satire had he completed his "Imitation of Horace. Satire 4." This eighteen-line fragment, when read in the context of its original, raises a tantalizing question about Byron's relationship to Charles Churchill. Horace, establishing his place in the Roman satiric tradition, acknowledged himself the successor of Lucilius, whose models he identified as the bold writers of old Attic comedy, but was highly critical of Lucilius's harsh, unpolished verse. Byron,

substituting Churchill for Lucilius in the "Imitation," attributed
Churchill's ability to write stinging satire to what had been learned
from Dryden, George Villiers, and Samuel Foote but then belittled Churchill's rough, prosy verse.[18] Yet there is no evidence
that Byron was ever a disciple of Churchill, as Horace actually
was of Lucilius. Indeed Byron later reproached Churchill, who
had drawn heavily on Dryden's *Absalom and Achitophel* for his
political satire and on *MacFlecknoe* for examples of caricature
and invective, for having preferred Dryden to Pope.[19] Even so,
Churchill displayed a rugged vigor, a defiance of governmental
(as well as critical) authority, and a gift for vituperation that evidently appealed to the coarser aspects of Byron's nature, just as
Butler's and Swift's less refined satires did. If Churchill ever
served as a model, it was before the more cultivated strains of
Dryden, Pope, Samuel Johnson, and Gifford curtailed Byron's
youthful brashness.

In addition to the English tradition of satire, there was the
more clearly defined Roman tradition consisting of three Latin
poets who had considered themselves in direct line of descent
from Lucilius. Horace, Persius, and Juvenal (and occasionally
their French adapters such as Nicolas Boileau) had served as
models for English satire, and no educated Englishman of Byron's
day could have escaped their study at a public school or university. Although Persius was too moralistic to appeal to Byron,
there is evidence that Byron made limited use of his substance.
The other two Roman satirists (with bolstering inspiration from
such English imitators as Dryden, Pope, Johnson, and Gifford)
were among Byron's principal models throughout his poetical career. Imitations and echoes of Juvenal's first satire in *English
Bards* were meant to link Byron with the Roman satirist famous
as the scourge of decadent society and literature. Similarly, *Hints
from Horace* advertised Byron's connection, through Pope, with
the most influential arbiter of classical taste. As a continuer of
this time-honored tradition, Byron felt an obligation to rework
whatever of the old was still viable and readapt it to contemporary contexts.

As he matured, the Horatian and Juvenalian strains became
intricately intertwined, as they had been for most of his English
predecessors. They also provided complementary modes of looking at the world. Horace initially posed a problem because he

represented the equanimity, poise, and unruffled detachment that were incompatible with Byron's passionate, often volatile, temperament in youth. Horace's sometimes oblique and usually gentle approach to life seemed "by indirections" to "find directions out," and his satiric irony was so subtle that it cut in several directions. Then too, as Byron admitted in *Childe Harold IV*, the tedium of having Horace drilled into him at school produced a revulsion, and not until much later did he come to appreciate the understated charm of Horatian satire—the ability to prick the conscience and awaken the heart without ever wounding it (77.7–9). It was the example of Pope, who consciously strove to be "the English Horace," and Pope's Horatian imitations that compelled Byron to appreciate the excellence of the Roman poet whose correctness of language, perfection of form, and artistic control were combined with effortless ease and a gentlemanly, conversational tone. Horace's satiric persona, the plainspoken Sabine farmer with ingratiating humility and common sense, won readers to his viewpoint by representing the rational man whom all could trust. If Byron's early satires lacked the urbane polish of Horace's, they came somewhat closer in the use of personae who, as landed squires, served as Regency adaptations of the Horatian mask. Indeed Horace Hornem in *Waltz* advertised his literary paternity. By the time of the ottava rima satires Byron had achieved a sophisticated cosmopolitan air that was more compatible with the Horatian mode. His reference to "pedestrian Muses" in the Dedication to *Don Juan* clearly invoked the simple, truthful *musa pedestris* who inspired the "plain style" of Horatian satire. On the other hand, the Horatian maxim of *nil admirari* that characterizes Lady Adeline's "calm Patrician polish" suggests that withdrawal from emotional involvement amounts to a sterile rejection of life. Evidently the equanimity born of Horatian detachment was never completely congenial with the Byronic temperament.

Byron's letters and poetry show that he alluded more frequently to Juvenal's satires than to Horace's satires and epistles. In 1811 he claimed that Juvenal's tenth satire had always been his favorite and asserted that it might be read to a dying man "in preference to all the stuff that ever was said or sung in churches" (*BLJ*, II, 95). His lifelong admiration of Johnson's *Vanity of Human Wishes* and *London*, imitations of Juvenal's tenth and third satires, confirmed his belief in Juvenal as a moral philosopher (*BLJ*, VIII, 19–20). The fact that two of his friends, Francis Hodgson and William Gifford, published excellent translations of Juvenal also strengthened the tie. From the start Byron probably recognized a natural affinity between himself and Juvenal. The Roman poet's direct approach, his powerful invective encouraged by righteous indignation, his bitter irony, and his uninhibited treatment of even the seamier aspects of sexuality fascinated Byron all his life. Juvenal's compassion for the poor, oppressed as they were by the abuse of power and wealth, aroused Byron's social and political sympathies. Moreover, Byron could identify more readily with Juvenal's depiction of a decadent, corrupt society that had strayed from the path of moral, as well as literary, rectitude than with Horace's stable Augustan Rome. *English Bards* and *The Age of Bronze* are two of Byron's most clearly marked Juvenalian satires, though modulations of Juvenal's "grand style" and impassioned rhetoric are visible in every Byronic satire. Juvenal's epic aspirations for his humble genre and his poignant use of tragic satire, whereby good is overwhelmed by forces beyond its control, may also have been responsible for the deepening tone of *Don Juan's* later cantos.

Not until Byron discovered the comic possibilities of the ottava rima stanza did he avail himself of a more compatible artistic medium than the school of Pope had provided. Before his arrival in Italy, he knew what Ludovico Ariosto, Luigi Pulci, and Francesco Berni had achieved in the serious treatment of that stanza. On the Continent in 1816 he became acquainted with Giovanni Battista Casti's licentious narratives adapting ottava rima to burlesque uses. But it was John Hookham Frere's mock-heroic *Prospectus* (1817) that showed him the stanza's diverse potentialities for his composition of *Beppo*. The specific benefits to *Don Juan* of his subsequent study of Frere's Italian precursors—Pulci, Berni, and Casti—are debatable, but there can be no doubt that the casual stanzaic form, which freed Byron's natural exuberance and made a virtue of diffuseness, was the real key to his rebirth as a satirist. Combined with the liberated environment of Italy, it encouraged him to utilize talents that he had developed as letter-writer, raconteur, and man of the world. Because of its flexibility, it also permitted him to adapt skills that he had learned as an adherent to other satiric traditions. Above all, he was able to transfer his facility with the Popean couplet to the concluding couplet of the ottava rima, giving it a sting that it had never had before.

Not the least of its benefits was that it enabled Byron to resolve a problem that had vexed him throughout his career—the establishment of an authoritative persona who could, even while expressing different voices, convince without dogmatizing. The Augustan satirist could employ a persona embodying a system of values that readers were expected to endorse and could rest assured that any deviation from the accepted norms would be condemned. But in Byron's day no one system of values prevailed among the large reading public, and the morality to which the governing classes paid lip service obviously did not constitute the ethic by which they lived. Hence Byron faced a problem for which his satiric mentors offered no solution. He needed to create a satiric persona who, in the absence of a definite code of established truths, would construct private norms that he himself, as a fallible human being, did not invariably follow. The persona might well be at odds with the dominant standards of his society, but because he was honest and true to himself, his norm in a relativistic ethic would remain more acceptable than that which he attacked.

In a number of his early works, not only in satire, Byron grappled with this dilemma. In *English Bards* he self-consciously attempted a persona who, despite an admitted lack of qualifications, strives to be the guardian of his country's literature and morality. Subsequently in *Hints from Horace* Byron carried the tendency to undercut his persona's authority further by making him a bluff landed gentleman who, in his practical but unskilled way, tries to uphold at least an *appearance* of traditional rectitude in public morality and the arts. Understanding the need for greater coherence in his desultory comments, Byron in *Childe Harold* created two personae moderately independent of himself and of each other. By having Harold and the narrator confront one another with differing points of view, he constructed a more unified framework for his diverse and tonally inconsistent observations. In *Waltz* Byron's experiment with detaching and undermining his persona went so far that Hornem denies any moral basis whatever, proves himself a fool, and thereby invalidates himself as a satirist. Yet in *The Giaour* Byron made a notable advance toward resolving the problem of narrator, for there he created a single persona (implied if not explicitly developed) who as ballad singer could incorporate the voices of several speakers and relate the story from different viewpoints. Subsequently in monologues such as *The Prisoner of Chillon, The Lament of Tasso,* and *Mazeppa* Byron refined his skills in the use of a fictive narrator who controls the poem with a single voice.

But it was the ottava rima stanza that enabled Byron to develop a complicated, sophisticated persona capable of embodying numerous voices within himself, of sliding easily from one mood or subject to another, and of expressing divergent perspectives on the world. This stanzaic form, with its extraordinary versatility and flexibility, encouraged the persona to reflect, even in the midst of narration, on virtually anything that came to mind while never feeling obliged to make an irrevocable commitment. Indeed it invited Byron to dramatize antithetical and often unresolvable elements in his own nature through the projection of a captivating personality serving as the poem's center of consciousness. Its inherent weakness, as Byron no doubt learned from observing his predecessors' use of the form, lay in permitting artistic liberty to lapse into anarchy. Byron avoided that pitfall in his ottava rima satires—*Beppo, Don Juan,* and *The Vision of Judgment*—by creating in each instance a persona who shapes and controls the poem with his unifying presence. Through the resolution of artistic problems that had troubled his earlier development, Byron in these particular poems reached the height of his powers and attained his most notable success. Looking backward from the vantage point of this accomplishment, one also sees that most of his prior endeavors led, in one way or another, toward this culmination—a truly unique contribution to satiric poetry.

CHAPTER 2

EARLY SATIRIC POEMS AND
ENGLISH BARDS AND SCOTCH REVIEWERS

ALTHOUGH Byron's earliest excursions into satire are not in themselves significant, they deserve attention because they foreshadow many of the motives, ideas, and techniques that recur in his more mature works. If they seem to be crude experiments directed toward the establishment of an authentic satiric voice, they also reveal an early diffidence toward satiric utterance. Lines from "Childish Recollections," for example, express a desire to avoid the negative approach and leave to "keener bards" the questionable "delight in Satire's sting" (ll. 77–80). Even so, the cloying Romanticism prevalent in *vers de société* when Byron began to write produced a strong revulsion in him. It was partly in opposition to what he considered the falseness of the Romantic vision of life that his satiric spirit arose.

Despite Byron's claim that his "first dash into poetry" was a sentimental love poem (*BLJ*, IX, 40), his biographer Thomas Moore asserted that Byron's earliest "rhyming" was satiric verse prompted by slights and insults.[1] According to the oral account gleaned from the poet's nurse, May Gray, an elderly woman who visited Mrs. Byron in Nottingham repeatedly taunted the highly sensitive boy with a demeaning expression. Deeply resentful, young Byron, then about ten years old, told his nurse that the visitor had infuriated him and thereupon recited two doggerel couplets ridiculing the old crone's beliefs about soul migration:

> In Nottingham county there lives at Swine Green,
> As curst an old lady as ever was seen;

And when she does die, which I hope will be soon,
She firmly believes she will go to the moon. (*CPW*, I, 1)

Whether these lines represent Byron's earliest poetry is problematic, but they are certainly in the spirit of the epigrammatic verse that he would from time to time dash off against people who angered or hurt him. From the beginning, satire was a way of settling the score, exposing absurdity, or degrading his opposition.

Somewhat later he used this same denunciatory vein in behalf of politics. His poem in reply to a newspaper slur on the late Whig statesman Charles James Fox begins with a vituperative attack, totally unrelieved by any trace of comic distancing, on the anonymous Tory poet responsible for the insult: "Oh! factious viper! whose envenom'd tooth, / Would mangle still the dead, perverting truth" (*CPW*, I, 42). Although Byron would in time discover subtler and more effective means of countering both personal and political enemies, he never completely overcame the inclination to blast them with verbal abuse; that art apparently came naturally to him.

Byron's extreme sensibility, which caused him to feel psychic pain so sharply that he retaliated against those who offended him, also impelled him to react intensely to those he loved. It is not surprising, therefore, that his earliest collections of poetry (1806–08) should juxtapose occasional pieces celebrating the sweet sadness of love and others expressing mocking derision. The former variety is highly imitative of *The Poetical Works of the Late Thomas Little* (1801), which Byron claimed to have known by heart at age fifteen.[2] The satiric ones, however, could not have been modeled on the gentle raillery of Moore's pseudonymous poems but indicate, rather, the early impact on Byron of the English Augustan tradition. Nor were these seemingly incompatible modes always reserved for separate poems. As "Childish Recollections" and "The First Kiss of Love" show, they were sometimes used in conjunction, with traces of cynicism reflecting the poet's ambivalence even in sentimental lyrics. This ingrained combination of satire and sentiment (which critics would later term a dialectical interplay of Classic and Romantic) produced from the very outset of Byron's literary career a poetical voice with two modulations.

The conflict between the two is sharply visible in poems that deal with what the poet loosely termed "truth," a concept which, as Robert F. Gleckner has observed, is crucial to the function of satire as Byron viewed it.[3] "To Romance" associates deceit, affectation, and "sickly Sensibility" with the realms of romance, which the young poet vows to abandon "for those of Truth." "Answer to Some Elegant Verses" carries the defense of his artistic realism further by asserting, as Byron would continue to claim about his satires, that his muse is "the simple Truth." Although one senses that Byron did not quit the world of "golden dreams" without some regret—and one may indeed question whether he ever completely forsook it—the important point is that he resolved to forgo the childish habit of seeing the world as one would like to *imagine* it. He would instead look reality squarely in the eye. In the juvenilia, then, the dialectic between romantic idealism, on the one hand, and satiric truth, on the other, is already established. So also is the dual nature of Byron's satiric purpose. Though born of a negative impulse, his satire aspires to the positive goal of freeing mankind from the illusions that falsify life.

If Byron found Romantic idealism incompatible with his own temperament, he was also aware, implicitly at least, that the accepted code of standards which characterized Augustan satire was no longer operative and that, if there was to be any norm, it had to be determined by his own judgment. Thus a few of the early poems challenge the artificial conventions of society and literature with shrewd pragmatism. The poem "To a Lady, Who Presented to the Author a Lock of Hair, Braided with his Own, and Appointed a Night, in December, to Meet him in the Garden" ridicules false notions of courtship. Though a nocturnal garden assignation might have served for Romeo and Juliet in December, it can do nothing but hinder the progress of love in a cold climate. Similarly, "To the Sighing Strephon" laughs at the foolish man who has almost died for unrequited love and recommends instead an unsentimental variety of gratification. Unlike the typical Augustan satirist, Byron in each instance offers an unconventional solution, knowing that many of his readers will reject it.

Coupled with the enunciation of characteristic ideas and points of view was Byron's early experimentation in poetic forms and techniques encountered through his education. Several inherited literary models served as vehicles for the expression of his satiric bent. One of the simplest forms, the mock-epitaph, which had long flourished in both Latin and English, could be adapted, as Byron did in his "Epitaph on John Adams of Southwell," to show off his verbal wit at the expense of the dead. It might also be employed, as he did in the "Epitaph on Mrs. [Byron]," to express his wish that someone toward whom he felt strong antipathy were in the grave. Referring to his overbearing mother, then still in good health, as one "Prone to take Fire, yet not of melting Stuff," the poet as caricaturist focuses upon her most vulnerable frailty—her volatile and ungovernable temper. Characterizing her rages as "worse than Ocean's roar," he commends Death for having graciously halted them. The poem suggests that Mrs. Byron contributed more than has been realized to the molding of a young satirist, for she evidently possessed a gift for invective that presaged her son's. She was inclined to loose a hurricane of abuse before subsiding into a resigned calm, much as he did in youthful tantrums and would later do, in a more sophisticated way, through satiric art.

Another illustration of a traditional form adapted to satiric purpose is the epigram "Damaetas." In the style of Martial and the Greek Anthology, it offers an unfavorable portrait of a debauched youth who, as the Countess Guiccioli's manuscript copy proves, is a projection of Byron himself. As such it is one of his earliest examples of self-satire. It is also an interesting adumbration of the title character in Canto I of *Childe Harold*, which, as Jerome J. McGann has pointed out, is considerably more satiric in the original draft than in the printed text.[4] The satiric epigram, however, was not a form that Byron often attempted, possibly because it required a conciseness of phrase and obliquity of approach that were not customarily his. Years later he told Lady Blessington that he had never succeeded to his satisfaction in an epigram and that this failure was mortifying because he knew Greek and admired Greek epigrams, which expressed "by implication what is wished to be conveyed."[5]

While some of the poems in Byron's early volumes qualify as "parodies" in the generic sense of the term, they are of the sympathetic, rather than the reductive, variety—the sort that exaggerates stylistic features of the original but does not necessarily seek to demolish its model's content. Far from depreciating their originals, Byron's versions may actually be regarded as good-humored tributes, such as those parodies on which William Hazlitt would later comment in his lecture "On Wit and Humour" (1818).[6] Such forms of mild distortion were only one step removed from Byron's liberal translations and imitations of the classics. This tendency to imitate a model, partly with respect and partly with tongue-in-cheek humor, evidently began with Byron's school exercises and would remain part of his satiric technique, to be used in *Don Juan* when he parodied the Decalogue or Sappho's address to Hesperus.

Sometimes Byron showed a predisposition to imitate specific poems as vehicles for expressing personal aversion. "To Miss H[ouson] An ancient Virgin who tormented the Author to write something on her *sweet* self," a faint parody of Southey's poem "The Old Man's Comforts" ("Father William"), displays a satirist's delight in puncturing the overblown compliments poets were expected to write for their friends. In this instance Byron was employing only gentle raillery since the "ancient Virgin" was just fifteen. Far more acrimonious is "A Parody upon 'The Little Grey Man' in Lewis' *Tales of Wonder*," which heaps insults upon some desperate spinster who apparently hoped to trap Byron into matrimony.

The depictions of academia at Harrow and Cambridge reveal Byron attempting the more sophisticated techniques of accomplished Augustan satirists, even though these poems suffer from the same unjustifiable vehemence that mars other early denunciations. In a highly declamatory imitation of Pope's style, the poem "On a Change of Masters, at a Great Public School" exaggerates the significance of the replacement of Joseph Drury with George Butler as headmaster of Harrow. In mock-heroic fashion Byron, a friend of Drury, likens this academic succession to the supplanting of a caesar by a barbarian. Grandiloquent language and emotionally charged names such as schoolboys use for masters ("Probus" for the friend, "Pomposus" for the enemy) heighten the extremes of feeling so that the reader is left with no neutral ground. Through the use of barbed phrases and succinct couplets, the satirist loads the case for his loyalty and his prejudice. The fact that Byron later became reconciled to Butler and regretted several poetic attacks on him as "Pomposus" (*BLJ,*

I, 154–55) does not weaken the poem, but it does show that, after overreacting and venting his spleen, Byron could deplore the rashness of his initial response.

Two other academic romps deserve mention because they show Byron advancing techniques he would someday use with mastery. "Thoughts Suggested by a College Examination" successfully employs both high and low burlesque—to magnify an insignificant proctor to godlike stature and to depreciate the overvalued academicians. It also shows Byron striving toward a variety of irony at which he would become adept—that of extending praise in one line and withdrawing it with qualifications in the next: "Happy the youth! in Euclid's axioms tried, / Though little vers'd in any art beside" (ll. 9–10). More daring in its experimental nature is "Granta, A Medley," which drew bitter sarcasm from the *Edinburgh* reviewer Henry P. Brougham. Its novel multiple rhymes, such as "historic use" and "hypothenuse," prove that Byron was interested in fantastic rhyming long before he encountered Italian comic epics. More notably, though, this mediocre poem in quatrains marks the first emergence in Byron's career of a distinct satirical persona, in fact one who even undercuts himself as Byronic personae would be made to do more adroitly in the mature satires. Assuming the traditional role of the blunt, honest man, the persona humbly concedes that he ought not "scribble longer" (l. 93). Through informal diction and detachment he achieves a tone of relaxed nonchalance, ultimately dismissing the entire Cantabrigian subject because of fatigue.[7]

Byron was not one, however, to dismiss with similar nonchalance what he regarded as unfair criticism of his poetry. Apparently some elderly ladies in Southwell had been so outraged by the suggestive poem "To Mary" in his *Fugitive Pieces* (1806) that they pronounced him a "*most profligate Sinner*" and a "*young Moore*" (*BLJ*, I, 103). Byron, having followed the Rev. J. T. Becher's advice to destroy as many copies of that volume as he could, indignantly protested against what he viewed as prudish, inept censure. Byron's rejoinder, "To a Knot of Ungenerous Critics," employs an allegorical fable in which his detractors, having sought the aid of Fiction (Falsehood), are routed in combat by Truth, the poet's patron. Byron's allusive quotation from Pope's "Epistle to Dr. Arbuthnot" shows, by virtue of its context, that

anuscript, but after the latter rejected it as too harsh,
nd a less reputable entrepreneur, James Cawthorn,
l to print a thousand copies. Byron continued to send
ndations and additions to the text even while it was
ed, so that the anonymously issued first edition con-
lines when advance copies reached the poet on

fear that Cawthorn had printed too many copies
founded, for on 17 April Dallas informed him that
ed unsold. The satire caused a reasonable sensation
praise from Gifford. It was favorably noticed in the
e of the *Gentleman's Magazine*, which hailed the young
English "Patriot." The *Antijacobin Review* in its March
ed the anonymous satirist as Gifford's successor and,
s Tory bias, applauded his attacks on Whigs such as
nd and Jeffrey. Hence Byron decided, while waiting to
his Mediterranean tour, to enlarge and emend the
second edition, which would bear his name. Having
lines of his own for Hobhouse's contribution on
expanded the prose preface, as well as the introduc-
ncluding portions of the poem, and added numerous
ons and a postscript for additional broadsides. By 10
ad an edition of 1,050 lines ready for publication.
Dallas urged suppression of the vitriolic attacks on
d Hewson Clarke, who had abused Byron in the *Sati-*
yielded only in softening some of his language. Sub-
while Byron was traveling in Mediterranean lands,
found it sufficiently profitable to publish the third and
tions (both reprints of the second) in 1810. After re-
England in July 1811, Byron incorporated other
ns in a second issue of the fourth edition (1811). Al-
made still more alterations for a fifth edition running
ines, he suppressed further publication in 1812. The
lous Cawthorn had to be prevented by injunction from
at last edition, of which only a few copies survived, but
e ensuing years he continued surreptitiously to turn
us copies of previous editions.[14]

intense reaction to the *Edinburgh*'s review of *Hours*
was justifiable, although he had probably provoked

the unjustly maligned youth saw himself in the role of Pope retaliating against Lord Hervey's calumnies.

In a more cavalier response to other unprofessional critics,
"Soliloquy of a Bard in the Country," Byron reveals a willingness
to poke fun at himself as well as his detractors:

> When Peers are Poets, Squires may well be Wits;
> When schoolboys vent their amorous flames in verse,
> Matrons may sure their characters asperse. (ll. 16–18)

Whereas poets such as Dryden, Pope, and Thomas Gray brushed
aside petty disparagement, Byron's rhetoric, like his pretense to
invulnerability, lacks conviction. As both these salvos indicate, he
was extraordinarily sensitive to adverse criticism and quite willing to strike back with acerbic wit even while, like Pope, claiming
reluctance to fight. He was obviously training himself in the bel-
licose arts of satire and needed only a major impulse to provoke
further deployment of his incipient skills. In unwittingly providing this impulse, the *Edinburgh Review* could hardly have anticipated that a bard so little known would rise to challenge the
world's most powerful critics.

THE STIMULUS that transformed Byron into a notable satirist
was Henry P. Brougham's unsigned review of *Hours of Idleness* (1807) in the January 1808 issue of the influential *Edinburgh
Review*. Brougham damned the entire volume. With sarcasm and
mordant irony, he attacked its contents as puerile effusions so
mediocre that the poet could not plead, as his defense, either his
minority or his nobility. In conclusion Brougham predicted that
Byron's youthful poems were the last that readers would "ever
have from him." Instead of silencing Byron, however, this censure spawned a poetical rejoinder in the hybrid form of satire
prevalent at that time.

Although the Augustan variety of satire, characterized by formality, decorum, self-assurance of one's own rectitude, and terse
precision of language, had ceased to be the dominant literary
mode,[8] the satiric spirit had by no means gone underground in
the early nineteenth century. It clearly existed, usually in a sub-
ordinate role, in the works of the greatest Romantic authors—
William Blake, Jane Austen, Walter Scott, Moore, Thomas Love

Peacock, Percy Bysshe Shelley, John Keats, and even William Wordsworth. That the tradition of Pope was still alive, however altered or diluted it had become, is also clear from the unquestioning allegiance paid to it by the *Edinburgh Review* (begun in 1802) and later by the *Quarterly* (founded in 1809). One might actually assert that the satiric spirit was nourished by the caustic reviews (including, by 1817, those of *Blackwood's*) that afforded anonymous critics the dreaded power, to which Augustan satirists had aspired, of functioning as arbiters of morality and taste. At the same time, ephemeral poetic satires on the shortcomings of literature continued to be written and, like the reviews, were often tinged with political bias.

Thus when Byron decided to compose a satire on the unworthy writers of his day, he had a living tradition on which to draw. Among those poems imitative of *The Dunciad* from which he learned much were Charles Churchill's *Rosciad* (1761), William Gifford's *Baviad* (1791) and *Maeviad* (1795), and T. J. Mathias's *Pursuits of Literature* (1794–97). Helpful suggestions may also have come from Churchill's *Apology Addressed to the Critical Reviewers* (1761), *The Prophecy of Famine* (1763), *The Times* (1764), and the Dedication to the *Sermons* (1765). Inspiration for thrusts against poets such as Southey and Erasmus Darwin probably derived from *Poetry of the Anti-Jacobin* (1799). Though the immediate impetus for an attack on the literature of his day may well have come from Lady Anne Hamilton's *Epics of the Ton* (1807), Byron could have read numerous other attacks on contemporary writers and reviewers in poetical satires such as the *Rolliad* (1784), *The Children of Apollo* (c. 1794), E. S. Barrett's *All the Talents* (1807), and *The Simpliciad* (1808).[9] One has only to consider this collection of now-obscure works to realize that, however erroneous Byron's critical opinions may appear in the light of modern evaluations, his early views coincided with opinions still prevailing in those conservative literary circles that had not yet accepted Romantic tenets.

While in London in October 1807 Byron began his poetic satire against the abuses perpetrated by contemporary writers, and on 26 October he informed his Southwell friend Elizabeth Pigot that he planned to have the poem of 380 lines published a few weeks hence.[10] His Cantabrigian friend John Cam Hobhouse

had in 1806 drafted a satire, in
deriding extravagant excesses i
addressed it, in its final form, to
long enough to stand alone, B
quired of Ben Crosby, the Lo
lisher Samuel Ridge, whether h
anonymous publication of Hol
then grown to over 400 lines, i
After reading them, Crosby re
work might bring suits of libel.[1
the *Edinburgh Review* was prepa
February 1808 its January issue
review of *Hours of Idleness* reach
directly with his satire's publica
scope to include Francis Jeffrey
be the author of the scathing
practices of the *Edinburgh*, and
redaction, according to Byron's
pleted at Newstead in Septemb
had contributed fourteen lines
much emended work, Byron or
intention to publish the poem,

Since his friend Robert Char
in publishing than he, Byron,
his seat in the House of Lords i
over to him.[13] What Dallas rec
sion of "British Bards, A Satire
by Samuel Ridge and extensi
manuscript by the poet. Dallas,
ommended changing the title t
and offered, in addition to crit
of his own for insertion. At first
mendation to include a couple
self (to confound speculations
that couplet, as well as Dallas's
title he selected, *English Bards*
invention, designed possibly to
and to suggest the peculiar rela
Dallas first approached his ow

with
Dalla
who
Dalla
being
taine
Marc
By
prove
few r
and w
Marc
poet a
issue
showi
Lord
embar
poem
substit
Bowle
tory a
interp
May h
Thoug
Jeffrey
rist, By
sequen
Cawtho
fourth
turning
emend
though
to 1,07
unscru
pirating
during
out spu
Byro
of Idlen

Brougham's hostility more by a supercilious, dilettantish preface advertising both his youth and his station in life than by his jejune compositions. Conceding that he had been "cut to atoms" by the review, he had first written his friend Hobhouse that he would "submit in Silence" (*BLJ*, I, 159). He must have realized, ironically, that some of his juvenilia were as inept as the poetry he derided in "British Bards." Hobhouse subsequently noted, possibly with some exaggeration, that Byron "was very near destroying himself" at that time.[15] Much later Byron told Thomas Medwin: "When I first saw the review of my 'Hours of Idleness,' I was furious; in such a rage as I never have been in since."[16] The denunciation was particularly crushing not only because of the *Edinburgh*'s prestige but also because of its literary and political affiliations. It adhered, as did Byron, to traditional, commonsensical taste as its literary norm and Whig doctrines as its political ideal; and Byron, a member of the Whig Club at Cambridge, had planned, upon assuming his seat in the House of Lords, to align himself with the party for which the *Edinburgh* served as spokesman. Hence he was faced with the alternatives of becoming a Whig peer in disgrace with his own party or of proclaiming the injustice of its semi-official organ. Though profoundly discouraged by either prospect, he was not, as he later recalled, a man who would permit his talents to "be snuffed out by an Article." In 1821, after the death of Keats, whose physical decline was supposedly triggered by two merciless reviews, Byron conceded to John Murray that "a savage review is Hemlock to a sucking author" but asserted to Shelley with greater bravado that the effect of the *Edinburgh* on him had been "rage, and resistance, and redress—but not despondency nor despair."[17] That he, a fledgling author, should dare to oppose the most prestigious review of his day on its own territory and in its own scathing terms attests to his indomitable spirit—a courageousness that established him as the symbol of Promethean opposition to all forms of tyranny.[18] Therefore, even though Byron had been no particular admirer of Keats's poetry, Shelley in *Adonais* included Byron as the "Pythian of the age," the champion who had bearded the Scottish critical wolves in their own den, among the chief mourners at the dead poet's bier. Whatever Byron's shortcomings may have been in his critical evaluations of contemporaries, pub-

lication of *English Bards and Scotch Reviewers* served notice that
one man of letters would not tolerate bad poetry or submit pas-
sively to arrogant criticism.

Much of Byron's animus toward the *Edinburgh* stemmed from
the militant Scottishness of its reviewing policy. Scotland, after
having been scorned for centuries as the most backward area
of Britain, had since the mid-eighteenth century experienced
an intellectual renaissance; by the early nineteenth century it
seemed determined to establish its capital city as the undisputed
Athens of the North and exert its cultural dominance over the
entire island. The *Edinburgh Review* was often regarded in Scotland as a major contributor to national distinction. John Gibson
Lockhart, using the persona of Dr. Peter Morris, asserted in
1819 that two men—Scott and Jeffrey—had "done more than all
the rest of their contemporaries put together, for sustaining and
extending the honours of the Scottish name."[19] That the *Edinburgh* under Jeffrey's guidance had an intensely nationalistic bias
and favored what Byron called a "Scottish taste" (l. 503) was obvious to anyone who read it. In a generally favorable review of
Scott's *Marmion* in 1808, Jeffrey taxed its author with introducing
"scarcely one trait of true Scotish nationality or patriotism . . . ;
and Mr Scott's only expression of admiration or love for the
beautiful country to which he belongs, is put . . . into the mouth
of one of his Southern favourites."[20] While Jeffrey showed not
the slightest hesitation to evaluate English works, he made it
clear that only another Scot could fully appreciate a Scottish
work. Later he asserted of the poet-turned-novelist: "He is above
all things national and Scottish. . . . His countrymen alone, therefore, can have a full sense of his merits."[21]

Such exclusiveness, combined with a pontifical air, did not win
many friends south of the Tweed, and English authors resented
being judged by a foreign autocrat adversely disposed to Sas-
senachs. Wordsworth not only compared Jeffrey to Buonaparte
and Robespierre but, in an unusually bold outburst, threatened
to kick him in the "breech."[22] Though the nostalgia for Scotland
expressed in some of Byron's early poems might have been expected to endear him to *Edinburgh* critics, Byron felt, no doubt
with some justification, that his misuse of the term *pibroch* (which
Brougham pounced upon to prove him an outsider) and his pride
in an English title had aroused Scottish enmity. Hence in *English*

Bards he suavely undercuts Scotia's pride in Jeffrey, as well as the critic's self-appointed mission, by ironically having Caledonia's goddess hail him as "Boast of thy country, and Britannia's guide" (l. 501). And it is definitely from the viewpoint of an English antagonist that Byron dubs Jeffrey the "chieftain of the critic clan" and his reviewing accomplices "the oat-fed phalanx." Indeed the acrimony toward Pictish Scots in Byron's satire is strong enough to encompass Lords Elgin and Aberdeen, whose taste in Grecian marbles (those "Phidian freaks") is deemed equally Scottish and equally bad.

In time Byron regretted most of his rash criticism. With more mature judgment, he began to realize not only that his strictures had magnified flaws to the obliteration of merits but also that many of his comments were downright unjust; and in 1816 he so labeled them in a copy of the fourth edition. "The greater part of this Satire," he wrote while in Switzerland, "I most sincerely wish had never been written—not only on account of the injustice of much of the critical and some of the personal part of it—but the tone and temper are such as I cannot approve." [23] The venomous assault on "The paralytic puling of Carlisle" (l. 726), who in "British Bards" had been glowingly likened to Pope's Roscommon but who had subsequently slighted his young cousin and legal ward, was one for which Byron later sought to make amends, not so much because his satire had been groundless but because it had been in bad taste. Moreover, upon befriending some of the people he had lambasted—notably Scott, Moore, and the Hollands—he found *English Bards* a source of embarrassment. Once his social and political aspirations in London became linked with eminent Whigs of the Holland House set, he was quite amenable to the suggestion, tactfully conveyed in March 1812 by Samuel Rogers, that Lord and Lady Holland would be pleased if publication ceased, and thereupon he suppressed the inchoate fifth edition (*BLJ*, IV, 320–21). A preliminary reconciliation with Jeffrey occurred after the *Edinburgh* for February 1812 favorably reviewed *Childe Harold* and Byron wrote an apology for his earlier outburst. In his equally gracious reply Jeffrey, without revealing the identity of the offending reviewer, assured Byron that his lordship's resentment had "hitherto been misdirected." [24] In Canto X of *Don Juan* Byron attempted, even while taking another fling at lawyer-critics such as Brougham, against whom he had several verifiable grievances, to make Jeffrey final amends. By 1822 he was happy to admit his Scottish ties and join in a health to "Auld Lang Syne":

> And though, as you remember, in a fit
> Of wrath and rhyme, when juvenile and curly,
> I railed at Scots to shew my wrath and wit,
> Which must be owned was sensitive and surly,
> Yet 'tis in vain such sallies to permit,
> They cannot quench young feelings fresh and early:
> I "*scotched*, not killed," the Scotchman in my blood,
> And love the land of "mountain and of flood."
>
> (*Don Juan* X.19)

Many readers who know *English Bards* only from anthologized excerpts fail to grasp the overall significance of Byron's attack on contemporary writers. Certainly the norm he implies is the neo-classical tradition, but to have defined it more explicitly than he did would have altered his role from satirist to polemical critic. The Preface to the first edition makes unequivocally clear that he does not deny either "the real talents" or the "considerable genius" of some of the poets he censures. On the contrary, he hopes to improve their standards by correcting the "mental prostitution" of their abilities and by liberating them from coteries that uncritically overrate their merits and ignore their faults. Certainly one of the main charges Gifford leveled against the Della Cruscans in his *Baviad* and *Maeviad* was that they wrote namby-pamby poetry praising one another for composing their own variety of poetry, and some members of that group also evoke Byron's spleen in *English Bards*. But the worst offenders, who have defied accepted tradition to the extent of codifying their radical aesthetic notions in a manifesto by Wordsworth, are the Lakers, and here too Byron's views had been anticipated by the critics. Jeffrey, in his review of *Thalaba* (1801), for example, conceded that Southey and cohorts were extremely talented but, because of their conspiracy against sound poetical theory and language, deserved "a larger share of our censorial notice, than could be spared for an individual delinquent."[25] Indeed he began his review of the poem by declaring: "The author . . . belongs to a *sect* of poets, . . . and is looked upon, we believe, as one of its chief champions and apostles." Similarly, a review of Southey's *Madoc* in the *Critical Review* for January 1806 included a slur on its author's poetical coterie. In the collection entitled *Poetry of the Anti-Jacobin*, the poem "New Morality" also referred to "Coleridge and Southey, Lloyd, and Lambe and Co." as a band of revolutionary bards. Therefore it can be suspected that, in *English Bards*, Byron includes even Charles Lamb and Charles Lloyd, Jr. (ll. 903–10) in this "lowly group." In Byron's opinion these eccentrics have organized themselves into rebellious splinter groups preoccupied with minutiae that are of no concern outside their immediate circles:

> Each country Book-club bows the knee to Baal,
> And, hurling lawful Genius from the throne,
> Erects a shrine and idol of its own.
> (ll. 138–40)

In short, poetry for such bards has become a private, in-group phenomenon. As Byron later declared of James Hogg, "he, and half of these Scotch and Lake troubadours, are spoilt by living in little circles and petty societies."[26]

To counter such provincial narrowness, Byron assumed the public voice of a righteously indignant man addressing, as well as speaking for, all of society. But not until he wrote the enlarged Preface to the second edition did he feel strongly the need to defend himself as a public-spirited reformer in the manner of traditional satirists. With his valiant refusal to be "bullied by reviewers" none could quibble. But his claim to "have attacked none *personally* who did not commence on the offensive" is equivocal. If it is taken to mean that he had no *personal* animosity except toward critics Francis Jeffrey and Hewson Clarke, then it also implies that he condemned selected poets primarily because, knowingly or unknowingly, they had threatened the aesthetic principles he deemed essential to the general literary welfare. His main purpose, if one accepts his rhetoric in the expanded Preface, was not personal but social: to cure pestilential rhymers and eradicate ophidian reviewers.

Like Pope, in his Dialogue II of "Epilogue to the Satires," Byron defends satire on the grounds that it restrains where nothing else can, causing offenders to "shrink from Ridicule, though not from Law" (l. 36). In Gifford's hands, it could "Make bad men better, or at least ashamed" (l. 830). Since Byron's own satiric powers, as he suggests, may be inadequate to eliminate social crimes, he promises to concentrate on literary offenders. Even while calling on Truth to "rouse some genuine Bard, and guide his hand" (l. 687), he volunteers himself as one trained by critics' tactics and uncorrupted by "distempered dream" (l. 24). Nor is he afraid to indulge in self-satire on his own presumption, for like "great Jeffrey" he appoints himself "Judge of Poesy" and, ironically, turns legalistic reviewer. Modestly admitting that his creative endeavors may be more flawed than those of Dryden, Pope, and Gifford, whose tradition he invokes, he feels nevertheless impelled by public duty to overthrow the tyranny of reviewers who have established their hegemony over an enslaved literature. Whereas the first edition of *English Bards* ends with a prophetic warning that degenerate letters will lead to the fall of a great nation, the second is greatly enhanced by a new conclusion emphasizing the satirist's role as champion of his people.

Although the neoclassical satirist usually strove to reveal only his public personality—that of the simple, honest man—and sometimes assumed an almost incredible mask of rectitude, Byron makes no such pretensions. Using a persona whose voice is close to his own, he presents even the vulnerable side of his nature without worrying whether it may undermine his qualifications or his satiric authority. One such frank admission occurs after a passage attacking the moral corruption of his day, as Byron concedes that he too has erred in heeding passion rather than reason:

> E'en I must raise my voice, e'en I must feel
> Such scenes, such men destroy the public weal:
> Altho' some kind, censorious friend will say,
> 'What art thou better, meddling fool, than they?'
> And every Brother Rake will smile to see
> That miracle, a Moralist in me! (ll. 695–700)

His candor is all the more ingratiating because it is combined with humility: his avowed mission is to chasten only until a more virtuous bard may arrive on the scene to apply the lash that even the erring Byron will feel. His earlier role as puerile poet, he declares, was that of "A school-boy freak, unworthy praise or blame" (l. 49), and equally self-abasing are his prefatory references to his writings as "scribblings" and to himself as "a country practitioner" substituting for "the regular physician." Much of this self-deprecation is probably rhetoric. Yet it is certainly a far cry from the usual assurance of formal Augustan satirists, though one should not forget that the Earl of Rochester proclaimed himself a sinner satirizing other transgressors or that Horace railed against his acquaintances for peccadillos he readily acknowledged in himself. Evidently Byron felt that confessions strengthened rather than weakened one's authority, for he told Lady Blessington: "I maintain that persons who have *erred* are most competent to point out errors."[27] The integrity of *English Bards* depends in large part on an unassuming persona who dominates the scene of corruption not with moral superiority but with winning openness and common sense. If we find it difficult to comprehend how Byron could have exalted men such as Rogers, Gifford, Henry Kirke White, and Martin A. Shee, we must also keep in mind the relative insignificance that the persona assigns himself with respect to firmly established poets.

It was while disciplining his talent in preparation for *English Bards*, according to Moore, that the young poet developed his "enthusiastic admiration" for Pope.[28] Of the many verbal echoes of Pope in this first formal satire there can be no doubt, and it appears that Byron strove in particular to emulate Pope's neat grammatical control and epigrammatic style. Moreover, in the structures of his rhetoric, as A. B. England has maintained, Byron most conspicuously shows himself the heir of Popean moral satire.[29] For example, he relies on the analysis of Lord Hervey's antithetical character in the "Epistle to Dr. Arbuthnot" when satirizing the moral confusion in Scott's Marmion through a series of unresolved contradictions:

> Now forging scrolls, now foremost in the fight,
> Not quite a Felon, yet but half a Knight,
> The gibbet or the field prepared to grace;
> A mighty mixture of the great and base.
>
> (ll. 167–70)

Such imitation served not only as a tribute to its Popean model but also as a way of acknowledging the tradition Byron meant to further.

Careful study of Pope, who had made a systematic defense of his mission as satirist, also led to closer acquaintance with the tradition on which he had particularly relied—that of Roman satire. When Byron read Owen Ruffhead's *Life of Alexander Pope*, he wrote in his copy, inscribed "Cambridge, A.D., 1808," that "Imitators of Horace and Juvenal were Boileau and Pope—of one as well as of the other of whom it may be said—Même en imitant toujours original."[30] From this critical biography he also learned of Pope's intent to be part of the Roman satiric tradition and to give it eloquent expression in his *Imitations of Horace.* Pope's adaptations of his primary mentor reflected the content, tone, style, or simply the manner of the Horatian originals, but in such a way that each product became a new creation as well as a modernization and a loving criticism of its model. While most of the impetus derived from the gentlemanly conversations and epistolary discussions of Horace, there were also instances where Pope, by the process of "contamination," interwove both vituperation and moral philosophy more typical of Juvenal and Persius. Pope's success in playing off imitation against original pointed the way to what Byron might accomplish within this same tradition.

But whereas Pope's contemporaries could identify with Horace's Augustan Rome, early nineteenth-century Englishmen, because of the defiance of law and morality by wealthy aristocrats and even royalty, felt greater affinity with the debauched imperial city under Nero and Domitian. Byron, in his determination to attack the corruption he had observed at the highest social level in England, realized that his times required a more vehement scourge than Horace. Juvenal, with his *saeva indignatio*, was apparently a more congenial model for Byron, as he was for other contemporary poets, who frequently translated, imitated, and parodied his works. Although Byron probably knew Johnson's adaptations of Juvenal's Satires III and X (*London* and *The Vanity of Human Wishes*), as well as Dryden's translation of Juvenal, it was not until 1807, during his second period of residence at Cambridge, that developing friendships with Hobhouse and Francis Hodgson confirmed his devotion to the satirist who became his favorite Latin writer. Hodgson's translation of *The Satires of Juvenal* appeared late that year, as did also the second complete edition of Martin Madan's *New and Literal Translation of Juvenal and Persius; with Copious Explanatory Notes.* Byron acquired the 1807 edition of Madan's extremely helpful work, which both Gifford and Hodgson acknowledged in their translations of Juvenal, and proceeded to draw from it.[31]

In the second and subsequent editions of *English Bards* Byron documented his imitations of specific passages from Juvenal's first satire by printing in footnotes the Latin that served as his model. Though he was careful to avoid a slavish adaptation of the original or of Madan's tortured prose translation, it can be shown that Madan's notes had a subtle impact on his phraseology. In one instance, for his lines "While these are Censors, 'twould be sin to spare; / While such are Critics, why should I forbear?" (ll. 87–88), Byron cited Juvenal's "Stulta est clementia, cum tot ubique / Vatibus occurras, periturae parcere chartae" (I.17–18), which Madan had translated as: "It is a foolish clemency, when every where so many / Poets you may meet, to spare paper, that will perish."[32] Byron's wording of the last clause (l. 88) bears less resemblance, however, to that of Juvenal or to Madan's enigmatic rendition than it does to the latter's explanation—that others "will write upon it if I do not; therefore there is no reason why I should forbear." In his footnote citation of Juvenal, Byron, expecting his readers to comprehend the Latin, deleted the word *Vatibus*, evidently because he was transferring the idea to critics on the grounds that "Our Bards and Censors are so much alike" (l. 92). It was this reapplication of Juvenal to something new that was expected to give his classically educated readers a pleasure not only of recognizing the allusion but also of seeing how it could be applied in a contemporary context.

Other links to the classical tradition have already been adduced. In particular, Claude M. Fuess and Mary Clearman have suggested connections to Juvenal's first satire.[33] It is also apparent that Byron's style, with its strident denunciations, emotional intensity, and occasionally grandiose diction, is closely akin to Juvenal's. And while Byron evidently strove to imitate Pope's technical skills in the couplet, though without achieving his master's compactness, it can certainly be demonstrated that he was invoking the entire scope of English Augustan satire from Dryden to

Churchill and Lady Anne Hamilton. Commentators have often cited Byron's mock invocation to his "grey goose-quill" (ll. 7–26), which he exhorts, "Then let us soar to-day," as an allusion to Pope's "Epistle to Dr. Arbuthnot" (l. 249); however, one might also point to a poem in *Poetry of the Anti-Jacobin*, beginning "On grey goose-quills sublime I'll soar," as an even closer parallel.[34] Obviously, much of the style and content in this tradition was a common possession among its practitioners. If one is to understand Byron's disdain for his contemporaries who had broken with classicism to utter new thoughts in experimental ways, one must remember that in *English Bards* he presented himself as both heir and defender of an esteemed, though evidently waning, tradition.

Had Byron wished to concentrate only on the corruption of contemporary literary taste without regard to its social context and without use of a connecting fable such as Pope invented for his *Dunciad*, the first satire of Persius might have served as the ideal prototype. Yet Gifford had already exploited that possibility for his *Baviad: A Paraphrastic Imitation of the First Satire of Persius* (1791). Moreover, to show how contemporary authors could be pilloried in the framework of an appropriate model, Gifford had conspicuously imitated Horace's Satire 10 of Book I in his *Maeviad* (1795). Hence Juvenal's first satire, which seems to have been fashioned after Persius's first, was the most appropriate remaining choice for a fledgling satirist eager to declare himself the direct descendant of the classical tradition of English satire. Since Byron was apparently interested in candidly portraying literature as the reflection of a degenerate society, Juvenal's first actually provided him with a model even better suited to his purposes than anything of Horace or Persius. But contrary to what some scholars have asserted about its having been a preliminary "general plan" or "blueprint" for *English Bards*, Juvenal's first must be regarded largely as an afterthought in the accretion of Byron's poem. The Juvenalian impact on the first edition of *English Bards*, as well as on its antecedent "British Bards," was negligible.

It seems likely that after publication of the first edition of *English Bards* and before departure on his Mediterranean tour Byron decided to bring his satire more conspicuously into line with not only the English Augustan but also the Roman tradition while at the same time improving its coherence. Though Madan's commentary on Juvenal's use of *farrago* (I.86) to explain the contents ("a mixture, an hodge-podge—as we say, of various things mixed together") might have justified the disorganized nature of Byron's early versions, Juvenal's structure was far more cohesive than his modest deprecation of it as a catchall implied. Possibly to give *English Bards* a similar unity of purpose, Byron added, after a thorough study of Madan's work, the first 96 lines of the final text to expound both his reasons for writing satire and his views on the debasement of contemporary society. Two other insertions—notably the sections on gambling and the conclusion asserting the poet's militant determination to eliminate evil through satiric truth—may well have been inspired by Madan's copious notes (I.88ff., 149ff.), which are much more impressive than Juvenal's brief comments on those subjects.

Even Madan's prefatory "argument" for Juvenal's first satire strikes me as a much more appropriate resume of Byron's earliest satire in its second and subsequent editions than Gilbert Highet's skeletal outline of Juvenal's poem, which Clearman held up to *English Bards*.[35] As Madan explains,

> Juvenal begins this Satire, with giving some humourous reasons for his writing: such as hearing, so often, many ill poets rehearse their works, and intending to repay them in kind. Next he informs us, why he addicts himself to satire, rather than to other poetry, and gives a summary and general view of the reigning vices and follies of his time. He laments the restraints which the satyrists then lay under from a fear of punishment, and professes to treat of the dead, personating, under their names, certain living vicious characters. His great aim, in this, and in all other satires, is to expose and reprove vice itself, however sanctified by custom, or dignified by the examples of the great. (I, 2–3)

The first statement of this passage could serve as topic sentence for Byron's first poetical paragraph (ll. 1–6). The second suggests Byron's third poetical paragraph (ll. 27–62), in which the poet expresses the hope that his castigation will improve both corrupt society and debased literature. Madan's phrase "vices and follies," though common in the English satiric tradition, may well have been the impetus for the first two couplets of this section (ll. 27–30). Surely the governmental restraints on Roman satirists alluded to in the third sentence had their counterparts in the savagely unjust attacks of Scotch reviewers. Though Byron evidently did not begin his satire with Juvenal's plan in mind, he discovered after publication of the first edition that, with an added introduction and a new conclusion based on the fourth sentence of the above extract, he could use Madan's outline to provide an orderly framework for his previously chaotic substance.

That Byron's borrowing from Juvenal and Madan did not completely resolve the inherent structural deficiencies to the satisfaction of all critics, however, is obvious from the frequent and not unfounded charge that *English Bards* is only loosely strung together. But while its diatribes against objects as disparate as contemporary drama, opera, gambling, and Cambridge may not fit comfortably into an integrated whole, its assault on the lawyer-critics of Edinburgh has an undeniable unity, fused as it was by the intense heat of anger. With a sidelong glance at Pope's *Essay on Criticism*, Byron gives ironic advice to critics, deploring their inadequate literary preparation, eagerness to find faults, erroneous notions of wit, ill tempers, disrespect for truth, and evident desire to usurp "the Throne of Taste" (ll. 63–84). These "Northern wolves," cowardly by nature, are seen to fall upon a victim as a pack and then hide through anonymity. Byron suggests that it is actually the Holland House set, with political clout and financial patronage, that controls the journal's policies even to the extent of having Lady Holland edit the manuscripts. Though a few barbs are hurled at lesser contributors such as "blundering Brougham," Jeffrey inevitably bears the brunt of the attack: a mock-encomium likens him to the infamous "hanging judge" Jeffries, whose ghost predicts that Jeffrey will be elevated to the bench for party service and ultimately to the gallows.

Yet the most devastating attack on Jeffrey (and probably one of the most successful portions as poetical satire) is the mock-heroic account of the aborted duel between Jeffrey and Moore. Contemporary newspapers had made much of the allegation that when this actual duel was interrupted the two pistols were found to be unloaded. Byron's high burlesque, transforming this embarrassing incident into a myth of epic proportions, ridicules not only the apparent fraudulence of the combat but also the impotence of both critic and bard. Through fantastic metaphors and personifications of Edinburgh landmarks, the reader is made to understand that Scottish honor depends on Jeffrey's victory, assured by the supernatural intervention of Caledonia's "kilted Goddess," who

> hovered o'er
> The field, and saved him from the wrath of Moore;
> From either pistol snatched the vengeful lead,
> And strait restored it to her favourite's head.
> . . . .
> 'My son,' she cried, 'ne'er thirst for gore again,
> Resign the pistol, and resume the pen;
> O'er politics and poesy preside,
> Boast of thy country, and Britannia's guide!
> For long as Albion's heedless sons submit,
> Or Scottish taste decides on English wit,
> So long shall last thine unmolested reign,
> Nor any dare to take thy name in vain.'
> (ll. 490–93, 498–505)

Implicit in this prophecy of Scottish critical sovereignty is the assumption that the deplorable situation stems largely from English weakness.

Byron's animus toward contemporary poets, though less easily justified than that toward critics, is related to a gloomy, almost Spenglerian view of his country's literature that, at age nineteen, he recorded in his 1807 account of authors he had read. "English living poets I have avoided mentioning," he wrote. "We have none who will not survive their productions. Taste is over with us; and another century will sweep our empire, our literature, and our name, from all but a place in the annals of mankind." [36] His disrespect for contemporaries stemmed largely from a belief that they had renounced the cumulative wisdom of the past without offering any valid standards of taste to replace it. In *English Bards* his ridicule of Southey's *Thalaba* begins with the premise that it had been "written in open defiance of precedent and poetry." [37] Byron does not endorse only the neoclassicists, as his praise of William Cowper, Robert Burns, and Henry Kirke White shows, but he thinks innovators who "deviate from the common track" run the risk of failure or public neglect. There are, as Pope suggested in his *Essay on Criticism*, a few original geniuses who can bypass accepted precepts and still attain those "nameless graces which no methods teach." But the satirist, whose prerogative it has always been to take a negative approach to whatever falls short of success, is not bound by the critic's obligation to evaluate overall achievement. Thus Byron, though capable of measured judgments, felt free to take greater liberties in his satires.

When Byron reviewed Wordsworth's 1807 *Poems* for *Monthly Literary Recreations* (July 1807), he certainly, without ranking Wordsworth among the immortals, provided a balanced view of merits and defects.[38] When he wrote satire, however, he apparently felt obliged to be mordantly witty about literary shortcomings and eccentricities that he considered symptomatic of a national malaise. His attack on Wordsworth in *English Bards* is biased and disregards the experimental nature of the *Lyrical Ballads*. Yet even dedicated Romanticists can hardly deny that there is some truth to what Byron so cleverly expressed in the following epitome:

> Next comes the dull disciple of thy school,
> That mild apostate from poetic rule,
> The simple Wordsworth, framer of a lay
> As soft as evening in his favourite May;
> Who warns his friend 'to shake off toil and trouble,
> And quit his books, for fear of growing double';
> Who, both by precept and example, shows
> That prose is verse, and verse is merely prose,
> Convincing all by demonstration plain,
> Poetic souls delight in prose insane;
> And Christmas stories tortured into rhyme,
> Contain the essence of the true sublime:
> Thus when he tells the tale of Betty Foy,
> The idiot mother of 'an idiot Boy';
> A moon-struck silly lad who lost his way,
> And, like his bard, confounded night with day,
> So close on each pathetic part he dwells,
> And each adventure so sublimely tells,
> That all who view the 'idiot in his glory',
> Conceive the Bard the hero of the story.
>
> (ll. 235–54)

Most of what Byron contended about Wordsworth and other Romantic poets had already been charged. The anonymous author of *The Simpliciad*, who often applied the epithet "simple" to them, had begun his poem with a mock-dedication to Wordsworth, Southey, and Samuel Taylor Coleridge as leaders of the so-called "Anti-Classical School" and had also ridiculed Scott and Moore. Byron's attack on the poet now regarded as the leader of the Romantic movement is essentially a metrical adaptation of what Jeffrey, in his review of *Thalaba*, had asserted about the new simplicity, antisocial inclinations, and homely language of these poets.[39] The first Wordsworth poem specifically attacked by Byron, "The Tables Turned," is one that Jeffrey had previously ridiculed in the same review. Moreover, Byron's accusation that Wordsworth had actually proved his verse and prose to be indistinguishable echoes Jeffrey's denunciation of the tenets in the Preface to *Lyrical Ballads* (1800) and of *Thalaba* as "prose, written out into the form of verse" (p. 73). Byron's censure of Scott's supernaturalism, "stale romance," and hasty composition for financial gain had been voiced not only in critical journals but in Lady Anne Hamilton's *Epics of the Ton*; and the artificialities in *The Lay of the Last Minstrel* had been condemned by E. S. Barrett in *All the Talents*.

Byron's unsympathetic interpretation of Romantic theory and practice differs from the now-forgotten utterances of heavier-handed critics because he perceived and exploited possibilities for comic distortion, especially where high seriousness had been intended. In one irreverent metaphor he pulled the rug from under Southey's glorified Joan of Arc: "A virgin Phoenix from her ashes risen" (l. 210). By refusing to see the addressee of Coleridge's "To a Young Ass" as anything other than a long-eared animal, he reduced that poem to absurdity. Using the techniques of caricature, he would often select a distinctive feature (such as Bowles's sentimental delight in bells or Moore's fascination with the mildly erotic) and, through exaggeration of that characteristic, make an author appear absolutely ridiculous. Byron's deliberate misprision of Romantic principles, which, ironically, would soon predominate over those he was championing, sets him apart as the one great poet of his day still clinging to neoclassical ideals.

Aside from the fact that he was unimpressed by the style of Romantic poetry, he evidently felt that it lacked edifying and inspiring substance. Romantic poets, as William H. Marshall has suggested, were not in Byron's view fulfilling their vatic obligations as guardians of a distinguished national tradition.[40] By concerning themselves with inconsequential issues, they had trivialized English poetry. The conservative majority of Byron's day was inclined to agree with this assessment of contemporary poets. That his judgment was also thought sound in reputable literary circles can be seen from remarks by an anonymous reviewer in the *Gentleman's Magazine* for March 1809:

> [*English Bards*] is unquestionably the result of an impassioned yet diligent study of the best masters, grounded on a fine taste and very happy natural endowments. . . . many years have passed since the English press has given us a performance so replete with mingled genius, good sense, and spirited animadversion.[41]

What continues to distinguish Byron's achievement, however, is not merely his discernment of the vulnerable features of early Romantic poetry and Scottish criticism. Rather, it is his ability to encapsulate their weaknesses in memorable poetry. The tags he attached to his contemporaries retain their original vitality largely because of the punch and pithiness of his phraseology. Not since Pope had anyone skewered his satiric victims as cleverly or impaled their idiosyncrasies so aptly: Coleridge ("The bard who soars to elegize an ass"), M. G. Lewis ("Apollo's sexton"), Bowles ("The maudlin prince of mournful sonneteers"), and Moore ("mend thy line, and sin no more"). Not only the bards but also their fictive creations—the Idiot Boy, Marmion, and Madoc—are imaginatively brought to life through the vigor of Byron's language, which sometimes even parodies the style of the original compositions. If *English Bards* lacks the emotional control and technical perfection of Pope at his best, it nevertheless shows that Byron had learned to polish a couplet or a phrase to achieve a stinging impact. He had not yet resolved or even addressed some other artistic problems, but *English Bards*, largely because of its cleverness of wit and exuberance of style, still illustrates irrefutably the talents that established his reputation as a satirist to be reckoned with.

～ CHAPTER 3 ～

SATIRES OF THE LONDON YEARS

THE SUCCESS of *English Bards* encouraged Byron to seek further inspiration in classical satire. His next such endeavor, *Hints from Horace*, fashioned after the Latin poet's *Epistola ad Pisones de arte poetica*, was originally conceived both as a sequel to *English Bards* and as a response to Hobhouse (referred to as Moschus), who had addressed Byron in an imitation of Juvenal's eleventh satire. Though the ancients had not considered the *Ars Poetica* a satire in form, there was ample precedent among neoclassical critics for regarding it as satiric in spirit, tone, and rhetorical intention. It is unlikely that Byron would have caviled at this generic amalgamation, since Pope himself had designated both Horatian *sermones* and *epistolae* as "satires." [1] The two forms dealt with the same topics in an informal, conversational manner and differed primarily in the immediate presence or absence of the person addressed. *Hints from Horace*, with its *sermo merus* style, was in theory an excellent sequel to the stridently Juvenalian *English Bards*. If the earlier satire diagnosed absurdities of the literary scene, the later offered practical advice on how to effect a cure.

Byron probably would not have turned to a Horatian poem as a model had he not chanced upon a copy of Horace's poetry in the library of the Capuchin convent where he was living in Athens. Three days after beginning his *Hints from Horace* he wrote Hobhouse on 5 March 1811: "I have begun an Imitation of the 'De Arte Poetica' of Horace (in rhyme of course) & have translated or rather varied about 200 lines and shall probably finish it for lack of other argument" (*BLJ*, II, 42). Since the last page of the earlier Lovelace manuscript is dated 11, 12 March, the first draft of *Hints* had presumably been completed by that time.[2] On 18 March Byron informed Hobhouse that he was engaged in polishing the work—he studiously used Horace's phrase "Limae Labor," knowing that his friend would recognize it—and added that he had adapted his imitation "entirely to our new school of Poetry, though always keeping pretty close to the original" (*BLJ*, II, 43). If printed, *Hints* was to have, like Hobhouse's imitations published in 1809, the corresponding Latin text alongside the English. From the first, as Byron conceded, he was "very fond" of this work. By 20 March he had finished a corrected manuscript copy of it, and by 14 June a second copy, enlarged to 796 lines, had been completed.

En route back to England, Byron wrote James Cawthorn from Malta on 9 May (and again on 7 July) concerning publication of the poem (*BLJ*, II, 44, 57–58), and he lost no time in delivering the latest manuscript of *Hints* to his publisher upon returning to London on 14 July. The following day he wrote Hobhouse, to whom he planned to dedicate the new satire, that he would show him the fair copy of it as soon as it could be transcribed by Cawthorn's amanuensis (*BLJ*, II, 59–60). So proud was Byron of his imitation of Horace that, when visited by Dallas on 15 July, he confidently declared satire his "*forte*" and said nothing about his manuscript of a travel poem in Spenserian stanzas.[3] Byron gave Dallas a copy of *Hints*, asking him to supervise its immediate publication; but Dallas, upon reading the poem, was "grievously disappointed," though he felt obliged to conceal his true feelings. Although Byron was very diffident about the merits of *Childe Harold's Pilgrimage*, Dallas induced him to allow publication of that work before *Hints*.

The first two cantos of *Childe Harold*, even in manuscript, do not qualify as sustained satire, but they do represent a contribution to the advancement of Byron's satiric techniques. Although the thematic materials—such as nature and art, imagination and reason, the vanity of human ambitions, and the triumph of time over man's achievements—were already commonplace, Byron's mode of presenting them was innovative. In 1814 he wrote Murray that if ever he had done "anything original it was in" that poem (*BLJ*, IV, 107). Certainly the employment of two personae, Harold and the narrator-poet, vastly enriched the mode of satiric presentation that would be tried again in *The Curse of Minerva* and refined in *Don Juan*. If the initial attempt to present diverse perspectives was occasionally muddled by failure to keep the dramatic voices of Harold and the narrator sufficiently differentiated, Byron nevertheless learned much in this early work about how to pit two personae against each other.[4]

Central to Byron's explicit intent was his separation of the narrator-poet from the title character, who was invented largely to give the travelogue unity. In a passage canceled from the manuscript Preface, he advertised his determination to establish a safe distance between his fictional character and himself by stating that "where the author speaks in his own person he assumes a very different tone from that of" Harold (*CPW*, II, 4n). The primary advantage of a divided perspective was that each persona could embody a particular set of responses that Byron wished to dramatize. Harold, as the degenerate scion of a once-distinguished lineage, symbolizes the present debasement of a once-glorious past: he is the equivalent of the ruined cultures and edifices encountered on his pilgrimage. Misanthropic and debauched, he is ridiculed in the opening stanzas for his self-indulgence and cynicism by a narrator who terms him "a shameless wight" but who obviously enjoys mocking bourgeois morality with accounts of Harold's wickedness. Harold often serves as a straw man against whom the narrator, in the posture of a corrective satirist, directs his sarcasm. Byron did not remain consistent, however, in either the degree of separation or the confrontational nature of his personae. At times each utters pronouncements unrelated to the orientation of the other; at times their expressed ideas reflect similarities. Yet even when Harold and the narrator tend to merge in the second canto, Harold serves as a negative standard against which the reader can perceive alterations in the narrator's point of view as his growing awareness of human misfortune brings about progressive disillusionment. Whatever the fluctuating relationship between the two personae, their different responses, all of which in reality are fictionalized projections of the mobile poet's own personality, provided Byron a novel means of playing off conflicting attitudes without ever having to reconcile their tonal or philosophical inconsistencies.

These diverse views lead not only to an unresolved irony but also, as the narrator himself asserts, to a rejection of absolute truth in favor of more sophisticated perceptions of it. The "truth" rather naively sought by the persona in *English Bards* is now acknowledged to be far more complicated, though some of the old dichotomy remains in the narrator's claim in *Childe Harold* that he is led on "By pensive Sadness, not by Fiction" (II.36.4). Melancholy thought not only becomes the impetus to the search for truth but justifies the highly subjective reflections and speculations. Even if truth is as elusive and indeterminate as Pontius Pilate implied, Harold's pilgrimage can nevertheless be seen largely as a quest for better apprehensions of that desideratum in its worldly manifestations. Among the reliable truths that the poem does incorporate are truth of human feeling, truth of man's lapsed condition as opposed to idealistic fabrication, and truth of history even though imagination may not accurately revive it. The narrator's negative interpretation of Socratic skepticism ("All that we know is, nothing can be known"—II.7.2) is only the beginning of his quest, for by acknowledging that nothing can be known with certainty, he, like Socrates, opens his mind to a critical, objective analysis of all accepted wisdom in the hope of acquiring sounder knowledge. And it is this critical, often satiric, approach in *Childe Harold* that provides a means of countering falsehoods, especially those that have obscured the realities of mankind's plight.

Not only the thought of *Childe Harold*, but the form as well is infused with satiric elements. The poem's subtitle, "A Romaunt," can be justified only in a moderately parodic sense, particularly since Byron asserts in his "Addition to the Preface" that real knights of old were no more chivalric than his "vagrant Childe," despite what medieval romances led one to believe. Much in Canto I suggests that Byron began his poem in 1809 with the idea of poking fun at travel literature, topographical poetry, and possibly other genres, for Harold is so unlike the typical romaunt hero as to be almost a caricature. The Gothic delineation of his depravity, emphasized at the beginning of the poem, borders on ironic raillery. Yet Byron was apparently eager to place *Childe Harold* generically within the eighteenth-century Spenserian tradition of reflective poetry unified by a single traveler making desultory comments on whatever he encountered along his route. In the Preface Byron defended his potpourri of diverse moods by quoting James Beattie's praise of the adaptable Spenserian medium, which allowed the poet to be "either droll or pathetic, descriptive or sentimental, tender or satiric, as the humour strikes" (*CPW*, II, 4). There was indeed good precedent for the incorporation of satire in the tradition of Spenserian meditative poetry as it had evolved under the guidance of Ludovico Ariosto, James Thomson, William Shenstone, and Beattie. A number of allusions to the *Odyssey*, moreover, suggest that Byron was also thinking of parallels with this oldest of travelogues showing how a man might develop psychologically through the fullness of experience, and McGann has asserted that the "whole treatment of the trip to Albania is a serious parody of the conventional epic descent to the underworld" (*CPW*, II, 288).

But however tongue-in-cheek Byron's approach to inherited literary modes may have been, *Childe Harold* initially incorporated passages that were boldly satiric in spirit. Although the first fair copy (*MS. M*) was not so preponderantly satiric as has sometimes been asserted, it contained some libelous personal attacks that Byron, obviously concerned about the obstacles to ultimate publication, completely excised or drastically toned down before turning it over to Dallas for transcription and verbal polishing.[5] Byron subsequently removed additional passages from Dallas's transcript as well. Examination of the deleted passages suggests that Byron resembled a free-swinging journalist who pulled no punches until, on second thought, he realized his copy was too offensive to be published with impunity.

The expurgated passages deemed too mordant or too indiscreet for conventional readers and fearful publishers attack, from the viewpoint of an indignant moralist, the perpetration of various wrongs. The sanctimonious attack on William Beckford's "unhallowed thirst / Of nameless crime" (I.22var.), like the reference to Turkish homosexuality (II.61.5–9var.), touched on a subject forbidden by the legitimate press. The stanza designating a priest as "churlish," his belief in immortality as "phantasy," and his heaven as a place from which his sins would bar him (II.8var.) was far too strong. Derogatory references to both religion and politics displeased publishers William Miller, who rejected *Childe Harold*, and John Murray, who ultimately accepted a mollified version. In 1811, when *Childe Harold* was being submitted for publication, some of Byron's political satire seemed almost unpatriotic, for by then the success of Wellington (Arthur Wellesley) against the French in the Peninsular War had partially atoned for the earlier Tory blunders, which Byron in the manuscript version had assailed with decidedly Whig bias. Even shortly after the Convention of Cintra, his scornful attack on British negotiators would have been too specific—naming men such as the four Wellesleys, Sir Hew Dalrymple, John Hookham Frere, and Lord Holland in stanzas that also included a stinging reference to Lady Holland's scandalous past (I.24var.*a*, 87var.*a,b,c,d*); and the sneering condemnation of those ineffectual protestors who allowed such leaders to go unpunished would have struck incongruously at the very people (e.g., William Cobbett) who shared Byron's antagonism (I.24var.*c,d*). Unfortunately, expunging references to those British leaders whom Byron expected Sir John Carr to praise in a forthcoming Spanish travelogue also blunted the point of Byron's jests about Carr's plodding Baedekers—precisely the kind of composition *Childe Harold* was not to be. Similarly, removal of an oblique slur on Elgin's adulterous wife eliminated the passage containing Byron's ironic invitation to other pilferers of Greek art (II.13.4–9var., 14var.*a,b*).

Some of the satiric phrases and longer passages were allowed to remain since they served to underscore a response, offered tonal variety (particularly as relief from the lugubriousness of Harold), and were successfully incorporated into the poem. The three revised stanzas (I.24–26) substituted for the original attack on the Convention of Cintra still constituted censure of the British leaders who at the conference table permitted the defeated French invaders to evacuate peacefully instead of being forced to surrender. But rather than name the culprits in the revised version, Byron began with a mock-Spenserian allegory ironically blaming a wicked fiend of the Cintran castle for converting military heroes into diplomatic fools. On the other hand, military glory on the Spanish battlefield is mocked as a deluding dream, sought by "Ambition's honour'd fools" (I.42.1) and celebrated "in worthless lays" (I.43.9), since in reality battle's chief victor is death. Splenetic Juvenalian outbursts against the venality of women's love (I.9.6–9) and the sexual lewdness of Seville and Cadiz (I.46,65–67) serve to emphasize the fallen condition of society. While the designation of religious faith as a comforting delusion (II.8) may be more skeptical than hostile in tone, the fling at asceticism (I.20.9) and the denunciation of an institutionalized religion turning "Foul Superstition" into "sacerdotal gain" (II.44.5–9) express unequivocal religious satire that did not please Murray (*BLJ*, II, 91). The harsh criticism aimed at both the Portuguese and the Greeks, however, is less a satiric condemnation than a specific illustration of the decadence displayed by any people who resign themselves to foreign tyranny. The much lighter buffoonery concerning London cockneys who on Sundays take the air in rural suburbs and indulge in various "fooleries" (I.69–71) is partly ridicule and partly an indirect means of convincing British readers not to take a pharisaical attitude toward Spanish desecration of the sabbath.

Two of the most successful satiric passages are carefully woven into the fabric of Byron's philosophical observations. The attack on Elgin is appropriately worked in after the lament that imagination cannot restore the ravages of time (II.10.4–7), for despite Elgin's pretense to being the preserver of Greek art, his despoiling of the Acropolis has surpassed the destructiveness of both time and barbaric conquerors. In the context of larger issues in the poem, denunciation of Elgin's misdeeds serves rhetorically as shocking evidence of Athena's lost powers and the enslavement of Greece:

> But most the modern Pict's ignoble boast,
> To rive what Goth, and Turk, and Time hath spar'd:
> Cold as the crags upon his native coast,
> His mind as barren and his heart as hard,
> Is he whose head conceiv'd, whose hand prepar'd,
> Aught to displace Athena's poor remains:
> Her sons too weak the sacred shrine to guard,
> Yet felt some portion of their mother's pains,
> And never knew, till then, the weight of Despot's chains. (II.12)

In an even more intricate way the narrator employs satire in the bullfight episode (I.71–80) to underscore adverse judgments along with praise. The Sunday ritual begins ironically with prayers to the Virgin ("the only virgin there") and proceeds to the fascinating but dehumanizing spectacle of the bullring. The narrator's repugnance to the torment of dumb animals, the callousness of spectators, and the frenzied delight in bloodshed is mixed with admiration for the intrepidity of the bullfighters and the ritualistic drama of the pageantry. But the rituals mask contemptible human traits; and the bullfight, as the narrator interprets it, dramatizes in microcosm the unwholesome as well as the admirable qualities associated elsewhere in the poem with Spanish character and culture. It brings into focus the acceptance of bloody deeds, savagery, and vengeance along with pride in a distinguished heritage, love of liberty, vigor, and bravery. The artistic gain obtained through functional assimilation of this and the other remaining satirical passages into the version that Murray published on 10 March 1812 outweighs the vitality lost through excision of the splenetic outbursts that had appeared in the manuscripts of *Childe Harold*.

Even as Byron amended the text of *Childe Harold*, he continued to revise his Horatian satire, but for some time he could not make up his mind whether to publish *Hints* singly or in conjunction with another edition of *English Bards* (*BLJ*, II, 74, 80). Moreover, he was not sure that Dallas could be entrusted with the assigned task. He had determined that a skilled Latinist such as Hodgson or Henry Drury was needed not just to correct the proofs but to correlate the parallel passages of his imitation and Horace's original in the typesetting so that no reader would "lose sight of the Allusion."[6] Meanwhile he continued to send Cawthorn further emendations, some (like the passage on Jeffrey) containing vitriolic sarcasm, and simultaneously to stall publication of *Hints*. Ultimately he decided to include it, as well as *The Curse of Minerva*, with the proposed fifth edition of *English Bards*. But when that edition was suppressed in 1812, *Hints* had not progressed beyond several sets of proofs printed between August and November 1811. The phenomenal success of *Childe Harold I* and *II* in 1812 caused his concern for *Hints* to wane.

Not until Byron, while living in Ravenna, took renewed interest in reevaluating Pope with respect to nineteenth-century poets who were depreciating the great Augustan did he revive the idea of publishing *Hints*. On 23 September 1820 he asked Murray to get that poem from Hobhouse and send him a proof of it with the Latin (*BLJ*, VII, 179). He was proud of having followed, however fortuitously, the Horatian rubric to withhold one's composition nine years before making it public.[7] Had he been closer to the text of *Hints*, he might not have asserted: "As far as versification goes it is good—and on looking back to what I wrote about that period—I am astonished to see how *little* I have trained on. I wrote better then than now—but that comes from my having fallen into the atrocious bad taste of the times—partly." (Strange though that observation may appear from Byron at the height of his powers, one must consider that in 1820 many critics were denouncing *Don Juan* as a retrogression in his poetical skills.) To avoid further antagonism he was willing, as he wrote Murray, to delete from *Hints* some offending passages and specific names but wished to add some observations on Pope in notes to what, in a letter to Hobhouse, he had called "that Popean poem" (*BLJ*, VII, 114). Both Hobhouse and Murray recommended drastic revisions "to suit the times," but when the first portion of Murray's proof arrived on 11 January 1821, Byron saw "little to alter" and fulminated against Murray's "cutting and slashing."[8] When the remaining portion of Murray's proof reached Ravenna on 1 March, Byron objected that it contained neither the requested Horatian text nor the note on Pope (extracted from his unpublished "Reply to *Blackwood's*") but retained the attack on Jeffrey that had been expressly marked for cancellation (*BLJ*, VIII, 88). Adjustment of Horace's Latin to his English text he considered of utmost importance because by this time he judged the poem's "principal merit" to be its closeness to the original. His claim that the Horatian imitation and the Pulci translation were "by far the best things of my doing" must have struck Murray as deliberate perversity. In Byron's mind, however, *Hints* had assumed the stature of a poetical manifesto in which he, like Pope in the *Essay on Criticism* and *Imitations of Horace*, had articulated his criteria for literary judgment. When he withdrew from Murray as his publisher, *Hints* had still not been published. Though selections from it appeared in Dallas's *Recollections of the Life of Lord Byron* (1824) and in Moore's *Letters and Journals of Lord Byron: With Notices of His Life* (1830), the entire poem, with corresponding Latin, was not published until Murray's 1831 edition of Byron's poetry.

Byron's extraordinary attachment to *Hints* may also be attributed to the unusual effort it cost him. Horace had not always been a favorite of Byron, certainly not during his school years; yet all educated people in his day studied the *Ars Poetica* on the assumption that it represented the most persuasive exposition of good taste ever codified. In the eyes of classicist critics it demonstrated eloquently and conclusively that the doctrines of imitation, decorum, tradition, style, unity, and character could be deduced from sound principle. It was therefore an essential text for all aspirants to good writing and sound criticism. Byron, however, recalled unpleasantly the task of translating this critical epistle, which he described in a letter of 4 September 1811 to Dallas as "the most difficult poem in the [Latin] language" (*BLJ*, II, 90). His visit to Horace's beloved Mount Soracte in 1817, as commemorated in *Childe Harold IV*, revived an abhorrence of "The drill'd dull lesson" that had erected a barrier against his appreciation of Horace. By that time, however, he conceded that the fault had been largely his own. In the Sabine setting he was willing to acknowledge the Latin poet's distinction as a lyricist, moralist, satirist, and even a critic who could "prescribe his art" (stanzas 74–77). Occasional quotations from Horace in letters to Hobhouse and the fact that two of Hobhouse's imitations published in 1809 were Horatian suggest that this friend may have played a role in causing Byron to see the most urbane of Latin poets in a kindlier light than had Harrovian masters.[9] That he had finally grasped the essence of Horatian satire is shown by his reference to its "Awakening without wounding the touch'd heart" (*CHP* IV.77.8), but when he composed *Hints*, he still did not find the Horatian spirit highly congenial.

Although Byron probably consulted more than one translation of the *Ars Poetica* before calling his own poem finished, there is no indication that he had access to or leaned on any in Athens. The only English version of it that he is known to have owned when his library was auctioned off in 1816 was John Oldham's, contained in a two-volume edition of that poet's works. Oldham had adapted several poems by Juvenal, Horace, Martial, Ovid, and Boileau, calling them paraphrases, imitations, or allusions according to their degree of closeness to the originals. In the 1684 preface to his adaptation of the *Ars Poetica* he defended his novel device of making Horace speak as though he were living in seventeenth-century London and added: "I have been careful to avoid Stiffness, and made it my Endeavour to hit (as near as I could) the easy and familiar Way of writing which is peculiar to *Horace* in his Epistles, and was his proper Talent above any of

Mankind."[10] Oldham's imitation of the *Ars Poetica*, though much more verbose than Byron's version, is strikingly similar in its linguistic freedom. It seems more than coincidence that some of Oldham's concrete illustrations—e.g., the replacement of Horace's Rhine by the River Thames, an allusion to Billingsgate language, and "the lions of the Tower"—also appear in *Hints*. Byron, in the section justifying the coinage of new English words, cites as precedents Chaucer, Spenser, Dryden, and Pope; Oldham had cited all of them except Pope (as yet unborn) for the same illustration. Moreover, where Oldham had written "a common Dauber may, perhaps, have Skill / To paint a Tavern-Sign," Byron wrote "But daub a shipwreck like an ale-house sign" (l. 32). Since the idea of the sign does not exist at all in Horace or in Byron's Mediterranean manuscript versions, this parallel is the most conclusive evidence that Byron consulted Oldham's version after his return to England.

It may also be significant that Byron's library in 1816 contained a copy of Richard Hurd's edition of *Q. Horatii Flacci Epistolae ad Pisones, et Augustum: With an English Commentary and Notes* (1766).[11] Though Hurd offered no translation, he provided commentary succinctly outlining the principal topics discussed by Horace and extensive notes elaborating on aesthetic, philosophical, and critical doctrines. Furthermore, his introduction and an appended essay, "A Discourse on Poetical Imitation," may have contributed not only to Byron's understanding of the classical tradition but also to his interpretation of the *Ars Poetica*. In an effort to categorize Horace's *sermo epistolaris* generically, Hurd had declared the "Didactic epistle" to be "the true and proper offspring of the Satire" (I, viii). All poetry, from his Aristotelian perspective, was imitation, and every supposed original merely a copy of something that existed elsewhere; hence the function of genius was to select, rearrange, refashion, and reexpress wisely (II, 118). The objects worthy of imitation he regarded as "a common stock, which experience furnishes to all men" (II, 175). In Hurd's judgment, an "anxious dread of imitation in polite and cultivated writers" was the principal cause of "a thorough degeneracy of taste in any country" (II, 230).

Agreeing with this view, Byron believed that his contemporaries who strove to express what they believed to be the uniqueness of their experience had severed their poetry from those experiences common to all humanity and had therefore vitiated the state of letters. Rather, the creative artist's obligation was to adapt well-proven themes to his age and idiom so that through ingenious technique, form, and perspective they became the property of another creator and another society. Ideally, then, according to Byron, the classical tradition should be a flexible and evolving phenomenon—not a rigid mold but an organic development to be modified by each individual artist who shaped it to his own purposes. The general principles would remain, but if the Horatian goals of *prodesse et delectare* were to be fulfilled, specific illustrations had to be translated into their modern equivalents. Oldham had certainly modernized Horace, and Sir William Soames's adaptation of Boileau's *L'Art poétique* (1683) had shown how even a French rendition of the *Ars Poetica* could be retransplanted into an English literary setting. Pope's "Epistle to Augustus," one of two Popean imitations of Horace from which Byron actually quotes in his *Hints*, provided a more immediate precedent for bringing Horatian literary criticism into a later scene. Byron himself epitomized the classical theory of imitation as follows:

> 'Tis hard to venture where our betters fail,
> Or lend fresh interest to a twice–told tale;
> And yet perchance 'tis wiser to prefer
> A hackney'd plot, than choose a new, and err:
> Yet copy not too closely, but record
> More justly thought for thought, than word for word;
> Nor trace your prototype through narrow ways,
> But only follow where he merits praise. (*Hints*, ll. 181–88)

A comparison of these lines with the corresponding ones in the *Ars Poetica* (ll. 128–35) shows how well Byron practiced the theory he was expounding.

Such adaptation of the original is typical of Byron's best imitations in *Hints*. Several of Horace's most famous *sententiae* appear virtually unaltered, in language as succinct and pointed as Pope himself might have expressed them:

> Two objects always should the poet move
> Or one, or both, to please, or to improve.

> Fiction does best when taught to look like Truth.

As Pictures so shall Poems be. (ll. 529–30, 535, 569)

Byron's aphoristic style was perhaps even more felicitous when he permitted a freer paraphrase of the original, as in "that Bard for all is fit, / Who mingles well Instruction with his Wit" (ll. 541–42). But his adaptations were not always so successful. Sometimes when he relied on English loan words to suggest his original, the result was a distortion. When, for example, he rendered Horace's "Aut famam sequere aut sibi convenientia finge" (l. 119, "Either follow tradition or invent what is self-consistent"), he allowed the desire for structural balance to override meaning in "Or follow common fame, or forge a plot" (l. 167). In a few instances—e.g., in the assertion that Southey's "epic mountains never fail in mice" (l. 196) and in "Our Muse—like that of Thespis—kept a Cart" (l. 438)—Byron's strained attempts at wit depend upon allusions so farfetched that without the underlying Latin his meaning is lost. Overly strict adherence to Horace's arrangement of subject matter also trapped Byron in a collection of desultory topics upon which he could superimpose no unifying progression of thought.

If Byron felt obliged to leave most of Horace's maxims intact, he nevertheless allowed himself free rein in the replacement of substantiating evidence, even to the extent of exposing his personal prejudices. Where Horace had used the "obnoxious itch" as an emblem of something to be avoided, Byron substituted "the Scotch fiddle" (l. 765). Although Horace usually recommended Greek models to improve Roman taste, Byron revealed a xenophobic bias:

> An English subject for an English Muse,
> And leave to Minds which never dare invent,
> French flippancy, and German sentiment. (ll. 450–52)

Whereas Horace had endorsed new words provided that they sprang from a Greek fount and were used sparingly, Byron asserts, with more irony than approval, that "New words find credit in these latter days, / If neatly grafted on a Gallic phrase" (ll. 79–80). And Byron's animus toward Southey surfaces again in his oblique adaptation of the Horatian injunction against hasty publication:

> And print not piping hot from Southey's school,
> Who, ere another Thalaba appears,
> I trust will spare us for at least nine years. (ll. 614–16)

Nor did Byron have any qualms about letting his own predilections override his mentor's: though Horace had insisted upon wisdom, particularly moral philosophy, as the essential prerequisite for a writer, Byron cast philosophy overboard and instead advocated thorough mastery of one's topic (ll. 489–92).

Other subjective comments show Byron to have been more openly autobiographical than Horace. In the first three manuscripts of *Hints*, he called attention to his own deformity with the words "one leg perfect, and the other lame" before changing the lines to "Now this to me, I own, seems much the same / As Vulcan's feet to bear Apollo's frame" (ll. 55–56). He also parenthetically declared Tyrtaeus to have been "As lame as I am, but a better bard" before altering the line to "A limping leader, but a lofty bard" (l. 642). The attacks on Jeffrey, the *Eclectic Review*, and Methodists are, in a quite un-Horatian manner, very personal expressions of wounded pride. Brougham's initial assertion that Byron's *Hours of Idleness* represented the kind of poetry that "neither gods nor men are said to permit" caused that allusion to the *Ars Poetica* to be forever associated in Byron's mind with reviewers' "columns," and hence his adaptation in *Hints* reads: "For middling poets' miserable volumes / Are damn'd alike by gods, and men, and columns" (ll. 585–86). Also charged with personal rancor are the ironic praise of "Longman's liberal aid" and the assertion that monetary considerations govern Longman's press (ll. 545–46) because he had rejected *English Bards*. Only in playful self-raillery does Byron, either in oblique reference to himself as "Some rhyming peer,—we have several of the sort" (l. 722) or in happy reminiscences of his association with Hobhouse (ll. 339–48), approximate the ingratiating nature of Horace's autobiographical revelations.

Byron was more often successful in capturing the Horatian plain style that rhetoricians deemed most suitable to instruction. The pose of humility, whereby he facetiously undercuts his own authority ("blunt myself, [I'll] give edge to others' steel," l. 484), might be thought typically Byronic were it not strictly Horatian too. Yet Byron, posing as the bluff landed gentleman with a strong sense of public, though not necessarily private, morality, carries the modesty one step further when he asserts that from Horace he will "show the pleasing paths of song, / And from my own example—what is wrong" (ll. 487–88). Though Byron does not always achieve the "graceful negligence" that Pope found so engaging in Horace, at times his phrasing does have the casual charm of Horatian diction. He attains the relaxed air of gentlemanly causerie in the couplet, "Laughed into Lethe by some quaint Review, / Whose wit is never troublesome, till true" (ll. 35–36). Byron's translation of "Maxima pars vatum" as "The greater portion of the rhyming tribe" shows greater linguistic nonchalance than Horace ever had. Indeed Byron's "King's Coll.," "brass" (for money), and "he'll see the dog a peer" contribute to the air of a plainspoken, upper-class Englishman salting his conversation with colloquialisms. Especially in explaining the various stages of human life in terms of an English gentleman's environment, Byron achieves a conversational mode and ironical detachment:

> Launch'd into life, extinct his early fire,
> He apes the selfish prudence of his sire;
> Marries for money, chooses friends for rank,
> Buys land, and shrewdly trusts not to the Bank! (ll. 241–44)

Above all, he succeeds in creating a satiric personality that dominates the literary scene. Byron's continued fondness for this poem may have derived, as Leslie A. Marchand postulated, from the fact that "in scope and range, if not in style, the *Hints* anticipated the free form of *Don Juan*."[12] Some passages of this poem reflect a naturalness that Byron's poetry did not achieve again until *Beppo*. Though *Hints* may have been an experiment that failed, its stylistic freedom in language paved the way for future success.

By weaving in and out of the Horatian framework while contributing his own originality to the inherited material, Byron proved the vitality of the tradition he was defending. A more sensible view of linguistic evolution can hardly be presented than his:

> If you can add a little, say, why not?
> As well as William Pitt and Walter Scott;
> Since they by force of rhyme and force of lungs

Enrich'd our island's ill-united tongues;
'Tis then, and shall be, lawful to present
Reforms in writing, as in Parliament. (ll. 83–88)

In place of Horace's prescriptions on meters most suitable to particular verse forms, Byron substitutes a completely Anglicized
equivalent (ll. 105–66) emphasizing the theme of propriety
throughout. Horace's analysis of the *iambus* or light foot becomes
Byron's praise of the tetrameter couplet used by Samuel Butler
and Walter Scott (ll. 397–410). Instead of Horace's Aristarchus
as the prototype of an honest critic, Empedocles as an example
of the mad poet, Aeschylus as the outstanding tragedian, and
Homer as the archetypal epic bard, Byron cites Dr. Johnson,
Eustace Budgell, Shakespeare, and Milton. Similarly, the deus ex
machina becomes the ghost of Gothic drama. At times genial wit
so unmistakably Byronic illuminates a readapted subject, as in
the following excerpt, that one can hardly imagine the germ
of the idea had originated in the *Ars Poetica*:

Orpheus, we learn from Ovid and Lempriere,
Led all wild beasts, but women, by the ear,
And had he fiddled at the present hour,
We'd seen the lions waltzing in the Tower. (ll. 623–26)

There were, however, passages in the *Ars Poetica* for which
Byron could find no modern counterpart, and he also added a
few for which there had been no precedent in Horace. Byron
rightly deemed Horace's discussion of the dramatic chorus,
musical accompaniment, and the satyr play unadaptable to the
nineteenth-century stage. In place of it he substituted a general
criticism of contemporary drama (ll. 289–380), advocating plays
that produce "good fun" and denouncing Methodistic drama
critics. His special derision was reserved for Italian opera, which
cartoonists such as Thomas Rowlandson and James Gillray had
also satirized. As in *English Bards*, he condemned opera not just
because it seemed foreign but because it was associated with fantastic stage illusions, silliness, and alleged immorality. In one
instance Byron radically altered the tone of the *Ars Poetica*.
Whereas Horace credited a respectable, admirable Muse with
the glorious achievements of poetry (ll. 391–407), Byron blamed
a wily coquette for inspiring the prostituted literature of his day:

The Muse, like mortal females, may be woo'd,
In turn she'll seem a Paphian, or a prude;
Fierce as a bride, when first she feels—affright!
Mild as the same, upon the second night!
Her eyes beseem, her heart belies, her zone;
Ice in a crowd, and lava when alone:
Wild as the wife of alderman or peer,
Now for his Grace, and now a grenadier! (ll. 649–56)

What might seem to be a burlesque of the original is actually part of Byron's plan for bringing Horace up to date.

Although Byron at the time most of *Hints* was written had not achieved Horatian finesse, subtlety, or well-mannered control, the poem nevertheless incorporated much ingenuity of which he could justly be proud. It represented, above all, a clarification of his literary tastes and prejudices. Of necessity its low-key approach precluded the flashy rhetoric and pyrotechnics of his Juvenalian *English Bards*. Yet its casual style allowed him freedom to range over a variety of contemporary topics and helped pave the way for the more relaxed, conversational approach that would characterize his mature art.

WHILE living at the Capuchin convent in Athens, Byron was inspired by an early surge of Philhellenism to begin *The Curse of Minerva* in March 1811, though most of the poem was not completed until November, after his return to England. The immediate stimulus for this satire was the poet's firsthand acquaintance with the devastation which Thomas Bruce, seventh Earl of Elgin, had wrought in despoiling the Athenian Acropolis of its architectural sculptures so that they might be preserved in England.

Byron's earlier ridicule of Elgin's bad taste in *English Bards* had rested primarily on the assumed worthlessness of the mutilated relics. Denigrating them as "Mis-shapen monuments, and maimed antiques," Byron scoffed at their Phidian authenticity. At that time he was not alone in believing the vast expenditures of Elgin, Aberdeen, and other antiquarians to be misguided. Even though several English artists had extravagantly praised the Elgin Marbles since their first public exhibition in London in June 1807, they were a far cry from the restored classical statues that English connoisseurs were accustomed to importing from

Italy.[13] Richard Payne Knight, the most prominent art critic of
the day and a leading spokesman for the Dilettanti Society, had
publicly told Elgin in 1806 that his "overrated" marbles were not
Greek originals but Roman restorations. Subsequently Knight,
in his *Specimens of Ancient Sculpture* (1809), conceded that the
sculptures may have been executed by Greek journeymen from
Phidias's designs but still thought their artistic merit dubious.
What is more difficult to account for than Byron's aesthetic judgment in *English Bards*, however, is his personal acrimony toward
Elgin. A seemingly innocuous footnote referring to statues "with
and without noses" (for l. 1027) is actually a cruel jest at the expense of Elgin, whose face had been disfigured by the loss of his
nose. Byron apparently knew to what that loss had commonly
been attributed because later he quoted, in conversation with
Thomas Medwin, Martin A. Shee's couplet on Elgin: "Noseless
himself, he brings home noseless blocks, / To show what time has
done and what—the [pox]."[14]

After Byron had seen the results of Elgin's depredations and
heard of the means by which his agents acquired the marbles, his
indignation assumed a different form. When he wrote the note
to the Elgin stanzas (11–15) in Canto II of *Childe Harold* on
3 January 1810, he deplored that the former British ambassador's agents had destroyed, "in a vain attempt to tear down,
those works which have been the admiration of ages." If his respect for ancient architecture had increased, so too had his hatred of Elgin, whom he likened to Verres, the Roman governor
who greedily plundered Greek art in Sicily during Cicero's day.
By this time Byron also emphasized the ignominy of stealing
from a defenseless nation, and in the published text of Canto II
he expressed extraordinary contempt for "the modern Pict"
who disgraced Britannia by bearing "The last poor plunder
from a bleeding land." The original manuscript version of these
stanzas embodies some of Byron's most biting satire on Elgin and
his band of "classic Thieves." There too, though not in the printed
version, Byron alluded to the scandalous divorce proceedings
that had proved Elgin a cuckold. In a similar vein, Byron's Latin
epigram on Elgin, written at approximately the same time, jested
about the difference between Pygmalion and Elgin.[15] Whereas
the former desired a statue as his wife, the latter ravished a statue
and lost a wife.

In all these comments Byron was clearly less concerned with the aesthetic merits of the marbles than with the dubious ethics by which they had been acquired. In a letter to Prof. E. D. Clarke, a Levantine traveler who knew and detested Elgin, Byron admitted to having "little of the antique spirit, except a wish to immolate Ld. Elgin to Minerva & Nemesis" (*BLJ*, II, 157). Elgin, he realized, was cunning in taking advantage of the Turks' desire to befriend England after the French invasion of Egypt. The ambiguous Turkish firman granted Elgin's agents permission to take any stones with inscriptions or sculptures on them, but it did not license the wanton stripping of buildings such as actually occurred on the Acropolis. Moreover, the right of Turkish overlords to grant a British ambassador the antiquities of Greece seemed highly questionable.[16] Whether the marbles were by Phidias, his workmen, or later copiers, Byron was firmly convinced that they belonged to the Greek people. Lord Elgin's assumption was, of course, quite the contrary, and he feared, with some justification, that if he did not rescue the spoils for England, Napoleon's agents would secure them for his growing collections in the Louvre. Believing that neither contemporary Greeks nor Turks could be relied upon to care for the treasures of antiquity, he became virtually obsessed with the idea that it was his duty, no matter what his own financial losses might be, to preserve them for posterity and improve British taste in the arts. Hobhouse, Byron's friend and fellow traveler in Greece, also justified the plundering of Greece in the hope that these specimens of Greek sculpture would effect a renaissance of English art and architecture.[17] But in Byron's view the basic issue was not whether the marbles would be better protected in London, especially since many of them suffered irreparable damage en route, or whether more people would benefit from their being displayed there, but rather the fact that Elgin was trafficking in stolen goods. Hence his indignation at the injustice expressed itself most vehemently in a satire denouncing Elgin's barbaric exploits.

A number of circumstances brought Byron's feelings on this subject to the creative boil. Since he happened to be in Athens while the last cases of Elgin marbles were awaiting shipment, his ire was no doubt inflamed by the controversy raging there between the faction supporting Elgin's principal agent, the Neapolitan artist Giovanni Battista Lusieri, and that favoring the French consul, Louis Fauvel, who was trying to prevent shipments to England.[18] Byron was personally more intimate with Lusieri than with Fauvel; yet his sympathies lay with those who opposed removal of ancient treasures. His bias against Elgin was further heightened in Athens by renewed acquaintance with John Galt, who had written a mock epic, "The Atheniad; or the Rape of the Parthenon," the manuscript of which he lent Byron.[19] In Galt's poem the Olympian deities avenge the degradation of Minerva and her shrine by punishing Elgin ("Brucides") for his personal life as well as his neglect of official duties.[20] The account of Venus's revenge is represented by asterisks in the 1820 version and is suppressed by Juno's interdiction in the 1833 version, but the former contains an anecdote explaining how Elgin lost his nose. Having been led by Bacchus to a "stranger's bed," Elgin is followed by Cupid, who in token of venereal disease burns off the adulterer's nose, leaving him "like an antique bust." In addition to ideational similarities between Galt's "Atheniad" and Byron's *Curse*, there can be no doubt that Galt's likening of Elgin to Eratostratus, "the bold youth that fired th'Ephesian dome," became the basis, as William St. Clair has pointed out, for Byron's comparison of Elgin to "the fool that fired the Ephesian dome" (l. 201).[21]

When Byron left Greece a month after having begun his poem attacking Elgin, he sailed from Piraeus to Malta on the same ship that carried Lusieri and the last large consignment of Parthenon marbles. Having been asked to relay a letter from Lusieri to Lord Elgin, he had an opportunity to meet Elgin, who was eager for firsthand accounts of his Athenian agent, but Byron evidently chose not to do so. On 31 July 1811 Byron wrote Hobhouse: "Lord Elgin has been teazing to see me these last four days, I wrote to him at his request all I knew about his robberies, & at last have written to say that as it is my intention to publish (in Childe Harold) on that topic, I thought proper since he insisted on seeing me to give him notice, that he might not have an opportunity of accusing me of double dealing afterwards" (*BLJ*, II, 65–66).

Because the second manuscript of *The Curse* bears the date 17 November 1811 and because certain references in the latter part of the poem allude to events that occurred between June and December, as McGann has shown (*CPW*, I, 445–46), Byron probably completed his poem about the time he wrote Hobhouse (17 November) that it was intended to be part of the "monstrous vol. of Crown Octavo" including *Hints from Horace* and the fifth edition of *English Bards* (*BLJ*, II, 131). With the cancellation of *English Bards* that collection came to nought. According to Moore, Byron subsequently withdrew *The Curse* because of "a friendly remonstrance from Lord Elgin, or some of his connexions."[22] Byron apparently told Edward Everett in 1815 that his "satire upon Lord Elgin" would never "be given to the World" because a particular friend of Elgin's had asked that it be suppressed.[23] Nevertheless, at the same time that *Childe Harold* was being printed, Byron had Murray's printer, Thomas Davison, set up *The Curse* in type so that by 27 May 1812 he had eight copies of the latter for private distribution among his close friends (*BLJ*, II, 178). For the next edition of *Childe Harold*, Byron requested that the opening lines of *The Curse*, under the title of "A Fragment," be included as one of several short pieces,[24] and Murray agreed. Yet these "floating" lines were withdrawn before the next edition of *Childe Harold* could be run off, and they were used later to begin the third canto of *The Corsair* (1814). In April 1815, however, there appeared in the *New Monthly Magazine*, to Byron's vexation, a garbled and abbreviated version of *The Curse*, probably based on one of the privately printed copies. The first complete piracy also appeared in 1815 with the Philadelphia imprint of De Silver. Despite other piratical editions, Byron never again authorized a printing of *The Curse*, and about the time when the artistic and political tide had turned in favor of the British government's purchase of the Elgin marbles, he wrote to Murray disowning the poem, especially in that "miserable & villainous copy in the Mag[azine]."[25] Whatever his reasons for suppressing the work, he apparently did not recant in his attitude toward Elgin's deeds. In his first reply to William Lisle Bowles (*Letter to ****** [John Murray]*, dated 7 February 1821) he reaffirmed his original position: "I opposed, and will ever oppose, the robbery of ruins from Athens, to instruct the English in sculpture" (*LJ*, V, 547).

The Curse of Minerva expresses far more, however, than Byron's opposition to Elgin's deeds; the words of both the vengeful goddess and the English traveler enunciate the poet's strong convictions about retributive justice. Despite the eclipse suffered by the other Olympian deities, Nemesis is obviously still powerful. Byron sees the personal misfortunes that have already befallen

Elgin—the scandal of his divorce, the loss of his wife, and his son's epilepsy—as well-deserved punishment for his guilt and predicts public contempt for his efforts to profiteer on his "pilfer'd prey." The emphasis on Elgin's Scottishness as an evil influence undoubtedly reflects Byron's own bias, as well as the kind of general condemnation of Scotland expressed in Churchill's *Prophecy of Famine*. It also suggests that Byron may not have completely forgiven Jeffrey or the *Edinburgh Review* and still felt a desire to even that score. But the English persona's attempt to pin Elgin's mean, sophistic, and mercenary traits on Scotland alone is rejected by Minerva, through whom Byron then widens the scope of his attack to encompass current British foreign policy. The poem concludes with the prophecy that the ruin Britain has visited on others in her quest for "lawless gain" will ultimately redound to herself and her "tyrant empire." Unfortunately, Byron felt too intensely about these matters to convert Minerva's diatribe into properly distanced satire. His subjective fervor, expressed in turgid oratory, is unleavened by either cleverness or humor.

Despite the lack of epigrammatic wit that enlivens some of Byron's earlier works, this poem improves upon its predecessors in other respects. It is better unified than previous satires: it concentrates on two related objects of attack, Elgin and Britain, and the preliminary meditation and ensuing dialogue are contained within a limited time-space framework. Although Byron's earliest manuscript version shows that he initially conceived of the meditation as less "real" than the dialogue ("But soon a vision, if it bear the name / Recalled me back to truth"—canceled ll. 63–64), he evidently realized that "visionary truth" involved a contradiction that would undermine his theory of satire. He therefore eliminated it and, in so doing, further tightened the structure. Even the highly romantic description of sunset witnessed from the Acropolis is not incompatible with satire, for, as Gleckner has observed, the gradual extinction of light over the ruins symbolizes not only Greek decline but two other declines to be prophesied by Minerva.[26] According to Byron's cyclical interpretation of history, the paradigm of Greek rise, fall, and possible revival is one that nations undergo. Thus the introductory elegy to the glories of ancient Athens serves not only to recall the brilliant light of Greek civilization, Athenian freedom, and Socrates. It also emphasizes the radical difference between *then* and *now*; for Apollo's altars are no longer respected, Greece's enslaved sons are inferior to their ingenious ancestors, and even Minerva appears as a battered wreck in the ruins of her own temple. Under such deplorable conditions, only the poet's imagination revives the greatness of the past.

The Curse also marks technical advances in the use of two personae who confront one another and, through them, in the presentation of different perspectives on the truths with which Byron wanted to deal. The products of Greek intellect in ancient days are seen to be as real as the present-day ruin of Greece; the power of Minerva to inspire her native sons in both wisdom and the arts of war is as irrefutable as her inability to prevent the spoliation of her holiest shrine. Her ultimate authority is such, though, that just as her patronage of the Greeks was able to inspire intellectual and military achievement, her withdrawal of support from the British nation will result in another inescapable reality. The first persona, an English traveler, comprehends these undeniable truths and retains them in a state of paradoxical irresolution, but he has only a narrow view of his own complicity in Greece's despoilment, even though England has become the repository of the Greek treasures. Minerva, the adversarial persona, considers the Englishman's refusal to acknowledge Elgin as a compatriot to be mere hairsplitting and condemns all of Britain for this and other imperialistic misdeeds. Though Byron was unable to handle these divergent viewpoints on reality involving past, present, and future as adroitly as in his later ottava rima satires, his experiment in *The Curse* is an important step toward the management of more complex ironies.

THE PHENOMENAL reception accorded *Childe Harold* in the spring of 1812 thrust Byron into social and political prominence at the same time that waltzing became the rage of fashionable English society. Though Byron asserted in *Waltz: An Apostrophic Hymn* that the popular German dance had been imported into England about the time of Austerlitz (1805), James Gillray's cartoon *Waltzer au Mouchoir* (1800) indicates a slightly earlier immigration date. Gillray's *Le Walsel: Le Bon Genre* (1810) suggests that, within a decade, the dance had climbed the social ladder without losing any of the vulgarity originally associated

with it. In every country into which it had been introduced, however, there were outcries against its lasciviousness, and in *Waltz*
Byron recalled not only Werther's moral qualms about its seduc-
tiveness but also Madame Genlis's proscription of the dance from
Parisian ballrooms (ll. 147–52). As early as *English Bards* (1809),
Byron had ridiculed "thin-clad daughters" leaping in the "loose
waltz" (l. 661), and R. B. Sheridan, in two short poems—"The
Walse" and "The Waltz," the latter of which can be dated about
1811—expressed a tone very similar to Byron's. Yet by the time of
Jane Austen's *Emma*, written in 1814–15, the proper landed gen-
try evidently considered a domesticated variety known as "country dance waltzing" to be highly respectable.[27]

The shift in attitude toward the waltz resulted largely from its
popularity in court circles. It became generally acceptable
through the patronage of the Prince of Wales, who upon becoming permanent Regent in February 1812 openly forsook whatever traditional values he may have retained, along with his
Whig friends, and dedicated himself to pleasure with the abandon of a voluptuary hurling himself into the dance. A craving
for novelty, as Byron asserted in *Waltz*, characterized the times,
and the Prince's innovative reign brought new military uniforms,
new laws, a new government, new coins, new wars, new victories,
and new mistresses (however old). As a result, "Morals and min-
uets, Virtue and her stays, / And tell-tale Powder" were all passé
(ll. 161–83). If the Whigs and old-fashioned respectability were
out, the Regent and the waltz were clearly in.

Lady Caroline Lamb, who shared the Prince's love of waltzing
and was eager to be in the vanguard of fashion, held morning
waltzing parties at Melbourne House in 1812, and at one of
these, on 25 March, Byron first met his future wife, Annabella
Milbanke, who impressed him by not participating. When he
soon afterwards formed a liaison with Lady Caroline, he insisted
that she was not to waltz.[28] Whatever the rationale, he evidently
associated that German dance with disreputable behavior, and
his only objection to Bessy Rawdon, with whom he became
friendly at Cheltenham during the autumn of 1812, was that she
waltzed (*BLJ*, II, 216). He pointedly inquired of Lady Melbourne whether her niece, Miss Milbanke, ever waltzed, adding:
"It is an odd question—but a very essential point with me" (*BLJ*,
II, 218).

Byron's intense dislike of waltzing probably stemmed from several causes. No doubt its intoxicating gyrations, which required smooth shifting of weight in what he himself termed "slippery steps," posed difficulties for the lame poet that precluded successful participation. What Marchand has called "prurient Puritanism" may also have been behind his antipathy.[29] But the chief reason for the antagonism expressed in his poem was that the waltz symbolized the meretricious spirit of the early Regency. After long years of devotion to the Prince, the Whigs found themselves perfidiously rejected by him the moment he had the power to be of assistance. Hence Byron and his Whig friends had no qualms about retaliating against the political and social world dominated by Carlton House and polluted by a gross old libertine with German connections. The waltz, then, became merely the latest symptom of Germanizing influences that, under the auspices of the Hanoverian royal family, had infected English cultural and social life.

In August of 1812, when Byron went to the fashionable spa of Cheltenham—primarily to be among distinguished Whig friends such as the Hollands, Melbournes, Jerseys, and Moira connections—waltzing must have been an integral part of the social life. His comments on the dance were the inevitable outgrowth of that aristocratic milieu. After the Hollands returned to London in early September, Byron moved into their Cheltenham house and in the subsequent weeks there composed *Waltz*. On 17 October he wrote from Cheltenham that he was making Murray a present of his new poem, allegedly in the style of *English Bards*, but stipulated that it had to be published anonymously. On 23 October he informed Murray that the new satire had grown to somewhat more than 200 lines and also contained "an introductory letter to the Publisher" (*BLJ*, II, 228–29, 234).

When Byron claimed that *Waltz* was in the style of *English Bards*, he probably meant to place it within the Popean tradition of mocking couplets and caustic footnotes. Curiously enough, although critics had bestowed lavish praise on the Spenserian stanzas of *Childe Harold's Pilgrimage* in 1812, he tried repeatedly to return to the couplet form that he had previously considered his forte. Several poems dating from the autumn of 1812—his "Address, Spoken at the Opening of Drury-lane Theatre," the "Parenthetical Address, by Dr. Plagiary," eight imitations of epigrams by Martial, and "[Verses on W. J. Fitzgerald]"—all show him struggling to achieve the succinctness and pointedness essential to couplet form. Even so, Byron was obviously aware of the shift in his poetic directions, for after laboring on revisions in his Drury Lane Address and while embarking on his *Waltz*, he wrote Lord Holland from Cheltenham: "Latterly I can weave a nine line stanza faster than a couplet, for which measure I have not the cunning."[30]

Since the poetical portion of *Waltz* does not completely emerge as the dramatic utterance of the persona developed by the prefatory letter, it seems likely that Byron added the introduction as an afterthought in order to create a fictitious author and explain, in retrospect, how circumstances had called the poem into being.[31] The character of Horace Hornem, in addition to intimating cuckoldry through his surname, harks back to William Wycherley's Horner, as well as a host of country gentlemen depicted by Henry Fielding, Tobias Smollett, and Oliver Goldsmith, and is reminiscent of the "True Briton" who served as Byron's persona in *Hints from Horace*. Surely the name Horace suggests the Sabine farmer and Roman satirist who preferred the simple rural life and, as his Satire I.2 suggests, enunciated a practical, rather than an ethical, code of sexual conduct. If the Roman Horace could recommend greater satisfaction from consorting with unattached rather than married women, then Horace Hornem could invoke an equally utilitarian ethic about the gratifications and genealogical benefits of the waltz. His own domestic tranquility had not been threatened by the dance until his wife and daughters insisted upon spending the winter in London. There he was horrified to discover at a ball that his wife's arms were "half round the loins of a huge hussar-looking gentleman," and that in this state of unabashed intimacy they went through dizzying motions that evidently served as an aphrodisiac. Yet once he himself became acquainted with the pleasures of waltzing, especially by overturning his wife's maid while practicing, he developed such admiration for it that he composed a hymn in its honor.

The epistolary introduction, in conjunction with the poem's conclusion, sweeps away any moral norm that might have existed, for the persona admits that, having sacrificed principle to pleasure, he is among the worst of sinners. According to the usual canons of satire, Byron might be said to have cut the ground from under himself. Indeed Robert D. Hume has argued "that as a satire the poem is distinctly ambiguous and that its technique foreshadows that of *Don Juan.*"[32] The apparent inconsistency results mainly from the ambivalence of the persona, who has gone from prudery to debauchery without becoming totally reconciled to the latter state. Yet herein is perhaps the cleverest aspect of the work—in showing the evil of the waltz to be so absolutely overwhelming that even the persona, an honest country gentleman of conservative nature, is swept away in three-quarter tempo, so corrupted by its influence that he rationalizes its benefits in order to continue its delights. The more involved he becomes with his subject, the more he becomes, ironically, the butt of his own satire. Only in the penultimate paragraph (ll. 230–47), in a decided wrenching of tone, does the persona emerge from behind his mask to become solemnly didactic, as though his conscience had temporarily been restored. Yet the conclusion returns, ever more strongly because of the preceding contrast, to ironic praise of the waltz as license for promiscuity.

Despite many humorous touches, however, the poem does not fully utilize the possibilities for comedy that might have been achieved through the perspective of a country squire observing the *haut ton* of court balls. As a depiction of social rituals gone awry, it actually resembles some of the satiric accounts in *Childe Harold*, such as the desecration of the Sabbath through Spanish bullfighting or English pleasure-seeking. As a mock-encomium, *Waltz* also recalls *Childe Harold* in the use of apostrophic techniques, though the former applies them negatively. Indeed it opens with three ironic apostrophes—to Terpsichore, patroness of the dance; to her "not too lawfully begotten" daughter, Waltz; and to the land of the latter's birth—before providing an account of the personified dance and her insinuating conquest of England. Waltz, in some ways comparable to Pope's personified Dulness triumphing over all, is ultimately embodied as a seductive prostitute who, through royal patronage, has reached the top of the social scale and is coarsening the fiber of the entire nation.

Some of the satire in *Waltz*, as William Childers has pointed out, is directed against the Germans who, in the eyes of many Englishmen, seemed to be corrupting English morality, literature, music, and society.[33] Hornem is conscious of this German impact not only in the outlandish name of Wilhelmina given an English child in honor of a German princess but also in the German pronunciation of "valtzing" that he encounters in London. All the popular German imports, the poet implies, have a debasing effect, whether they are musical compositions, pedantry, or August Kotzebue's dramas. But whereas German hock inspires only the head, Waltz awakens all one's limbs to wantonness. What makes this German influx all the more difficult to bear is that it has infiltrated the highest levels of court society. The royal Georges, whom Byron repeatedly called "Guelfs," were not far removed from Hanover. Their German wives and visiting relatives with unpronounceable titles, as well as those relatives' predilection for gaudy attire and German food, had often inspired Gillray's vicious caricature of unrefined, un-English ways. Since this German scourge had to be countenanced wherever the royal family was involved, one can understand Byron's ironic tribute

> To Germany, and Highnesses serene,
> Who owe us millions—don't we owe the Queen?
> To Germany, what owe we not besides?
> So oft bestowing Brunswickers and brides;
> Who paid for vulgar with her royal blood,
> Drawn from the stem of each Teutonic stud;
> Who sent us—so be pardoned all her faults,
> A dozen Dukes—some Kings—a Queen—and 'Waltz.'
>
> (ll. 47–54)

Byron's poem also reflects his growing political involvement at a time when the Whigs, upon realizing that the Prince had for the second time prevented their return to office, turned upon their surrogate monarch with unusual ferocity in order to discredit him.[34] The Regent's preference for married women who were "fat, fair, and forty," as well as his penchant for waltzing in military uniform (complete with boots and spurs), was well known.[35] In view of what ultimately happened to John and Leigh Hunt for publishing a libel on the Regent in their *Examiner*, Byron's direct address in *Waltz* was quite daring: "And thou, my Prince! whose sovereign taste and will / It is to love the lovely beldames still" (ll. 218–19). Moreover, reference to "princely paunches" and to a "hand reposing on the royal hip" (ll. 195, 197) offered an unflattering picture of the corpulent Regent as dancing partner. "The young hussar, / The whiskered votary of Waltz and war" (ll. 15–16) has usually been taken as an ironic allusion to the Regent, though it could also suggest his brother, the Duke of Cumberland, who often appeared in the regimentals of his German hussar regiment and, as a determined reactionary, was inimical to the opposition party.[36] And though the Whigs, to discredit the Prince Regent, sometimes allied themselves with the Princess of Wales, Caroline of Brunswick, they were well aware of the coarseness of her demeanor and the numerous scandals of her private life. Lady Charlotte Bury, in her *Diary of a Lady-in-Waiting*, recorded some of Princess Caroline's most ludicrous assaults on idiomatic English and observed that at fancy dress balls she (like the women in Byron's *Waltz*) was almost indecently clad. Byron's mention in a footnote of the "delicate Investigation" into cuckoldry in *The Merry Wives of Windsor* is an undoubted reference to the 1806 inquiry (actually called "the Delicate Investigation") into the Princess's adopted son, William Austin, who was rumored to be her illegitimate child (*CPW*, III, 402). A footnote allusion to Lord Yarmouth, in red as a "favourite," and now a "*favourite's*, colour" (*CPW*, III, 400–401), also struck dangerously close to the royal family because Yarmouth's mother, Lady Hertford, was then the Prince's reigning mistress and the Whigs had tried unsuccessfully in 1812 to dislodge the Hertfords from the royal household.

The power such people were capable of wielding determined to some extent the kind of satire *Waltz* had to be if it was to avoid charges of libel. Its attacks on the *beau monde* at play are therefore cast in an ironic mold, such that outrageous acclaim replaces the intended censure. The fallen Hornem, having himself been overturned through waltzing, becomes an appropriate character to demonstrate the inversion of traditional values. Thus Byron exalts the base and trivial, employing satiric techniques associated with the mock-heroic, and praises the personified Waltz in extravagant apostrophes and hyperboles justified by all the wrong reasons. In some instances his exaggerations collapse under their own weight; in others a tonal wrenching or an inappropriate analogy ironically undermines the compliment:

Not soft Herodias, when, with winning tread,
Her nimble feet danced off another's head;
Not Cleopatra on her galley's deck,
Displayed so much of *leg*, or more of *neck*,
Than thou, ambrosial Waltz. (ll. 87–91)

Praise of the Regent and his social set, if less flamboyant, is equally ludicrous in calling attention to scandals and penchants they did not want advertised. But it is primarily through subtle derogation of a newly fashionable dance—one Byron suspected of encouraging immorality, like the Regent himself, under cover of polite rituals—that the poem carries out its oblique attack on the debauchery of the Hanoverian royal family.

Since John Murray was always fearful of attacks on the Establishment, he was predictably hesitant about publishing *Waltz*.[37] The imprint for the first set of proofs actually bore the names of Murray and his printer S. Gosnell, but successive proofs indicate that the publisher decided not to have his name attached to this anonymous squib.[38] When *Waltz* appeared in February 1813, it bore only the names of Gosnell and the booksellers Sherwood, Neely, and Jones of Paternoster Row.[39] The poem received little critical attention—and that mostly unfavorable. The reviewer in the *Satirist* belittled the poem's literary merit and called attention to its political thrusts against Wellesley, Wellington, William Pitt, and the royal family.[40] An unequivocal warning appeared in the review by the *British Critic*.[41] Accusing the anonymous poet of "going out of his way to satirize" Wellington "and other persons whom it would have been much more proper not to have introduced," the reviewer suggested that the author was "not perhaps aware that political discontent is a crime as dangerous to encourage, as indecency."

Byron's fears that he might be prosecuted should his authorship be established were not unfounded. As Childers has shown, in September 1812 the Regent's private secretary, Colonel John McMahon, suspected Byron of providing libels on the Prince for the leading Whig newspaper, the *Morning Chronicle*, and promised the Regent to take action against any recurrence.[42] It is unlikely that Byron would have disclaimed such a witty, rollicking production as *Waltz* had there not been good reason to do so. In a letter of 21 April 1813 he denied rumors that he had written "a certain malicious publication on Waltzing" and instructed Murray to do the same (*BLJ*, III, 41).

M ANY of Byron's satires composed during his residence in London reflect the political, social, and personal turmoil of his life there. Often they are so charged with the poet's antipathies that they lack the equanimity characteristic of the most skillful satiric art. Even so, these productions of lesser quality provide insight into Byron's poetic development, particularly when considered against the background that inspired them.

Byron's early hopes for a Parliamentary career under Whig auspices gradually faded, but his contempt for the Regent did not diminish. In fact, his growing friendship with Moore, as well as with Leigh Hunt later, strengthened a shared antipathy toward the Prince and his Tory followers. (Although Fuess accused Byron of "double-dealing" in his cordiality to the acting monarch at a ball in June 1812 and of being flattered into a favorable impression, one must realize that the Prince was at times capable of displaying great cultivation and, additionally, that in the social circles in which Byron then wished to move it was necessary to be gracious to him.)[43] The trial and conviction of the Hunts for libeling the Prince in 1812 proved that acknowledged frontal attacks on him would not be tolerated. Yet the popular success of Moore's pseudonymous *Intercepted Letters, or the Twopenny Post-Bag* (1813), which went through twelve unhindered editions in its first year of publication, also showed that satire on the Carlton House coterie, including Col. McMahon, might be carried out with impunity provided it was clever, gossipy, and reasonably playful. Byron certainly understood the distinction, and on 19 May 1813, the day before being taken to meet Leigh Hunt in the Surrey Gaol, he wrote in a poetic epistle to Moore:

> To-morrow be with me, as soon as you can, sir,
> All ready and dress'd for proceeding to spunge on
> (According to compact) the wit in the dungeon—
> Pray Phoebus at length our political malice
> May not get us lodgings within the same palace! (*BLJ*, III, 49)

Apart from the Prince's scandalous amours, mistreatment of two wives, sybaritic extravagance, and gross appearance (all of

which Moore and Hunt had touched upon), the Parliamentary
Whigs were unable to forgive his perfidy. The Opposition had
long supported the Prince of Wales's self-indulgence, largely in
anticipation of political rewards when he officially came into un-
restricted power as Regent, and peremptorily rejected his proposal of a coalition government in mid-February 1812. The result was continuance of a completely Tory cabinet. The Prince
selected the occasion of his Carlton House banquet on 22 February to level such a scurrilous tirade against his former Whig sup-
porters, by whom he fancied himself monstrously abused, that
Princess Charlotte burst into tears. In an eight-line poem entitled "Lines to a Lady Weeping," Byron immortalized the scene
that resulted in the first open rupture between Whigs and the
Prince, denouncing the Regent but expressing confidence that
Princess Charlotte would succeed in effecting future amelioration. These lines, which appeared anonymously as "Sympathetic
Address to a Young Lady" in the Whig *Morning Chronicle* on
7 March, were not acknowledged by the poet until 1814, when
they were appended, with five other poems, to the earliest issue
of *The Corsair*.[44]

Immediately after the republication of Byron's "Lines" with
The Corsair on 1 February 1814, Tory newspapers began a violent
outcry protesting that a peer, a hereditary councillor of the
realm, should for the sake of party favor abuse the royal heir apparent in such manner.[45] But except for references to "A Sire's
disgrace, a realm's decay" and the expressed hope that tears
might "wash a father's fault away," there is nothing personally
derogatory in the poem. Indeed the tribute to Princess Charlotte's virtue and the patriotic belief that her people's smiles will
repay her tears more than compensate for the affront to her father. Byron had not feared to divulge his authorship because the
lines contained nothing that could be construed as a threat to the
monarchy; and the Regent, upon learning that the lines were
Byron's and not Moore's, as he had previously suspected, was
hurt rather than angered (*BLJ*, IV, 51). Even so, Murray, ready
as ever to turn political scandal into financial gain, had already
canceled the six poems from the enormously vendible *Corsair*
volume and proposed transferring them to his forthcoming seventh edition of *Childe Harold*.[46] Byron, however, assumed that
"Tory Murray" was yielding to protest and argued that such a

transfer would look "like shrinking & shuffling—after the fuss" the Tories had made about his "Lines." At the poet's insistence they were restored to their original position in subsequent editions of the *Corsair* volume.

Far more defamatory is Byron's ghoulish account of how the Prince, in an effort to determine precisely where Charles I was buried at Windsor, superintended the exhumation of Henry VIII's remains on 1 April 1813. Byron wrote several versions of an epigram commemorating the event and sent one in his letter of 7 April to Lady Melbourne, adding that she might give it to Lord Holland or anyone else.[47] The poem asserts fancifully that Charles's civil tyranny and Henry's domestic tyranny have been combined and revived in the Prince Regent (the "double tyrant"), who now comes to life as a vampire because the grave cannot prevent his royal predecessors from creating another of their own kind. Though Byron would not have dared publish this treasonable poem, he apparently feared no harm from private circulation, especially since he was planning to leave England again. Yet it apparently circulated more widely than anticipated, for on 12 March 1814 he wrote Moore: "I cannot conceive how the *Vault* has got about,—but so it is. It is too *farouche*; but, truth to say, my satires are not very playful" (*BLJ*, IV, 80). Concerning his plans for further ridicule of the Prince, he added in the same letter: "I have the plan of an epistle in my head, *at* him and *to* him. . . . As to mirth and ridicule, that is out of my way; but I have a tolerable fund of sternness and contempt, and, with Juvenal before me, I shall perhaps read him a lecture he has not lately heard in the C——t [Cabinet]."

Another political squib, less denunciatory only because less specific, is the two-line epigram entitled "Ich Dien," which laments the discrepancy between the Prince of Wales's heraldic motto and his actual practice of demanding that his country serve *him*. But the "Condolatory Address to Sarah, Countess of Jersey, on the Prince Regent's Returning Her Picture to Mrs. Mee" contains far more explicit gibes. Intended as a private missive, this poem was actually sent by Byron, as a friend, to the Prince's eclipsed mistress on 29 May 1814. Presumably passed along to the press by a domestic, it was printed with the poet's name (though without his permission) in the Tory *Champion* on 31 July 1814, and on the following day the Whig *Morning Chron-*

icle quoted it. Therein Byron assures the Countess that she has lost nothing in being jilted by "that vain old man," who at fifty-two still regarded himself as an irresistible lover. The poet's further description of the Prince as "Heir of his father's crown, and of his wits" has an especially malicious sting in view of George III's insanity. But the most devastating charge of all—that the Prince's behavior as a lover is consistent with his political despotism—is saved for the conclusion:

> That dull cold sensualist, whose sickly eye
> In envious dimness pass'd thy portrait by;
> Who rack'd his little spirit to combine
> Its hate of *Freedom's* loveliness, and *thine*. (ll. 47–50)

Yet Byron blamed the debased condition of politics not solely upon the selfish desires of the Prince and his Tory ministers but also upon the apathy of people in general. He wrote Lady Melbourne on 21 September 1813: "At Bugden I blundered on a Bishop—the Bishop put me in mind of ye Government—the Government of the Governed—& the governed of their *indifference* towards their governors which you must have remarked as to all *parties*" (*BLJ*, III, 117). Into that letter he incorporated a satiric poem deploring the political inertia into which his countrymen had fallen:

> 'Tis said—*Indifference* marks the present time
> Then hear the reason—though 'tis told in rhyme—
> A King who *can't*—a Prince of Wales who *don't*—
> Patriots who *shan't*—Ministers who *won't*—
> What matters who are *in* or *out* of place
> The *Mad*—the *Bad*—the *Useless*—or the *Base*?

For his last satire written during the London period, Byron turned from political criticism to censure of a purely personal nature. Unfortunately the poem, though unrivaled for genuine rancor and invective, deteriorates into name-calling. Directed against Lady Byron's former governess, Mary Anne Clermont, whom he regarded as a female Iago and blamed for many of the difficulties with his wife, "A Sketch from Private Life" was completed in draft form on 30 March 1816. On the same day Byron requested that Murray have fifty copies of it struck off "for *private distribution*" (*BLJ*, V, 58), since he was evidently determined to have his friends see Lady Byron's housekeeper as the one who, because of meddling and snooping, was largely responsible for the marital rupture. In a letter of 10 April to Lady Byron, the poet, after reiterating many of his charges against the informant whom his wife had introduced into their London home, assumed the voice of a Hebrew prophet and pronounced his curse upon the troublemaker (*BLJ*, V, 62–64). Meanwhile the privately printed copies of "A Sketch," along with others of "Fare Thee Well," did in fact circulate for almost two weeks before finding their way, presumably without the poet's authorization, into London newspapers eager to capitalize on the Byron domestic scandal.

Publication of "A Sketch" brought a storm of abuse down on Byron and vastly reduced his popularity during his last days in England. True though his accusations may have been, his image as a liberal peer was not enhanced by sneers about the former governess's humble origins ("Born in the garret, in the kitchen bred"). He was unable to see any good in someone who interpreted loyalty to her mistress as implacable hostility toward him. The reptile and insect imagery marks her as an untrustworthy creature whose petty concept of virtue has made her vicious:

> Quick with the tale, and ready with the lie—
> The genial confidante, and general spy. (ll. 9–10)

As a result of Byron's bold depiction, Mrs. Clermont emerges as the epitome of a venomous, unforgiving woman. Murray, after showing "A Sketch" to Samuel Rogers, Stratford Canning, and John Hookham Frere, assured Byron: "You have produced nothing better; . . . satire is your forte; and so in each class as you choose to adopt it."[48] Though Byron's abuse has generally been deemed excessive, his passionate hatred undoubtedly helped to fuse thought with feeling in succinct, epigrammatic couplets.

One other poem of this period deserves special attention, not because of outstanding achievement but because of its attempt to break new ground. Apparently Byron did not take "The Devil's Drive," dated 8 December 1813 in draft form, seriously enough to polish it or even complete it for publication. In his Journal of

1813–14 he described it with reasonable accuracy as "a wild, rambling, unfinished rhapsody."[49] Instead of the usual heroic couplets, the poem employs a much freer verse form—lines of variant length, irregular stanzas, original rhyming combinations, and a jaunty meter combining iambs and anapests. Desultory though the organization appears to be, the topics are loosely strung together by the devil's sightseeing itinerary, much as Byron's observations had been connected by Harold's travels and later would be by Juan's. Admittedly, many of the satiric objects—the Prince Regent and his sycophants, "the Haram so hoary," Methodists emphasizing faith to the exclusion of good works, political chicanery in Parliament, fraudulence in reviewing, and carnality in waltzing—had been ridiculed before, but here they are treated in a much lighter, sportive vein. The poem also contains Byron's first attack on the ravages of modern warfare and, significantly, foreshadows the siege of Ismail in *Don Juan*. At the battlefield of Leipzig the devil realizes that Europe's armies are doing his destructive work so well that he is not needed. The negative viewpoint allows the poet to praise ironically what he in fact deplores and, as an avowed friend of the devil (l. 232), to treat the entire satire in a cavalier fashion. In its more relaxed, conversational style and its humorous approach from an admittedly jaundiced perspective, "The Devil's Drive" signals Byron's first decided attempt to break out of the Augustan mold for a satiric poem. Flawed though its execution may be, the poem stands as a harbinger of the greater satires yet to come.

SATIRE IN A NEW VEIN: *BEPPO*

WITH the composition of *Beppo* Byron added a new and radically different dimension to his literary career. But he did so with little advance fanfare. In fact, on 15 September 1817 he wrote Murray from Venice that he was putting the final touches on Canto IV of *Childe Harold's Pilgrimage*, which he considered his greatest achievement, and that he was thinking of concluding his poetical career (*BLJ*, V, 264–65). Such a farewell to poetry, which he had uttered before, was not to be taken seriously since he had been at work on *Beppo* for the past nine days and would complete the first draft by 10 October. Yet this letter to Murray, which Gifford thought Byron's finest because of its critical enunciations, would in time assume the genuine importance of marking a watershed in Byron's development. It may well be that his veiled disappointment in Thomas Moore's long-awaited *Lalla Rookh* caused him to reiterate his conviction that "*all* of us—Scott—Southey—Wordsworth—Moore—Campbell —I—are all in the wrong—one as much as another—that we are upon a wrong revolutionary poetical system—or systems—not worth a damn in itself" (*BLJ*, V, 265). Having recently compared Moore's poems, as well as his own, with Pope's, he was firmly convinced of "the ineffable distance in point of sense—harmony— effect—and even *Imagination* Passion—& *Invention*—between the little Queen Anne's Man—& us of the lower Empire." Contemporary poetry, in his estimation, had evidently not fulfilled its promise. If he "had to begin again," he informed Murray, he would strive to imitate Pope.

The implications of this letter are more significant, however, than its reaffirmation of Pope's comparative stature. As Byron realized, he could no more start anew at almost thirty than the prevailing school of English poetry could reestablish Pope as a tutelary deity. The Popean tradition, however admirable in its own right, was dead, despite the efforts of William Gifford, George Crabbe, Samuel Rogers, and Thomas Campbell to resuscitate it. Ultimately awaking to what most of his contemporaries had earlier concluded, Byron, possibly without fully realizing the implications, was uttering an elegiac tribute to that tradition. Even though careful study of Pope might still teach one something about technical perfection, Byron's letter acknowledges that the possibility of imitating him, especially to the extent of reviving his kinds of poetry, was slight. What Byron, with his almost legalistic reliance on precedent, needed at this point was the light of another poetic tradition to guide him. Actually he had already found a new literary construct that permitted him a more complex perspective on reality. Its flexibility allowed him to combine a relaxed approach with the technical skills he had acquired through use of the formal couplet. Yet in the early autumn of 1817, he was not sufficiently sure of himself in the new mode to announce this breakthrough to his publisher.

Having been fluent in written and spoken Italian before ever arriving in Italy, he was acquainted with what Ludovico Ariosto and possibly Francesco Berni had achieved in the Italian ottava rima stanza.[1] Moreover, he had read with great care *Orlando in Roncesvalles* (1814), written by his friend John Herman Merivale in English ottava rima imitative of the last four serious cantos of Luigi Pulci's *Morgante Maggiore* (*BLJ*, IV, 12). He called Merivale's "measure . . . uncommonly well chosen & wielded," and he subjected his own first adaptation of that stanzaic form, in "Epistle to Augusta" (1816), to an equally sober treatment. Meanwhile, in May 1816, he was introduced to Giovanni Battista Casti's *Novelle Amorose* (sometimes entitled *Novelle Galanti* or even *Novelle Licenziose*). In Brussels Major Pryse Gordon gave Byron a copy of these bawdy tales in ottava rima, and the poet subsequently wrote him: "I cannot tell you what a treat your gift of Casti has been to me; I have almost got him by heart. I had read his 'Animali Parlanti,' but I think these 'Novelle' much better. I long to go to Venice to see the manners so admirably described" (*BLJ*, V, 80). Casti's light, uninhibited treatment of characters triumphing amorally over social and religious restraints was evidently highly compatible with Byron's Continental mood. But not until he encountered in Venice the first two cantos of John Hookham Frere's pseudonymous *Prospectus and Specimen of an Intended National Work* did he become aware of what could be achieved in the comic form of English ottava rima.

Frere was not only a friend of Byron but also a literary adviser of Murray, who published the mock-heroic poem purportedly by "the brothers [*frères*] Whistlecraft" in July 1817. Whether Frere's work, an imitation of Pulci's *Morgante Maggiore*, reached Byron that summer as a postal shipment from Murray (as E. H. Coleridge averred) or whether (as Marchand has suggested) it was personally conveyed to him in early September by William Stewart Rose, a friend of Frere, certainly Byron's association with Rose in Italy had an impact on the genesis of *Beppo*.[2] Byron soon became friendly with him and his Italian fiancée in Venice and in May 1818 wrote that he was "a fine fellow—and one of the few English who understand *Italy*—without which Italian is nothing" (*BLJ*, VI, 38). Rose was certainly an enthusiastic connoisseur of Italian literature and life, having anonymously published an abridged adaptation of Casti's *Animali Parlanti* as *The Court of Beasts* (1816). Fortunately his fascination with the Italian burlesque tradition coincided with and reinforced Byron's developing interest in the subject.

Byron's first mention of his new poem in that form appeared, a few weeks after its inception, in a letter of 12 October to Murray. "I have since written a poem (of 84 octave Stanzas) humourous," he announced, "in or after the excellent manner of Mr. Whistlecraft (whom I take to be Frere), on a Venetian anecdote—which amused me."[3] The anecdote, a brief account of a woman who had installed a lover in her house during her husband's absence only to have the supposedly dead spouse return, was told to Byron by Pietro Segati on 29 August, and the composition of *Beppo* was begun on 6 September.[4] By 23 October there were 89 stanzas, and Byron was declaring himself Whistlecraft's greatest admirer (*BLJ*, V, 269). When he wrote to Murray in March 1818 to prepare his publisher for the shock he might experience upon

first encountering the new Byronic mode, he further commented: "The style is not English—it is Italian—*Berni* is the
Original of *all.—Whistlecraft* was *my* immediate *model.*"[5]

Although Byron subsequently became better acquainted with
Frere's Italian prototypes—especially Pulci, Berni, and Casti—
and discovered Pulci to have been the real progenitor of that
style, the *Prospectus* (often called *The Monks and the Giants*) was all
he needed in the early autumn of 1817 to inspire the technical
innovations that he would master so superbly as to make them
appear to be his alone. Frere, having cast formal structure to the
winds and having gone so far as to advertise his planlessness,
had indulged in multiple rhymes, asides of various lengths, and
whimsical shifts of tone. He had approached Arthurian legend
not as an exalted subject but as material for good-humored burlesque in the vernacular. His use of a persona with limited education and a tradesman's practical outlook gave the story an unusual slant, for the attitude of two Whistlecraft saddlers toward
chivalric romance, very much like that of Sancho Panza, ironically undercut it with a rudely mundane perspective. Once Byron
realized the opportunities offered by this lesser poet, he needed
only to emulate them with his superior genius. Since they were
closely akin to those of a clever, gossipy raconteur and a fascinating letterwriter, he had only to adapt those skills which he had
been developing during his Continental exile to the highly flexible, almost amorphous form that Frere had mastered.

The greatest impact on his creative impulses, however, came
from the Italian environment itself, which encouraged the extraordinary liberation of his spirit that is recorded in letters detailing his observations on life there. Indeed *Beppo: A Venetian
Story* must be read as an attempt to capture the essence of Italian
life as it appeared to him after almost a year's residence in Venice. Although his overall view of Italians was far from uncritical,
at the time *Beppo* was being published he referred to the poem as
one "where I have said all the good I know or do not know of
them, and none of the harm" (*BLJ*, VI, 15). Often English authors had depicted Venice as the most wicked and licentious city
in Christendom. For instance, the prudish John Chetwode Eustace, whose *Classical Tour through Italy* (1813) Byron repeatedly
cited with disdain in Canto IV of *Childe Harold*, had deplored its

luxury, wantonness, and debauchery. Yet Byron's own appraisal of the city reflects unmitigated delight. He particularly enjoyed the Venetian dialect of Italian, with its voluptuous appeal—

> that soft bastard Latin,
> Which melts like kisses from a female mouth,
> And sounds as if it should be writ on satin. (44.1–3)

Later he would declare, in his "Reply to *Blackwood's*," that Italians were the only modern people having a poetic language (*LJ*, IV, 487). Even after having caught gonorrhea from a genteel Venetian lady during his second Carnival season, Byron continued to extol Venice as the most desirable place to live. Writing to his friend James Wedderburn Webster on 31 May 1818, he attributed this partiality to "the people the language & the habits of life" (*BLJ*, VI, 43). He warned Webster, however, that in order to find Venetians so extraordinarily pleasant it was necessary to "live with them in their own way—which is different of course from the Ultramontane in some degree." If one can believe Stendhal, Byron was also aided in his rapid adaptation to the Venetian milieu through a study of Pietro Buratti's satiric poetry and Carlo Goldoni's comedies. In Stendhal's opinion Venice was unique—"a distinct world, of which the gloomy society of the rest of Europe can form no conception," a place where "care" was "a subject of mockery" (*LJ*, III, 445). No doubt the permissive society of that city enabled Byron to discard many feelings of guilt relating to his own delinquencies, and in such an atmosphere he developed a more sophisticated view of human nature and of the human imperfections on which satire thrives.

It was not what Italians did that was so unusual but rather their more tolerant attitude toward others' peccadilloes—quite different from the English tendency to ostracize or make scapegoats of any violators of the social code. He wrote Augusta from Milan that morals there were lax and as an example cited a case of mother-and-son incest (*BLJ*, V, 125). Yet what amazed him was that the man who told him of that "Theban" connection, a highly respected citizen of Milan, "seemed to be not sufficiently scandalised by the taste or the tie." Upon settling in Venice, Byron discovered that *cicisbeism* within genteel limits was standard practice. Instead of being hypocritical or puritanical about such liaisons, as the English were inclined to be, the Venetians actually countenanced a socially acceptable polygamy allowing sexual variety. As Byron wrote Murray on 2 January 1817, "There is no convincing a woman here—that she is in the smallest degree deviating from the rule of right or the fitness of things—in having an 'Amoroso.' The great sin seems to lie in concealing it—or in having more than one" (*BLJ*, V, 156). Indeed Byron found this arrangement so compatible with his own nature that he domesticated himself in the house of a Venetian draper named Pietro Segati and became the *amoroso* of Segati's wife Marianna. Far from being jealous, Segati visited Byron and Marianna at La Mira in order to court another woman in the vicinity. What especially impressed Byron about these peculiar folkways, as many of his epistolary tales substantiate, was that the attachments of love often produced more enduring fidelity than the bonds of marriage.

Byron was exhilarated not only by the sexual tolerance and insouciance of Venice but also by the intellectual stimulus of its fascinating culture. The exotic setting was in many ways a greater catalyst to his imagination than the Levant had been. At the *conversazioni* of the Countess Albrizzi, generally dubbed "the de Staël of Italy," and of the Countess Benzoni he was able to consort with the literary and social lights of the city. In Venice he also enjoyed the theater, opera, masquerades, and the pre-Lenten Carnival. In Milan he had had the memorable experience of hearing a poetical recitation of an entire tragedy by Tommaso Sgricci, who had shown how an *improvisatore* could spur his Pegasus into what appeared to be spontaneous creativity. Byron wrote Moore that the improviser's fluency astonished him, and there is no doubt that Byron's encounter with the bardic tradition of oral poetry—differing markedly from the studied, deliberate perfection of Pope's formality—had an effect on his style.[6] It may also be significant that the heroine of Mme. de Staël's *Corinne*, which Byron certainly knew, is an *improvisatrice* who likens her extemporary poetic effusions to animated conversation stimulated, as it were, by preternatural enthusiasm.[7] Moreover, it is likely that Byron knew of the theatrical improvisation in which Venice indulged only during the Carnival season. Eustace, in his *Classical Tour*, described long farces in which "the actors seem to be obliged to have recourse to their own ingenuity for the dialogue, which, however, seldom flags for want of materials; such is their natural talent for repartee and buffoonery."[8] Making Laura's Count in *Beppo* a true Venetian, Byron designated him a patron of the *improvisatori*, as well as a poetic extemporizer in his own right.

In this generally uninhibited environment, where one was more likely to be commended than condemned for giving expression to impulses of the moment, Byron shook off his "sables" and abandoned the melancholy, manneristic style of whose monotony he, as well as his critics, had wearied.[9] *Beppo*, as he announced to Murray, would show "*the knowing ones*" (i.e., the publisher's literary consultants) that he could "write cheerfully" (*BLJ*, VI, 25). Above all, Italy had sparked in him a renewed fascination with life that is vividly recorded in his rollicking letters and animated poetry. In both of these forms he became aware of himself as a performing artist, very much like the improviser, who by means of his personality, showmanship, and unrehearsed ingenuity strove to hold his audiences spellbound through an uninterrupted, unimpeded monologue—one that appeared to have the immediacy and urgency of spontaneous creation. Moreover, his abilities, like those of the improviser, were further stimulated by interaction with his audience, since consciousness of their admiration inspired him to greater heights of impromptu discourse.

Since Murray had published a number of poetical narratives blending local color with sentiment (for example, Henry Gally Knight's *Ilderim: A Syrian Tale, Phrosyne: A Grecian Tale*, and *Alashtar: An Arabian Tale*), it is not surprising that, after reading Byron's letters, he should have requested one depicting Italians. "Give me a poem—" he wrote, "a good Venetian tale describing manners formerly from the story itself, and now from your own observations, and call it 'Marianna.'"[10] The content of *Beppo* thus had Murray's advance sanction, but Byron's diffidence about its style is obvious even from his first announcement of the poem. Though many astute critics, including Francis Jeffrey of the *Edinburgh Review*, would be quick to discern the stylistic similarities between the anonymous *Beppo* and Byron's previous works, Byron himself seemed convinced that he had taken a radical new direction. Many readers had so come to expect the lugubriousness of Childe Harold and the remorse of guilt-ridden heroes such as the Giaour, Selim, Conrad, Hugo, and Manfred that even some of his friends at first refused to believe him the author of *Beppo*.

Byron's uncertainty about how *Beppo* would be received is apparent from his offer to throw it "into the balance" in order to bring Murray round to the 2,500 guineas he was asking for Canto IV of *Childe Harold's Pilgrimage* rather than accept the 1,500 his publisher had offered (*BLJ*, V, 269). For the benefit of all concerned, he added, Murray "perhaps had better publish it anonymously." When Byron finally made a fair copy of the poem (by then grown to 95 stanzas) and sent it to Murray on 19 January 1818, he noted that it would not be suitable for Murray's proposed literary journal because of its biased political allusions. The poet insisted that it be published separately without his name, that nothing be altered, and that a scholar be employed to assure more accurate printing, especially of Italian phrases, than Murray's printer usually achieved (*BLJ*, VI, 7–8). When Byron received the proof in Venice, he was highly annoyed that some words had been inadvertently omitted, to the detriment of meter and sense, and that his slur on the Tory suspension of *habeas corpus* had been expunged.[11] His hope that Hobhouse might come to the rescue of his text may well have been realized, for Murray published the poem textually intact on 28 February.

Beppo was an instantaneous success, despite a few unfavorable notices such as those in the *Eclectic Review* and the *Monthly Review*. On 16 June 1818 Murray wrote Byron: "Mr. Frere is at length satisfied that you are the author of 'Beppo.' He had no conception that you possessed the protean talent of Shakespeare, thus to assume at will so different a character. He, and every one, continues in the same very high opinion of its great beauties. I am glad to find that you are disposed to pursue this strain, which has occasioned so much delight."[12] Not only were the 500 copies of the first edition soon sold out, but second and third editions had been printed before Byron could make some desired alterations and additions, including four new stanzas that he sent to Murray in March 1818. This tangible evidence of *Beppo*'s popularity was an especially welcome surprise, for, as Murray wrote Byron: "I have just put forth two more cantos of Whistlecraft—which the knowing ones think excellent, and of which the public think nothing, for they cannot see the drift of

it. I have not sold 500 copies of the first parts yet; and of 'Beppo'
I have sold six times that quantity in a sixth part of the time, and
before, indeed, it is generally known to be yours."[13] The fifth
edition, issued on 4 May, was the first to acknowledge Byron as
the author. By the end of the year *Beppo* had gone through seven
editions, and for the poem that Byron had merely thrown into
the bargain for *Childe Harold IV* Murray ultimately paid £525.

The only obstacle to the continued publication of *Beppo*
stemmed from Byron's frontal attack on William Sotheby as "bustling *Botherby*."[14] An entry in "Detached Thoughts" (1821–22)
indicates that the antipathy toward Sotheby dated from their
earlier acquaintance in London (*BLJ*, IX, 29). On one occasion,
when Byron was eager to pursue his own interests, Sotheby fawn-
ingly latched onto him and could be shaken off only through the
intervention of Byron's friend William Spencer. In recounting
the incident Byron used a modification of the last line from Horace's Satire I.9 to suggest similarities with the Roman work.[15]
One cannot grasp the implications of Byron's anecdote without
realizing how he cast himself in Horace's role, Sotheby as the obnoxious sycophant intent on using Horace to gain Maecenas's
favor, and Spencer as the rescuer. By projecting his own experiences into Horace's mold, Byron revealed the basis of his contempt for Sotheby's opportunism. Whether the implied Maecenas
in this case was the Drury Lane Committee or Murray, Byron evidently thought that Sotheby had pretended friendship only to
use him and then, as the diary entry records, dropped him the
moment those prospects faded.

The real catalyst for Byron's attack, however, seems to have
been an occurrence during his three-week sojourn in Rome in
the spring of 1817, when he received "an *anonymous* note containing some gratuitously impertinent remarks" on his poetry
and a copy of the *Prisoner of Chillon* volume containing derogatory marginalia (*BLJ*, V, 252–53). Sotheby, he knew, had been
one of the few Englishmen whose stay in Rome coincided with
his. Moreover, the handwriting and the affected diction of the
anonymous commentaries convinced him that they were Sotheby's. Byron was doubly indignant because he had previously recommended Sotheby's tragedy *Ivan* to the Committee at Drury
Lane Theatre (though to no avail, since it was rejected). Upon
returning to Venice, he wrote that he had seen no one in Rome

whom his publisher likely knew "except that old Blue-*bore* Sotheby—who will give a fine account of Italy in which he will be greatly assisted by his total ignorance of Italian—& yet this is the translator of Tasso" (*BLJ*, V, 229). In a subsequent letter to Murray Byron further scoffed at Sotheby as an unskilled translator of Christoph Wieland's *Oberon* (*BLJ*, V, 252). Not only did Byron regard him as personally tiresome, but he pronounced the anonymous insult "petty—mincing—paltry—dirty," as opposed to what might have been an honorable, open attack in print. Knowing that Sotheby had published a poem entitled *Saul*, Byron assumed his best mock-prophetic voice and warned: "Let him look to it—he had better have written to the Devil a criticism upon Hell-fire—I will raise him such a Samuel for his 'Saul' as will astonish him without the Witch of Endor" (*BLJ*, V, 253).

Since Byron had observed Sotheby in Italy surrounded by an insufferable entourage, he had evidence from personal experience for this highly charged lampoon in *Beppo*. Apparently Sotheby arrived in Rome accompanied by "a party of Blue-stocking Bi—women" similar to those whom he later guided "to the Abbate Morelli's at Venice—to view his Cameo" (*BLJ*, VI, 35). Such overzealous, intellectual women asking questions "in infamous Italian & villainous French" were always an abomination in Byron's eyes, and the poetical attack on Botherby suggests that, having failed in his bid for fame, Sotheby had settled for a vapid coterie of would-be intellectuals oohing and ahing over his worthless productions—

> Small "Triton of the minnows," the sublime
>   Of Mediocrity, the furious tame,
> The Echo's echo, usher of the school
> Of female wits, boy bards—in short, a fool! (73.5−8)

Aside from "Translating tongues he knows not even by letter, / And sweating plays so middling, bad were better," Sotheby (like his followers) ostentatiously assumed a professional air that was both narrow and unjustified. Byron, the professed man of the world rather than of letters, deplored this pretentiousness:

> One hates an author that's *all author*—fellows
>   In foolscap uniforms turned up with ink,

So very anxious, clever, fine, and jealous,
   One don't know what to say to them, or think,
   Unless to puff them with a pair of bellows. (75.1–5)

Thus what began as a particular personal animus culminated in the portrait of a universal type, and the technique of broadening the scope to include a whole species of frauds increased the relevance of the attack. For the satiric thrust Byron relied less upon biting words to convey his vituperation, as he had in *English Bards*, than upon ridiculous images. The result, though ostensibly good-humored, was even more devastating than labeling or name-calling.

Upon the appearance of *Beppo*, Sotheby, having had no doubt concerning the prototype for Botherby, protested to Murray, who had also served as his publisher. But Byron, claiming the right of self-defense, became increasingly indignant and fulminated to Murray: "Ask him from *me* in so many words—did he or did he not write an anonymous note at Rome . . . & let him be confronted with the note now in the possession of Mr. Hobhouse! He (Sotheby) is a vile—stupid—old Coxcomb—& if I do not weed him from the surface of the society he infests & infects—may—may—but I won't adjure a great power—for so scabby an object—as that wretched leper of literature—that *Itch* of Scribbling personified—Sotheby" (*BLJ*, VI, 24, 33). After Sotheby protested innocence to Murray with respect to the Roman missive, Byron, evidently unconvinced, again listed his objections and invited his adversary to seek redress any way he dared (*BLJ*, VI, 35–36). According to Byron's rationale, it was really Sotheby's friends, with their public lamentations and private laughter, who deserved blame, for malice was seen to lie primarily with those who identified Botherby as Sotheby. Furthermore, Byron contended, the legitimate literary world held Sotheby's "Blue-stocking Mummeries" in greater contempt than anything in print had yet suggested. However amiable and moral Sotheby himself might be, Byron felt a privately expressed obligation to expose the "wretched affectations & systematized Sophistry" of anyone with "false pretensions." Not only did he regard such individuals as "fair Game"; he felt that his "honest purpose . . . to extirpate—extinguish & eradicate" had "the blessing of God." Not even Pope, who in his "Epilogue to the Satires" asserted that he was wielding a "sacred weapon" permitted only to "Heav'n-directed hands" ("Dialogue II," ll. 205–15), had assumed a loftier mission for the satirist as divinely approved scourge.

On 23 April 1818 Byron informed Murray that if he wished to suppress *Beppo* "entirely at Mr. Sotheby's suggestion" he might do so (*BLJ*, VI, 35). But the poet, after reminding Murray that *Beppo* had been thrown gratis into a good bargain, refused to allow its publication "in a *garbled* or *mutilated state*." Subsequent editions of *Beppo* would have to include the "bustling *Botherby*" stanzas. Since Murray was able to sell Byron's poetry almost as fast as it could be printed but could scarcely give away Sotheby's collected *Tragedies* (1814) and *Ivan* (1816), the choice was not difficult. On 16 June 1818 he reassured Byron: "I have heard no word more from Mr. Sotheby; and as to my having ventured upon any alteration or omission, I should as soon have scooped one of my eyes out." [16]

A bardling such as Botherby, who could think of nothing but his own authorship, served as an excellent foil for the persona through whom Byron chose to present his vignettes of Venetian life. This narrator, "a broken Dandy," whose debts presumably drove him (like Beau Brummell and Byron's friend Scrope Davies) into Continental residence, is concerned with the arts of living, loving, dressing, eating, and talking well. Though superficial concerns are far from being his sole interest, he abides by the fashionable code of never scratching the veneer to uncover the ugliness beneath it. As a result, among Byron's works *Beppo* is perhaps most vulnerable to Goethe's charge of excessive *empeiria*, a mode of thought marked by the ultramundanity of perceptual concern. Johann Eckermann did not understand Goethe's objection until he had read *Beppo*, which in his opinion was characterized by "the predominance of a nefarious, empirical world, with which the mind that introduced it to us had in a certain measure associated itself." [17] What Eckermann failed to comprehend was the dramatic role of Byron's persona, who was meant to be not an aloof observer of a worldly society but rather an active participant in it and indeed its spokesman.

This persona relates a series of events that supposedly occurred thirty or forty years earlier, but the associational digressions that divert him reveal his inability to focus for long on any topic. He is, however, the most convincing of gossips. Though refusing to assert more than he can substantiate, he displays a mastery of innuendo. And to suggest something risqué, he resorts to double-entendre, as in reference to "carnal dishes" and "other things which may be had for asking." Since the ideals of his class demand that nothing (not even he himself) be taken very seriously, he strives to keep his commentary light and crisply flippant. An admitted snob, he draws the distinction between "mixed company" and fashionable society, which is known as "The World." At times he assumes a puritanical air, as when he declares: "And then, God knows what mischief may arise, / When Love links two young people in one fetter" (16.5–6). At other times, he combines a false naïveté with modesty:

> For my part, now, I ne'er could understand
>   Why naughty women—but I won't discuss
> A thing which is a scandal to the land,
>   I only don't see why it should be thus. (68.1–4)

The perceptive reader is expected to see through these hypocritical pretenses and ironies that serve the persona as social protection. Since by his implication we are all more or less sinners because we collaborate in polite dissembling, the poet's satire is directed not only against his persona but against all of us. One must consistently bear in mind that the persona in *Beppo*, like all of Byron's speakers, deliberately undercuts himself and therefore his own satiric authority.

Consequently there can be no absolute standards but only relative judgments, and in this respect Byronic satire makes a serious break with the neoclassical. Since no rigid code of ethics such as the Augustans presupposed can exist in the peculiar ethos of Venice, the terms "moral" and "immoral" are inapplicable in the usual senses. The narrator creates a willing suspension of belief in theoretical morality; hence judgments of right or wrong, if they are to be made at all, must be determined on the basis of individual cases, through practical consideration of benefits weighed against detriments. One might actually assert that Byron has so detached himself from any moral implication in this Venetian tale that he has ceased to be a satirist and has become a comic writer laughing at his story as well as himself.

And the narrator would corroborate such a view with his assertion that at his age he is more inclined "to laugh than scold" (79.7).
Yet while the refusal to acknowledge an absolute morality is indeed a rejection of the underpinning of Popean satire, the es-
pousal of comic detachment is largely the pose of an ironist such
as Swift would have understood. The discrepancies between different perspectives on "reality" in *Beppo* provoke laughter, but
they also expose, in a highly satirical way, the folly of restraining
the life force within externally imposed norms.

This comparative approach to morality, which causes the
reader to feel his bonds with common humanity, is especially
useful for making the satire widely acceptable, and indeed it
won the hearts of many readers who had hitherto been hostile to
Byron's poetry. The unidentified reviewer of *Beppo* in the *British
Critic* for March 1818, who had no hesitation about attributing
the anonymous poem to Byron, conceded that his august journal
had thus far "refused all commendation of our author's former
productions," but since he found in *Beppo* nothing morally objectionable, in addition to "satirical powers of no common description," he was quite willing to praise it.[18] Moreover, he asserted that since in *Beppo* the poet never directed his satirical
talent against virtue Byron might learn from this present success
not to suppose "that satire in order to be satire, should have
something sacred, or otherwise respectable, for its object." What
the pious reviewer failed to note was that the poet's ridicule,
though still directed against many of the same objects, had been
mellowed by irony, by tolerance of both man and his fallible institutions, and by comparisons that involved everyone in the satiric scene. Byron had evidently realized, in keeping with the
Horatian dictum of *solventur risu tabulae* (Satire II.1.86), that genial laughter could overwhelm barriers that were impregnable
to denunciation. Indeed, of his new approach, he had his speaker
in *Beppo* declare:

> I fear I have a little turn for Satire,
>   And yet methinks the older that one grows
> Inclines us more to laugh than scold, though Laughter
> Leaves us so doubly serious shortly after. (79.5–8)

Much of the poem's double-edged irony depends on series of
comparisons and contrasts. In each instance the speaker, unlike

most traditional satirists, refuses to assert that one aspect is all bad and the other all good but concedes rather that each has qualities to be recommended and deplored. Andrew Rutherford has probably overstated the case by claiming that *Beppo* is "based not on morality but immorality—on a hedonism which asks us to disapprove only of bores (social, intellectual, or religious) who would spoil the fun." [19] It seems to me, however, that Byron has tried to show how the practical Venetians reconcile the conflicting demands of spirit and flesh. Hence his moral norm is as slippery as the bottom of an old gondola, his praise as mixed as his blame. Venetian women, he implies, are probably no more beautiful than English women, but they seem to be so because they deliberately try to set their pulchritude off to best advantage and turn the game of love into an art. Venetian women of contemporary days are no more and no less virtuous than the unfortunate Desdemona, but Venetian husbands (if true Venetians rather than Moorish imports) would never kill a wife just because she had a lover. Instead of succumbing to the "green-eyed monster," modern Venetian husbands would resolve the situation more adroitly—simply by taking another wife—"or *another's.*" That this appraisal was an accurate representation of Venetian conduct seems certain from what Byron wrote after Segati learned of Byron's affair with his wife. "Jealousy," he informed Moore, "is not the order of the day in Venice, and daggers are out of fashion; while duels, on love matters, are unknown—at least, with the husbands" (*BLJ*, V, 166). Venetians might keep up the external appearances of marriage but seemed to be more practical than people elsewhere about respecting the necessary loopholes. In nine stanzas (41–49) Byron counterbalances his praise of Italy against his sharply qualified praise of England, and the ironic commendation of the latter further serves to emphasize the superior quality of life in the former. Turkish women are also contrasted ironically with Western European women, so that all the supposed deprivations of the "poor dear Mussul*women*"—"no romances, sermons, plays, reviews"—appear instead to make them more fortunate than their emancipated European counterparts.

The most extraordinary phenomenon of life in Venice, one on which the basic anecdote in *Beppo* rests, was the institution of *cavalier servente*. Much of the Count's behavior is evidently drawn from Byron's personal observation. The name of the title charac-

ter, as Marchand has suggested, may be a sly dig at Giuseppe
Rangone ("Beppe"), for thirty years the "serving gentleman" of
the overamorous Countess Benzoni, who at sixty had even made
some passes at Byron.[20] Whereas in most other cultures polygamy was usually a masculine diversion, it tended in Venice to be a
feminine prerogative. As the narrator observes,

> to every woman,
> (Although, God knows, it is a grievous sin,)
> 'Tis, I may say, permitted to have *two* men. (36.1–3)

With such a system often came the concomitant benefit of unusual fidelity in the man who submitted himself to being the domestic appurtenance of some *gentil donna*. Italians, Byron wrote
Moore, "have awful notions of constancy; for I have seen some
ancient figures of eighty pointed out as Amorosi of forty, fifty,
and sixty years' standing" (*BLJ*, V, 189). One of the most charming anecdotes in Byron's letters relates how a young Irish officer
named Fitzgerald became the lover of the middle-aged Mar-
chesa Castiglione but because of the Napoleonic wars was sepa-
rated from her for some twenty-five years. When he returned to
declare his undying constancy, according to Byron's account,

> The lady screamed, and exclaimed, "Who are you?" The Colonel
> [Fitzgerald] cried, "What! don't you know me? I am so and so," &c.,
> &c., &c.; till, at length, the Marchesa, mounting from reminiscence
> to reminiscence through the lovers of the intermediate twenty-five
> years, arrived at last at the recollection of her *povero* sub-lieutenant.
> She then said, "Was there ever such virtue?" (that was her very word)
> and, being now a widow, gave him apartments in her palace, rein-
> stated him in all the rights of wrong, and held him up to the admir-
> ing world as a miracle of incontinent fidelity, and the unshaken Ab-
> diel of absence. (*BLJ*, V, 147)

Similarly, the Count and Laura "made their new arrangement"
and despite an occasional squabble became

> a happy pair,
> As happy as unlawful love could make them;
> The gentleman was fond, the lady fair,
> The chains so slight, 'twas not worth while to break them:

The World beheld them with indulgent air;
  The pious only wished "the Devil take them!" (54.1–6)

While Byron's account of regulated adultery pokes gentle fun at Italians, it also satirizes the inflexibility of the marital code in his own country. When the narrator with mock-piety declares, "But Heaven preserve Old England from such courses," he merely pretends innocence about what everyone knows to exist. The same habits obtain in both countries, but the Italians are far less hypocritical in facing up to them with easy charm and social grace.

    The exuberant spirit of the Carnival dominates the atmosphere of *Beppo* in a kind of historical present, as though no other time were of equal importance. During his first Carnival season, Byron himself regarded it as an opportunity for purging the old life (his own as well as others') and establishing the new. As he wrote Murray on 2 January 1817, "The Carnival is commencing—and there is a good deal of fun here & there—besides business—for all the world are making up their intrigues for the season—changing—or going on upon a renewed lease" (*BLJ*, V, 155). In Venice the Carnival had indeed become a Christianized Saturnalia, a harvest home, and a symbolic return to the Saturnian Age of uninhibited innocence. Ironically, the narrator in *Beppo* can think of no way to restore the prelapsarian state except through inebriation. "Oh, Mirth and Innocence! Oh, Milk and Water," he apostrophizes,

> Ye happy mixtures of more happy days!
> In these sad centuries of sin and slaughter,
>   Abominable Man no more allays
> His thirst with such pure beverage. No matter,
>   I love you both, and both shall have my praise:
> Oh, for old Saturn's reign of sugar-candy!—
> Meantime I drink to your return in brandy. (st. 80)

    The function of the Carnival also has a curious parallel in the effect of the satirist's purgative art, for, as the narrator concedes, "Laughter / Leaves us so doubly serious shortly after" (79.7–8). From a purely psychological point of view, Byron seems to endorse the idea of pre-Lenten revelry as a time for abandoning

conventional restraints and for gratifying desires with impunity.
Yet the very word *Carnival* (*carne vale*) reminds merrymakers
that their celebrations will be followed by a temporary farewell
to pleasures of the flesh. Moreover, Byron's justification of the
Carnival has a strongly Blakean ring in its assumption that the
palace of moderation can best be reached via the thoroughfare
of excess, followed of course by a short driveway of renuncia-
tion. The Venetians, according to the narrator, found the ab-
stemiousness of Lent more tolerable after their overindulgence.
That the Carnival serves any valid theological function, however,
is as questionable as the skeptical satirist's tone implies:

> Some weeks before Shrove Tuesday comes about,
>   The People take their fill of recreation,
> And buy repentance, ere they grow devout. (1.3–5)

Yet here, as elsewhere in the poem, the narrator, even while indulging in jibes at religious practice, implies that Roman Catholi-
cism in Italy has not been unsound in adapting itself to the realities of human nature rather than trying to bend humanity to
religion.

By combining ironic praise with intimations of shortcomings,
Byron skillfully satirizes his two principal characters, subtly undercutting them at almost every turn. Though the Count evidently renders satisfactory service to Laura, there is something
degrading about his position as "supernumerary slave" and
something fraudulent about his supercilious air. Admittedly, he
has a genuine title; yet without adequate financial resources, he
can afford liberality only in his pleasures but never in his expenditures. However attractive Laura may find him, he is by general
consensus a coxcomb. He has labored to make himself a connoisseur of the arts, but the way he has set himself up as an arbiter of
musical performances has established him as an obnoxious critic.
While he dabbles in all the socially acceptable diversions and
hobbies, he remains a dilettante in every respect, including love:

> Then he was faithful too, as well as amorous;
>   So that no sort of female could complain,
> Although they're now and then a little clamorous,
>   He never put the pretty souls in pain;

> His heart was one of those which most enamour us,
>   Wax to receive, and marble to retain:
> He was a lover of the good old school,
> Who still become more constant as they cool. (st. 34)

But a cooling lover, like a shrinking dollar, is a diminishing asset, and there is something inherently suspect about "a perfect Cavaliero" who seems a hero to his own valet and a conceited fop to virtually everyone else. When Beppo returns, after an absence of over six years, the Count resignedly yields "pride of place" and even lends him smallclothes to wear. The fact that, according to the narrator, the Count and Beppo remain friends ever afterward is perhaps the most backhanded of compliments. It indicates that Beppo never regards his wife's lover as a menace to his happiness but only what Laura took him to be—a "vice-husband," with all that the pun on *vice* implies. In Venice three can sometimes live as cozily as two.

Laura, however, is not so distinctively Venetian as she is a particular kind of woman in upper middle-class society. Intent primarily upon gratifying her own pleasures, she has little loyalty to anything beyond herself but abides by the formalities that make a married woman's life secure and pleasant. When her husband leaves, she pretends extraordinary sorrow and later thinks of wearing widow's weeds. Yet the celibacy of widowhood is not for her, so she rationalizes moving a lover into her house on the grounds that she needs a kind of human watchdog. Nor does she worry that the reason is specious, because she has always lived in an artificial world requiring only surface justification. Though she thinks the cattiest thoughts about her friends, she outwardly engages in all the amenities of social convention. At the ridotto,

> She then surveys, condemns, but pities still
> Her dearest friends for being dressed so ill. (65.7−8)

And however critical may be her friends' thoughts concerning Laura and her *cavalier servente*, she understands precisely how far she can go without overstepping propriety. The only time she is caught off balance is when the Turk, whose stares flatter her vanity, identifies himself as Beppo. Instead of expressing delight, she reveals herself as a petulant, scolding woman whose pleasures have been abrogated by the untimely return of a husband to whose loss she had become well reconciled. Realizing that she herself has been in the wrong, she tries, by accusing Beppo of probable misdeeds in heathendom, to turn the blame upon him. Yet Laura's readjustment to marriage is rapid, for despite occasional behavior that infuriates Beppo, she makes the best of an arrangement in which her self-gratification overrides spiritual and emotional detraction. The masterful description of Laura after Beppo's return is achieved with only a few penstrokes.

The brisk, nonchalant style of *Beppo* is certainly one of its most innovative and commendable features. It is to the credit of Francis Jeffrey, who detected Byronic traits in *Beppo* and had no reason to like Byron after *English Bards and Scotch Reviewers*, that in his notice of "this extraordinary performance" in the *Edinburgh Review* for February 1818 he singled out for special praise "the matchless facility with which [the author] has cast into regular, and even difficult unification, the unmingled, unconstrained, and unselected language of the most light, familiar, and ordinary conversation."[21] Finding the poem to be distinct from both the tradition of Pope's epigrammatic wit and Butler's distorted burlesque, Jeffrey declared its "great charm" to be "in the simplicity and naturalness of the language." Though he disliked the "out-of-the-way rhymes and strange sounding words and epithets," he admired the anonymous poet's achievement, totally without poetical diction or a single inversion, of making common words fall into the right places as though by some happy fatality. Byron's manuscript shows this seeming naturalness and ease to be products of repeated revisions rather than of some lucky accident. Far from being "unconstrained" or "unselected," his language was the result of many experiments leading ultimately to choices he thought most suitable. Jeffrey might better have said that the style of *Beppo* combined some of the best technical features of the neoclassical tradition (both formal and informal) with the desired goals of Romantic style. For here certainly were what *appeared* to be "profuse strains of unpremeditated art." Whereas Wordsworth had striven to emulate the language of rustic life and Leigh Hunt the urban vernacular, Byron was determined to imitate the speech of a well-educated, articulate cosmopolite to achieve a wide variety of idioms. While Byron's language consciously includes all the fashionable affectations of the "Dandy" world, it has the advantage of fewer limitations. One feels that almost any word, out of virtually any context, might appear at any time.

That Pope's examples of technical skill contributed much to *Beppo* goes without saying. Consider, for example, the following passage:

> And Laura waited long, and wept a little,
>> And thought of wearing weeds, as well she might;
> She almost lost all appetite for victual,
>> And could not sleep with ease alone at night. (29.1−4)

The first line combines parallelism, balance, and structural alliteration with a superb sense of anticlimax. Yet the choice of language in "all appetite for victual," in contradistinction to the polished elegance of Pope's diction, debases the seriousness of tone and begins the undermining of Laura's sincerity. By the time the stanza concludes with its humorous couplet rhyming "*protect her*" with "connect her," the reader has been made aware of Laura's rationalization even though the narrator has never resorted to an outright analysis of her motive.

One of the most daring and artful uses of language to convey a meaning other than what the words themselves express occurs in the *anagnorisis* scene that shakes Laura out of her usual prepossession of spirit. Unpleasantly shocked to see Beppo just as she and her *amoroso* are going home, she suddenly realizes that her whole Carnival-like existence has, without the slightest warning, come to an abrupt halt. But her annoyance cannot be revealed directly or even conceptualized. Like a dramatist or dramatic monologuist, Byron has Laura inadvertently disclose her feelings amidst a barrage of questions—often involving broken speech patterns—that cloak with superficial chatter the unspeakable sentiments responsible for her dismay.

> "Beppo! what's your pagan name?
>> Bless me! your beard is of amazing growth!
> And how came you to keep away so long?
>> Are you not sensible 'twas very wrong?
>
> And are you *really*, *truly*, now a Turk?
>> With any other women did you wive?

> Is't true they use their fingers for a fork?
>   Well, that's the prettiest Shawl—as I'm alive!
> You'll give it me? They say you eat no pork.
>   And how so many years did you contrive
> To—Bless me! did I ever? No, I never
> Saw a man grown so yellow! How's your liver?" (91.5–92.8)

Like Pope, Byron also uses allusion in highly suggestive ways that prefigure similar practice in *Don Juan*.[22] As the heir to several European literatures, *Beppo* is rich in allusions which, capricious though they may seem, serve to aid the satiric effect by being partly inappropriate. Their function therefore is to emphasize not similarities but, again, the differences that heighten the irony. The return of Beppo travesties one of the most famous of all homecomings—that of Odysseus to Ithaca. But Laura, as the modern Penelope, has consistently entertained a practical, unsentimental view of continence and an absent husband. As the narrator snappishly observes:

> And really if a man won't let us know
> That he's alive, he's *dead*—or should be so. (35.7–8)

Though Beppo's later recounting of tall tales about his odyssey is authentically Homeric, his acceptance of his wife's lover reveals a distinct shift in morality from that of the heroic age. The contrast between what we would ordinarily expect of a man who returns "to reclaim / His wife, religion, house, and Christian name" and what actually does occur makes the conclusion of the story all the more surprising. Byron may actually have chosen the name of Beppo's wife, as Rutherford has suggested, with an ironic eye on the chaste, unattainable married woman for whom Petrarch sighed in vain.[23] Only a vestigial trace of the Avignonese Laura survives in her Venetian counterpart, who originally "was deemed a woman of the strictest principle, / So much as to be thought almost invincible" (26.7–8). "Almost" in this instance proves to be the key word. In the account of the couple's too sentimental parting, the designation of Laura as an "Adriatic Ariadne" provides another adaptation of classical myth to modern life. Laura, except possibly in her own mind, is not being deserted on the seashore by a faithless opportunist, and her devo-

tion is far from that of the mythical Ariadne. Yet knowledge that
Ariadne was found by the god Dionysus, who married her, pre-
pares the reader who recalls his Ovid for Laura's subsequent liaison with the Count.

Even more significant to the adumbration of the plot is the
narrator's deliberate misconstruction, largely with tongue in
cheek, of the tragedy of *Othello* (sts. 17–18). According to the
narrator's distortion of Shakespeare, Iago's representation of Venetian women, including Desdemona, is probably accurate and
therefore acceptable. If Desdemona did not take Cassio as her
lover, she nevertheless had every right to do so. Othello, by the
narrator's account, is totally in the wrong and consequently not a
tragic hero but a villain. Enlightened modern Venetian husbands bothered by their wives' presumed adultery would not
smother "women in a bed of feather" but would show an equal
liberation from "the matrimonial tether."

Another kind of satiric allusion in *Beppo* pokes fun at the
popular taste for superficial Oriental tales such as Byron himself
had produced and later regretted having written. More particularly it ridicules the insipid tales of Henry Gally Knight, which
Murray had published. By means of a mock-encomium exploiting the ambiguity of words like *easy*, *pretty*, and *delighting*, Byron
both characterizes and satirizes Knight's work:

> Oh! that I had the art of easy writing
>   What should be easy reading! could I scale
> Parnassus, where the Muses sit inditing
>   Those pretty poems never known to fail,
> How quickly would I print (the world delighting)
>   A Grecian, Syrian, or *Assy*rian tale;
> And sell you, mixed with western Sentimentalism,
> Some samples of the *finest Orientalism*. (st. 51)

In letters Byron was even more outspoken in his attacks on
Knight's "trash." When Murray sent him, along with his requested
tooth powder, Knight's *Phrosyne* and *Alashtar*, Byron ungrate-
fully declared that he would clean his teeth with the one and
wipe his —— with the other (*BLJ*, V, 262). Murray's request that
Byron spare Knight only provoked Byron to suggest, by means
of sly innuendoes, that the publisher must have pecuniary motives for defending such a wealthy poetaster (*BLJ*, VI, 26–29).[24]

To understand fully Byron's attack on English bluestockings, another prime target in *Beppo*, one must recognize a Popean allusion in the assertion that Turkish women "cannot read, and so don't lisp in criticism." Pope had written to Dr. Arbuthnot, undoubtedly with facetious exaggeration, that in a sense he had been born a poet—that is, he had "lisp'd in numbers"—and Byron, through oblique reference to this assertion, makes a jest about English female intellectuals, who arrogantly think they were born critics, uttering profundities even as infants. In Byron's view, Pope was justified in his daring presumption but the English bluestockings were not. Again, it is the inappropriateness of the allusion—the lack of parallelism where a parallel is suggested—that underlies the satire.

All these novel approaches to his art were fostered by the discovery of what he could achieve within the context of the comic ottava rima, which liberated his spirit, invited multiple rhymes, encouraged undisciplined divagations of thought, and provided an elastic container for virtually everything he wanted to incorporate. The stanza's sestet, permitting a variety of tempi dependent on verbal combinations, allowed the narrator to expatiate with ease on any subject and then, with a consolidating couplet, to bring all back under control. If, for example, a sestet were sentimental, the concluding couplet might either confirm or shatter the mood, possibly even curtailing its extravagance ironically with a cynical afterthought. Since categorical assertions were intolerable, sudden shifts in tone were possible without ever jarring the associational flow of thought. Thus the new poetical medium indeed made Byron the unique satirist he became through its use: it freed him to represent both the world and himself as no other form ever had. The loose structure that might have created a problem for another poet became a solution to many of Byron's artistic difficulties.

But the boldest innovation of all in *Beppo* is that which, like the sea working away at Venetian foundations, undermines the very basis of satire itself. The hedonistic and moderately devious narrator, displaying only a relative scale of values, so discredits himself that the traditional norm of satire vanishes. The story he tells involves individuals and a whole society that could never serve as positive examples for an apologue. Moreover, his digressive manner and preoccupation with trivia defy all the accepted techniques of narration; as he himself admits, "This story slips for ever through my fingers." And though the stanzaic form obviously requires considerable technical skill, Byron's adaptation of it is so breezy, with colloquial diction and sudden wrenchings of tone, that it seems the product of effortless ease. Quite understandably, therefore, it was difficult (even though Horace had asserted that his *sermones* were merely prose conversations adapted to a metrical pattern—Satire I. 4.40–65) for some readers in 1818 to accept *Beppo* as serious poetic art. Nor were they accustomed, amidst a chimerical illusion of improvisation, to hearing a poet in what seemed to be the very act of creation— much less to perceiving a narrator-commentator preempting both the center and the circumference of his artistic product. But in spite of all these obstacles to acceptance, English readers accorded it immediate acclaim even before the peremptory critics of the *Edinburgh Review* and the *British Review* assured them that, in spite of the poet and virtually in spite of itself, *Beppo* was a work of genius.

In March and April 1818, while the reception of *Beppo* was still uncertain, Byron had promised Murray that if his innovative experiment succeeded with the public he would in a year or two provide more "in the same mood."[25] But nothing came of Byron's first intention to compose a sequel depicting "the Italian way of life." On 7 July Murray inquired of him, "Have you not another lively tale like 'Beppo'?"[26] By then the infinitely more daring *Don Juan* was already under way.

CHAPTER 5

CHALLENGE AND RESPONSE IN
THE EVOLUTION OF *DON JUAN*

THE EXTRAORDINARY obstacles to the publication and acceptance of *Don Juan* served, in a Mephistophelean way, as
catalysts to the fulfillment of that work. While Byron's satiric tendencies gave impetus to its composition, the satire itself was so
offensive to many early readers that they strove to prevent the
poem's continuation. In doing so, they further convinced Byron
of their need for his corrective medicine. Having appreciated
the freedoms offered by life in Italy, he refused to believe that
puritanical elements in English society had brought about a ref-
ormation in manners, morals, or reading tastes.[1] Nor would his
Promethean spirit bow to attempts by Tory governments or the
Chancery Court, in the name of church and state, to repress
what they defined as licentious, blasphemous, and seditious publications. He also considered those friends who tried to hinder
the genesis of *Don Juan* to be either hypocritical or pusillani-
mous. Hence the more they tried to make him conform to bourgeois propriety, the more determined he became to expose the
sham of canting moralists. The louder the public objections to
his satire, the more convinced he became that England needed
his expositions of truth. Indeed the pharisaical reviewers who
condemned *Don Juan* offered an illustration of precisely what
Byron was attacking in British society, as well as an explanation
why he suddenly ceased to be the poetical idol of his day. Since
he was determined to conciliate his opposition only enough to
permit publication of *Don Juan*, an account of his struggles toward that end reveals the degree to which he valued his satiric
purpose.[2]

Byron's first allusion to the composition of *Don Juan* appears in a letter of 10 July 1818 to Murray, just seven days after he began working on it. From Venice he wrote that he had two stories, one serious, the other "ludicrous (a la Beppo) not yet finished—& in no hurry to be so" (*BLJ*, VI, 58–59). During the summer he devoted his creative efforts largely to these two poetical narratives—*Mazeppa* and *Don Juan*. Yet he was also working on his memoirs, having abandoned the autobiographical novel in which, according to Hobhouse, he had, in the manner of Florian (J. P. Claris), "adumbrated" himself as a young Spaniard named Don Julian.[3] By 6 September the first draft of the initial canto of *Don Juan*, consisting of 180 stanzas, was complete, and on 19 September Byron informed Moore that his new poem, encouraged by the success of *Beppo*, was "meant to be a little quietly facetious upon every thing" (*BLJ*, VI, 67–68). Significantly, it was to Moore, whose reputation for lascivious poetry was established before Byron ever began to publish, that he first acknowledged a fear that this poem was "too free for these very modest days." Even so, Byron was determined to try it as an experiment and discontinue it if it did not "take." In this earliest of letters describing the work, he emphasized the comic and satiric qualities of his composition. Its dedication, he pointed out to Moore, was to Southey, "in good, simple, savage verse." This letter's only quotation from the work—the protest that the poem is indeed an epic—suggests that Byron felt obliged to argue what was not immediately apparent and, moreover, that he was striving for a genre higher than that ordinarily accorded the mock-heroic.

A more businesslike and less literary introduction to the work appears in his first account of it to Hobhouse, to whom his manuscript of the first canto (by then grown to 200 octaves plus an extended dedication) was addressed at Murray's (*BLJ*, VI, 76–77). Since Lord Lauderdale was personally conveying the manuscripts of *Don Juan*, *Mazeppa*, and "Venice: An Ode" back to England with him, Byron took this opportunity to warn his London friends of what they might expect. To Hobhouse he also explained the underlying reason for his hostility toward Southey (referred to in the letter as "The Son of a Bitch"). He accused Southey of having spread rumors two years earlier about Byron's and Shelley's involvement in "a League of Incest" with Claire Clairmont and Mary Godwin, and he therefore felt justified in attacking the laureate's political apostasy. (When Byron prepared Murray for his remarks on Southey, he further attributed to that "dirty, lying rascal" an attack on Leigh Hunt and Shelley in the *Quarterly* of January 1818—*BLJ*, VI, 83.) Again Byron conceded that, in addition to its political bitterness, the poem was "*free*" (in the sense shared by the works of many great writers in England, France, and Italy), but he insisted that it contained "no improper words nor phrases—merely some situations—which are taken from life." For satire to be acceptable, he realized, obscenity had to be cloaked with euphemism. Implied in this letter of 11 November is Byron's assumption that *Don Juan* would be recognized as a realistic masterpiece and therefore would be forgiven its indelicacies. It was to be Hobhouse's obligation to read the manuscript and acquire the largest, or at least the fairest, price from Murray or, if the latter demurred, from some other publisher. Hobhouse was invited to consult Douglas Kinnaird or anyone else he chose about its merits, but Byron was determined that, should "the damned Cant and Toryism of the day" turn Murray against it, *Don Juan* would go to the highest bidder.

During the ensuing weeks, even while proceeding on the second canto (begun on 13 December), Byron sent Murray emendations and additions to the first on the assumption that it would ultimately be found suitable for publication by the literary synod of Albemarle Street. Murray's failure to respond to Byron's additions was rightly interpreted as an ominous sign, but the poet could not believe that his publisher and friend would reject it. On 22 February 1819 Byron wrote Kinnaird that he could not understand Murray's silence and even threatened to trouble him no further unless he improved his manners (*BLJ*, VI, 100). What he gradually realized was that his friends, led by Hobhouse, opposed its publication and believed that it was in his best interest for them to do so. On 27 December Hobhouse and Scrope Davies breakfasted together and read Byron's new poems. Hobhouse recorded in his diary: "I have my doubts about 'Don Juan'; the blasphemy and bawdry and the domestic facts overpower even the great genius it displays."[4] Actually it was Hobhouse's caveats that stopped Murray, who had hitherto been ready to advertise it immediately. Two days later Hobhouse was pleased to record that Frere "was decisively against publication" of *Don Juan* (*Recollections*, II, 109–10). Frere had argued that its immorality would undermine Byron's power to aid freedom, that its liberality would permit religionists to suppress freethinkers, and that its portrayal of Lady Byron would make him look bad. Similarly, the attack on Southey, he felt, would be more detrimental to Byron than to the butt of its satire.

On 2 January 1819 Hobhouse called on Murray to insist that *Don Juan* not be published. Hobhouse's diary entry reveals that Murray was not originally opposed: "He acquiesced, and I suppose is not sorry to be off from the violence and the attack on Bob Southey" (*Recollections*, II, 110). On 5 January Hobhouse, with the concurrence of Murray, Kinnaird, Davies, and Frere, wrote a long letter to Byron specifying cogent reasons for suppressing the poem. Though not averse to the attack on Viscount Castlereagh, he thought the satire against Southey, Wordsworth, and Coleridge wasted since those poets in his view had no reputation save among some fifty "crazy proselytes."[5] Privately Hobhouse recorded his fear that Byron might refer it to Samuel Rogers and Moore, who were praised in it, and that they, out of vanity, would support him (*Recollections*, II, 110–11). To his surprise, however, Moore, after breakfasting with Hobhouse, completely agreed with his host that "it could not be published." In his own diary entry for 28 January, Moore, after talking with Murray and hearing Hobhouse's judgment from Rogers, pronounced *Don Juan* "not fit for publication" and added, in one of the most deferential tributes to hypocrisy: "[Byron] seems, by living so long out of London, to have forgotten that standard of decorum in society, to which every one must refer his *words*, at least, who hopes to be either listened to or read by the world."[6] Strangely enough, Moore had reached these conclusions without ever having seen the manuscript. After reading it on 31 January he concurred that, because of its ridicule of Lady Byron and its "systematized profligacy," *Don Juan* was "as a whole not publishable."[7]

Before learning of these objections, Byron on 19 January adamantly insisted in a letter to both Kinnaird and Hobhouse that he would tolerate no "cutting & slashing," though he would permit deletion of the stanzas on Castlereagh and of the naughty pun on "a dry bob" by removing "Bob" after both "high" and "adry" in the Dedication (*BLJ*, VI, 91). Byron was still convinced that the merits of *Don Juan* would carry the poem through more or less in its entirety. Refusing to yield to contemporary moral cant, he pointed to the "indecency" of well-established classics that the moral public continued to read. Yet with a flippancy that was characteristic but not utterly sincere, he claimed that he cared less about applause and abuse than about the money he expected from the copyright. On the following day he wrote Murray even more pointedly that when he had asked Hobhouse to solicit critical opinion it was to evaluate "poetical merit" and not to defer to the hypocritical morality of people who still read Christopher Anstey's *New Bath Guide*, Moore, Matthew Prior, Chaucer, Fielding, and Smollett (*BLJ*, VI, 94). Again he insisted that he would suffer only those few specified deletions and announced, postscripturally, that the second canto of 206 stanzas was finished.

Only a few days later, Hobhouse's overwhelming insistence that *Don Juan* not be published reached Byron, and in a letter to Murray the poet grudgingly acquiesced, protesting nevertheless that it should ultimately stand or fall on its intrinsic worth rather than be squelched by finical notions of prudery (*BLJ*, VI, 94–95). Even so, Byron, determined to circumvent the London verdict, asked Murray to print fifty copies privately for distribution to friends, deleting only the lines on the "intellectual eunuch Castlereagh." On the same day, 25 January, Byron acknowledged Hobhouse's letter detailing the collective objections, but he still insisted that since he was so "fond of his bantling," he would have fifty privately printed copies (*BLJ*, VI, 95–96). To both Hobhouse and Kinnaird he claimed that loss of anticipated copyright money hurt considerably more than loss of fame. Half-playfully, he added to the latter: "I will see you all damned— before I consult you again—what do you mean now by giving advice when you are asked for it?" (*BLJ*, VI, 98). Even while sending Murray another addition to the first canto and conceding that his enthusiasm for the second canto had been dampened by adverse criticism of the first, he protested that *Don Juan* was "the most moral of poems—but if people won't discover the moral that is their fault not mine" (*BLJ*, VI, 99). Just as the Carnival dissipations were ending, however, his resolution strengthened. On 22 February he tactfully but ominously warned Murray of the probability that he would after all decide to publish *Don Juan* (*BLJ*, VI, 100). On the same day he was more explicit

to Kinnaird: "Tell Hobhouse that 'Don Juan' must be published—the loss of the copyright would break my heart" (*BLJ*,
VI, 100). And on 6 March he reaffirmed his determination: the
first canto would be published anonymously, and Kinnaird rather
than Hobhouse was entrusted to bargain with Murray not only
for it but also for the second canto and the ode "Venice" (*BLJ*,
VI, 101).

In Byron's opinion the second canto was "more correct" and
"at least equal to the first in the whole—as fun & poetry" (*BLJ*,
VI, 101). Far from submitting to "any more damned preach-
ments from Hobhouse" and his friends, Byron now condemned
their prudish judgment, demanded money for his poetic labors,
and staked his counters on the reading public's acceptance. After
Murray's failure to respond for three months, Byron toyed with
the idea of changing his publisher if "tradesman" Murray continued to balk (*BLJ*, VI, 103). On 3 April he peremptorily wrote
Murray: "You have had the second Canto of *Don Juan* which you
will publish with the first, if it please you" (*BLJ*, VI, 104). The
poet reexpressed his willingness to omit some words in the dedi-
catory attack on Southey and the stanzas on Castlereagh—but
no others—and Murray was permitted to judge whether anonymous publication would be advisable. Byron was resolved, however, not to write just to please his English readers. Having had
his fill of popular acclaim, as well as cant about morality, he rejected Murray's suggestion of a "great work" such as a conventional epic or something more acceptable to feminine readers
(*BLJ*, VI, 105–6). "I have written from the fullness of my mind,
from passion—from impulse—from many motives—but not for
their 'sweet voices,'" he wrote Murray on 6 April. Moreover, he
warned: "You sha'n't make *Canticles* of my Cantos." Byron was
proudly determined that the second canto, which by his erroneous count numbered 217 stanzas before being sent off on 3 April,
should suffer no mutilation. "By the Lord!" he wrote Kinnaird,
"it is a Capo d'Opera" (*BLJ*, VI, 114).

So certain was he of the first two cantos' ultimate success that
even after Murray agreed to publish them (admittedly, without
much enthusiasm), Byron assured him he need not do so against
his own inclination (*BLJ*, VI, 122). Knowing what a field day the
scalping critics would have, Byron rather looked forward to the
inevitable éclat. But in view of Murray's preference for anony-

mous publication, Byron decided to eliminate completely the Dedication to Southey, declaring: "I won't attack the dog so fiercely without putting my name—that is reviewer's work" (*BLJ*, VI, 123). Though Hobhouse after reading the proofs noted in his diary that he did not think the poem "so indecent or so clever" as he originally did, he evidently warned Byron again about its impropriety.[8] In response Byron protested to Murray that there was "*no indelicacy*" in *Don Juan* because, whatever the underlying thought might be, he had avoided objectionable language in conveying it (*BLJ*, VI, 125). In his most intractable mood, he refused to acquiesce to any of the suggestions Hobhouse made on the proofs and so informed him (*BLJ*, VI, 131). And despite irrefutable evidence to the contrary, he protested that Donna Inez was not meant to represent his "Clytemnestra," Lady Byron. Insisting on the literary merit of his composition and refusing to make any further alterations, he instructed Kinnaird to come to a specific agreement with Murray before publication or to transfer the manuscript to the highest bidder (*BLJ*, VI, 136–37). On 7 June Kinnaird wrote to Murray assenting in advance to whatever terms Murray, who had hitherto proved himself equitable, might propose. The publisher offered £525 for *Mazeppa* and £1,575 for the first two cantos of *Don Juan*; "Venice: An Ode" was to be thrown in gratis.[9]

The first two cantos of *Don Juan* were published on 15 July 1819. Although neither author's nor publisher's name appeared on the title page of this expensive quarto edition (which sold for £1. 11s. 6d.), there was no doubt in literary circles about the poet's identity. Quite some time before it appeared, in fact, the literary world of London had been anxiously awaiting Byron's new production. As early as 14 February Keats had written to his brother and sister-in-law in Louisville that "another satire is expected from Byron call'd Don Giovanni."[10] So widely had word of the anticipated poem been bruited about in the spring of 1819 that the pseudonymous Mr. Odoherty declared in the June issue of *Blackwood's*: "If Lord Byron does not publish Don Juan speedily, I will."[11] After *Beppo* no discerning reader of *Don Juan* could have mistaken the internal evidence that pointed to Byron as its author.

The moral outcry against the first two cantos of *Don Juan*, once the installment appeared in print, was not long in coming.

William Blackwood wrote Murray that he would not "on any account whatever" permit the poem to be sold in his shop and pointed to a note in the July issue of *Blackwood's Edinburgh Magazine* declaring that "a Work so atrocious must not be suffered to pass into oblivion without the infliction of that punishment on its guilty author due to such a wanton outrage on all most dear to human nature."[12] And the following issue of "Maga," even while calling *Don Juan* "the most admirable specimen of the mixture of ease, strength, gayety, and seriousness extant in the whole body of English poetry," roundly damned this "filthy and impious poem" for its depravity, its mockery of all that is noble, and its exposé of domestic scandal.[13] The two other most prestigious journals, the *Edinburgh* and the *Quarterly Review*, refused even to notice the first two cantos of *Don Juan* or, for that matter, any of the subsequent ones. Except for a feeble attempt by the Hunts' *Examiner* to defend the first installment,[14] British reviews, while occasionally admitting poetic merit, expressed strong disapproval. A few representative opinions will suffice. The reviewer in the *British Critic*, denying that it had even any satiric merit, condemned it as a "flippant, dull and disgraceful" work, "a narrative of degrading debauchery in doggerel rhyme."[15] The *Edinburgh Monthly Review*, conceding its "prostituted brilliancy," pronounced it an "enchanted repository of pollution."[16] The *Monthly Magazine*, while granting that the "flexibility of the English language was never exhibited so perfectly before," rated the moral qualities of *Don Juan* "very low."[17] The *New Monthly Magazine*, warning that *Don Juan* was all the more dangerous to public morality because of its appealing poetry, urged that it be "met by public scorn and reprobation."[18] No wonder then that Byron, in an 1822 comparison of himself to Napoleon, would declare: "Juan was my Moscow" (*DJ* XI.56.1).

Although Byron had asserted, soon after its publication, that if *Don Juan* were not well received he would discontinue it (*BLJ*, VI, 207–8), he had not yet faced up to the eventuality that its "indiscretions" might be sufficiently repugnant to prevent many readers' acceptance. Even while defending "license" as the soul of such writing and the "quick succession of fun and gravity" as the natural pattern of human experience, he minimized the venom of his satire by claiming, not quite ingenuously, that it should all be taken facetiously: "Do you suppose that I could

have any intention but to giggle and make giggle?—a playful satire with as little poetry as could be helped." Though by 20 August Murray's reports about its success had been less than enthusiastic, Byron was confident that he had never written better and
informed Hobhouse: "I wish you all better taste" (*BLJ*, VI, 212).
While his friends sincerely feared that *Don Juan* had failed, Byron wrote Kinnaird with complete self-assurance about his exu-
berant translation of life into art: "As to 'Don Juan'—confess—
confess—you dog—and be candid—that it is the sublime of *that*
there sort of writing—it may be bawdy—but is it not good English?—it may be profligate—but is it not *life*, is it not *the thing*?"
(*BLJ*, VI, 232). Nevertheless, Murray grumbled that the poem
was not selling well, in spite of the fact that by 29 October 1,200
of the 1,500 copies had already been sold (*BLJ*, VI, 237). By the
unusual standards of Byron's previous publications (Murray sold
10,000 copies of *The Corsair* on its first day) that figure was not
impressive, but it would have been a phenomenal success for almost any other poet.

Despite Augusta Leigh's claim that *Don Juan* was too "*execrable*"
to read (*BLJ*, VIII, 65), women were likely not so deterred from
it as Byron assumed, and at first the prudish clamor of middle-
class critics, like the banning of a book in Boston, helped more
than it hindered overall sales. Indeed the popularity of *Don Juan*
was sufficient to spawn continuations, parodies, and even cheap
piracies that cut into Murray's profits. By October two spurious
third cantos had been published, and Jean Antoine Galignani
was quick to pirate the first two cantos in Paris. In order to
defend his copyright against unauthorized printings, Murray
applied for an injunction from the Chancery Court. In mid-
November 1819 he was assured by authoritative legal opinion
that certain questionable passages in *Don Juan* were not offensive
enough to threaten the copyright and that the poem was actually
beneficial in showing the bad effects of Juan's "injudicious maternal education."[19] The Chancellor, Lord Eldon, concurred and
subsequently granted the requested injunction. Thereafter Byron turned a deaf ear to Murray's suggestions that indelicacies be
laundered.

Though the critical denunciation had admittedly dampened
his enthusiasm and undermined his confidence, Byron had begun the third canto on 17 September and on 26 October an-

nounced that it already contained about 100 stanzas. On 4 December, when he informed his publisher that the canto was completed in about 200 stanzas, the question of Murray's legal process was highly disturbing because he feared that, as in Eldon's ruling against Shelley on evidence of *Queen Mab*, the Court might declare his poem "*indecent & blasphemous*" and consequently, if his authorship were established, deprive him of guardianship rights over his daughter Ada (*BLJ*, VI, 252–53, 256). Indeed Byron later expressed fear that the parody of the Decalogue (*DJ* I.205–6) might alone be cause enough for revocation of his parental guardianship (*BLJ*, VII, 196). So sure was he that Murray's suit would fail that he offered to refund the money he had received for the copyright. Hence he would not discuss the third canto with Murray until he knew for certain that it was legally a "property."

By 7 February 1820 that question had been favorably resolved, and Byron informed Murray that he had made two cantos of what had been the third, though he would expect no more payment than for one; yet he did not send them off until 19 February because he felt they lacked "the Spirit of the first" (*BLJ*, VII, 34–35, 42). As he explained, "the outcry has not frightened but it has *hurt* me." On 23 April he reiterated his diffidence about the new cantos' merit, announced his erasure of six stanzas attacking Southey and Wordsworth (though he did not carry out the deletion), and insisted that the new cantos, consisting of 225 stanzas and a lyric of 96 lines ("The Isles of Greece"), be either rejected completely or published without further alteration (*BLJ*, VII, 82). Apparently Murray and his synod thought only half of the new installment very good, and on 30 April Byron wrote Kinnaird to assure Murray that he might publish or not as he wished and that no other publisher was being sought (*BLJ*, VII, 83–86). Yet on 22 June Byron, by then exasperated by Murray's indecision, asked Hobhouse to put his manuscripts into the hands of Longman or some other reputable publisher while stipulating, as he would again later to Murray, that Cantos III and IV had to be published anonymously to preserve his joint-guardianship over Ada (*BLJ*, VII, 121). Murray's favorable response of late June healed the breach. Though Byron first suggested withholding publication until *Marino Faliero* was ready (*BLJ*, VII, 124), on 7 August (and again on 24 August) he proposed that the new cantos be published with a second edition of the first two in order that, as he later explained, "they may make little noise—as they are not equal to the first" (*BLJ*, VII, 150, 162).

Byron's conviction that women disliked *Don Juan* because of its satiric views on love was confirmed by Teresa Guiccioli's observations, and to Murray he accounted for this phenomenon by asserting that "women hate every thing which strips off the tinsel of *Sentiment*—& they are right—or it would rob them of their weapons" (*BLJ*, VII, 202). Virtually in defiance of such disapproval Byron on 16 October began the fifth canto, the most misogynistic of all, while living in the Palazzo Guiccioli in Ravenna, and after scarcely more than a month (on 27 November) completed it. When he announced to Murray on 14 December that the fifth canto (then consisting of 151 stanzas) was being copied, he pointedly asked: "I want to know what the devil you mean to do?" (*BLJ*, VII, 250). He sent the canto (then 155 stanzas) on 28 December to Douglas Kinnaird, to whom Murray, if so disposed, was asked to apply and come to some decision (*BLJ*, VII, 255–56). Since the Whigs still supported the queen in her struggles against the king, Byron would later yield to Hobhouse's request that an offensive stanza (*DJ* V.61) containing a slur on Queen Caroline and her courier, Bartolomeo Bergami, be expunged (*BLJ*, VIII, 147–48, 192). On 19 January 1821 Byron conceded that Canto III might be dull but argued that the four other cantos compensated for it (*BLJ*, VIII, 65). On 16 February, when he agreed to leave the terms of payment for Cantos III–V in abeyance until the effect of publication became known, he outlined more extensively than ever before what Juan's roles in various countries might be and confidently assured Murray that the fifth was "hardly the beginning" (*BLJ*, VIII, 77–78). As Truman Guy Steffan has pointed out, this prospectus was partly designed to prod Murray into realizing that he could not drag his feet on an ambitious project.[20] With the composition of Canto V, which according to Shelley set Byron "not above but far above all the poets of the day,"[21] Byron evidently realized that he had returned to the fulfillment of his poetic destiny. *Don Juan* would be continued, no matter what carping critics and timorous publishers might say.

Not until after he had informed both Kinnaird and Murray on 9 March that a publisher named Fearman was interested in the three new cantos did Murray feel sufficient pressure to act (*BLJ*, VIII, 90–92). On 8 August 1821 Murray published Cantos III, IV, and V (the last without two of its 159 stanzas) in octavo— again without any indication of either publisher or author but again with the printer Thomas Davison's name. The immediate demand for copies was extraordinary; booksellers' messengers clamoring for their consignments of books from Murray filled Albemarle Street on the first day of publication.[22] From Ravenna on 16 August Byron taunted Murray by asking whether he were not afraid, as a result of publishing the "new Juans," of a vigilante group (the Constitutional Association of Bridge Street) that harassed publishers and booksellers of seditious and blasphemous works (*BLJ*, VIII, 181). Murray's offer of only 2,000 guineas for these three new cantos, *Sardanapalus*, and *The Two Foscari* was in Byron's opinion degrading, and on 23 August he wrote both Kinnaird and Murray that he would not accept it (*BLJ*, VIII, 185–87).

Upon reading the three cantos in print, Byron reassured Murray on 4 September that (in spite of gross misprints) they were excellent poetry, that the synod had been wrong, and that he regretted he was not continuing the poem (*BLJ*, VIII, 198). His ostensible reason for abandoning it was Teresa's insistence that this "abominable" production be halted.[23] In retort to Murray's assertion that Byron could rely on his publisher's honor for fair payment, the poet denied that honor could ever be relied on in commercial transactions (*BLJ*, VIII, 244–45). And when in a letter of 3 November he accused Murray of again playing "the Stepmother" by issuing the second installment without the publisher's name, he was well aware that Murray had profited greatly from *Don Juan* (*BLJ*, IX, 54–55). Increasingly annoyed by British condescension, he asked Murray to send him "no more reviews of any kind," for he did not wish to read them.

Though Byron expected 3,000 guineas for Cantos III–V and the plays *Sardanapalus*, *The Two Foscari*, and *Cain*, he did, however, follow Kinnaird's advice and on 28 November accepted Murray's offer of 2,500 guineas (*BLJ*, IX, 71–72). Yet the bickering over money and slovenly printing, in addition to Murray's coolness, had an abrasive effect on the relations between publisher and poet—one aggravated by Byron's conviction that the cantos contained distinguished poetry that in time would be honored.[24] Some of the puritanical attacks, Byron wrote Murray, had actually been invited by the latter's half-prudish decision to keep his name off the publication (*BLJ*, IX, 103–4). In this letter of 8 February 1822 Byron informed Murray that he was now agreeable to having his own name put on *Don Juan* but that, in view of attacks on Murray for publishing *Cain*, it would be to Murray's advantage if Byron sought another publisher.

Reviews of Cantos III–V offered less praise of the poetry and were just slightly less hostile toward the poet's implied outlook than those of the first installment. One of the rare commendations came from the *Examiner*, which applauded Byron's "careless contempt for the canting moralists."[25] *Blackwood's* conceded that in the new cantos Byron's powers had by no means abated but deemed his morality unregenerate.[26] The reviewer in the *British Critic* charged that Murray had admitted his just shame by not attaching his name to Byron's depraved, corruptive work.[27] William Roberts, whose *British Review* Byron had derided (*DJ* I.209–10), delivered a sanctimonious tirade in his journal against the "moral turpitude" and "mental prostitution" of this "pestilent production."[28] The *European Magazine*, attributing the moral improvement of the new cantos to Byron's having "felt the just severity of the critical lash," still found too much defiance of divine as well as human institutions.[29] The *Gentleman's Magazine* recognized the cantos' beauty and grandeur but concluded that, because of their licentiousness, they would "not of course be admitted into regular families."[30] The reviewer in the *Edinburgh [Scots] Magazine* declared the poem to be an "intermixture of ribaldry and blasphemy such as no man of pure taste can read a *second* time, and such as no woman of correct principles can read the *first*."[31]

Although such reviews led to Murray's declining interest in the publication of *Don Juan*, they had far less impact upon Byron. Feeling the need to release his literary creativity after his removal to Pisa in November 1821 and having been somewhat disappointed by the reception of his plays, Byron begged Teresa to lift the ban on *Don Juan*. By April 1822 (possibly before she had even relented) he had resumed composition of *Don Juan*,[32] and for roughly a year thereafter his literary efforts were consumed largely by that poem. Encouragement to continue the work came also from John G. Lockhart's anonymous pamphlet, *Letter to the Right Hon. Lord Byron,* purportedly by John Bull and published in April or May 1821. "John Bull's" assertion that "the Don sells, and will sell to the end of time" further strengthened his belief that he had not completely misjudged his audience.[33] On 8 July he wrote Murray that by autumn he might have three or four additional cantos because his "Dictatress" had granted permission "*provided always* it was to be more guarded and decorous and sentimental in the continuation" (*BLJ*, IX, 182). Ironically, the sixth canto, with its hilarious harem episode, is sexually one of the most daring of all, and though Teresa might not have understood all its implications, Murray certainly would have, despite its circumspect language.

Even while transferring *The Vision of Judgment,* the Pulci translation, and prose tracts to John Hunt for possible use in the *Liberal,* Byron evidently still expected Murray to remain the sponsor of *Don Juan.* Since Murray, in paying less for Cantos III–V, had pled that piracies had cut into his profits, Byron suggested to Kinnaird that if Murray published the ensuing cantos he should print concurrently some cheap editions to obviate piratical competition (*BLJ*, IX, 71, 187). When writing Moore a second time, on 8 August, about returning the Wellington stanzas that had been canceled from Canto III because his Tory publisher was likely to suppress them, Byron announced that he had completed three more cantos and was "hovering on the brink of another (the ninth)" (*BLJ*, IX, 191). That he was striving for the public's, as well as Teresa's, approval can be seen from his assertion to Moore that the new cantos were "as decent as need be" (*BLJ*, IX, 198), but his more explicit description to Kinnaird, conceding that they contained "satire upon heroes and despots and the present false state of politics and society," showed awareness of where the rub might arise (*BLJ*, IX, 196). By 10 September Byron had dispatched the four new cantos to Kinnaird, and on 18 September he expressed optimism about their sales "as they are full of politics—and some poesy" (*BLJ*, IX, 204, 209). On 9 October he informed Murray that Juan had been carried through a siege, thence to St. Petersburg, and finally to England (*BLJ*, X, 12). Moreover, Byron stated that he did not wish to break with his publisher, and he was certain there would be a reaction against critical antagonism toward *Don Juan*. Without altering his principles, he even offered to "make any allowance" to accommodate Murray in a professional way. On 24 October he further informed Murray, after harshly reproaching him for his dealings with Hunt, that Cantos X and XI were completed and copied (*BLJ*, X, 17–18).

Only a week later, however, Byron, having been forewarned by Kinnaird about Murray's reluctance, wrote John Hunt suggesting that, if the proper arrangements could be made with his agent Kinnaird, Hunt might obtain two dramas (then in Murray's possession) for inclusion in the *Liberal* and six new cantos of *Don Juan* (then in Kinnaird's possession) for separate publication, preferably in such a way as to forestall piracies (*BLJ*, X, 23–24). To Kinnaird he wrote on 2 November that he was "not at all sorry to be rid of" Murray, whom he thought "a sad shuffler," but realized it might be difficult to "dispose of the new Cantos elsewhere" (*BLJ*, X, 26). Upon completion of the twelfth canto in Genoa, he suggested to Kinnaird on 9 December various format possibilities for publication of the seven new cantos, proposing even that two volumes might be issued by different publishers (*BLJ*, X, 51). On 29 October Murray, by then not only fed up with Byron's association with Leigh and John Hunt (both of whom were anathema to him and his Tory cronies) but also annoyed by Byron's conditions and reprimands, had written that he would not publish the "outrageously shocking" cantos (VI–VIII) unless they were revised; moreover, he had urged Byron to regain a respectable reputation by restoring *Don Juan* to the good-humored tone of *Beppo*.[34] The comic was evidently more to Murray's commercial taste than the satiric. Byron replied on 18 November that he cared nothing about popular acclaim and would henceforth withdraw completely from Murray as his publisher (*BLJ*, X, 36). Having read the first half of what Reginald Heber had stated in the July *Quarterly* about his dramas, *Don Juan*, and the prostitution of his genius, Byron wrote Murray on Christmas Day 1822 that he was resigned to the prevailing hostility but assured him: "D[on] Juan will be known by and bye for what it is intended a *satire* on *abuses* of the present *states* of Society—and not an eulogy of vice;—it may be now and then voluptuous—I can't help that" (*BLJ*, X, 68). Immediately after announcing to Murray that John Hunt would likely publish the new cantos, Byron added: "I bear you no ill will for declining the D[on] J[uan]s—but I cannot commend yr. conduct to the H[unt]s" (*BLJ*, X, 69–70).

As his popularity in Britain waned, Byron, realizing that lasting repute would not rest upon the prestige of a publisher or be prevented by the hubbub of narrow-minded reviewers, came to rely increasingly upon posterity for the vindication of his own critical judgment of *Don Juan*. With the zeal of a crusading satirist he announced to Kinnaird on 2 May 1822 that he would not allow the "present Public" to "interrupt the march of my mind—nor prevent me from telling the tyrants who are attempting to trample upon all thought—that their thrones will yet be rocked to their foundation" (*BLJ*, IX, 152). It was some consolation to him that he was still highly esteemed in Germany, France, and America and that the Germans regarded *Don Juan* as "a work of Art."[35] Hence he tried to convince himself that such admiration compensated for British animosity and the consequent loss of sales.

Even so, though he had the highest respect for Hunt's integrity, the latter's somewhat tarnished reputation in the trade at first made Byron hesitate to engage Hunt as his publisher. In fact, on 28 November 1822 Byron inquired of Kinnaird whether James Ridgway might publish four or possibly six of the new cantos; the poet was willing to add the twelfth canto to make a sizeable second volume if the publication were to be so divided (*BLJ*, X, 42). Though reluctant to promise much in the way of alterations, he nevertheless offered, as he had never done with Murray, to be more amenable about objectionable passages. In any event, Hunt was setting up the cantos in type, and on 8 January 1823 Byron informed him that the twelfth canto had been sent to Kinnaird almost a month before and that he expected to receive proofs of the two volumes soon (*BLJ*, X, 80). Between 12 February, when he began Canto XIII, and 25 March, when he completed the first draft of Canto XV, Byron worked intently composing what would become three of his most brilliant cantos. On 31 March he informed Kinnaird that these newest cantos (through XV) had been sent to him and that, regardless of the critics, all the cantos were to be published immediately (*BLJ*, X,

132). On 9 April he asked Hunt to have Kinnaird send him proofs of these cantos, adding that the first nine of the unpublished ten were to be issued in three volumes (*BLJ*, X, 145–46).

Because Kinnaird was initially opposed to Hunt as anything more than printer, there was still some question as to who the publisher would be. Byron was puzzled by his agent's procrastination, for he had heard from a former clerk of Galignani that *Don Juan* was selling extremely well in Paris, "especially amongst the women." Actually Kinnaird knew that no other publisher was likely to pay what Murray had formerly paid, but he also thought publication under Hunt's aegis inadvisable while Hunt was awaiting trial for publishing *The Vision of Judgment*. On 6 May Byron completed the first draft of Canto XVI, which he sent off before 21 May (*BLJ*, X, 182). On 8 May he wrote fifteen stanzas (one canceled) of the fragmentary seventeenth canto, which was found among his papers in Greece after his death. On 14 July he sent Hunt the proofs he had read (through XV), but he had to entrust XVI entirely to Hunt since he expected to sail for Greece before proofs of it could reach him (*BLJ*, X, 212). Byron hoped that his Greek expedition might lessen the antipathy of the British reading public toward him (*BLJ*, X, 151, 199).

The business relations between Byron and Hunt were on the whole very satisfactory to both. On 8 January 1823 Byron warned Hunt, whom he had designated as his new publisher, not to be very sanguine about the profits of these later cantos because public opinion was marshaled against both of them (*BLJ*, X, 80), and indeed their financial rewards were not spectacular. Yet Byron was extremely generous in his dealings with Hunt, and Hunt did not quibble with what Byron wrote.[36] Knowing that Hunt, unlike Murray, could not offer substantial sums in advance for the copyright, Byron gave him 15 percent of the gross sales. Even before recommending on 23 December 1822 that Kinnaird make a publication agreement with Hunt, Byron had suggested that Hunt and his son Henry have their accounts audited quarterly in order to receive a reasonable profit. The poet, however, definitely wished to retain the copyright himself.[37] Though Byron received in all only a few hundred pounds from Hunt, who published all his subsequent works, the two men had enduring respect for one another.

In 1823 John Hunt, whose trial did not come to pass until the following year, published Cantos VI–XIV in three volumes—each containing three cantos and issued in three formats, the cheapest (an 18mo) designed to prevent piracies. The first volume appeared on 15 July, the second on 29 August, the third on 17 December. In August 1823 the copyright of *Don Juan* was ruled invalid by Sir John Leach, the Vice-Chancellor, after a piratical printer named William Dugdale asked to publish that work, which, upon reconsideration, was declared licentious if not libelous.[38]

Byron assumed that publicity arising from Hunt's prosecution would actually help his publisher's sales (*BLJ*, X, 66), but the contrary was probably the case. In 1823 the association of *Don Juan* with this publisher gave reviewers additional targets—the radicalism of the Cockney Hunts, their prosecution for seditious publications, and the possibility that they had tampered with Byron's text. Although Henry L. Hunt did what he could as editor of the *Literary Examiner* to give the nine cantos advance puffing in July, August, and November, his intended aid was to no avail. His insistence that the outcry against Byron was politically instigated because the poet had "embraced the cause of the politically oppressed" only emphasized the rift between Byron and the conservatives.[39] The poet's fierce invectives against the late Castlereagh in the Preface to Cantos VI–VIII and against Wellington in Canto IX were enough to make Tory critics froth at the mouth. The unfavorable reviews therefore harped on the new cantos' irresponsible jacobinism, as well as the old themes of obscenity, blasphemy, and profligacy. The *Gentleman's Magazine* declared Canto VI to be "fit only for the shelves of a brothel."[40] The reviewer of Cantos IX–XI for the *Edinburgh [Scots] Magazine* acknowledged that Byron was "sometimes a powerful satirist" in the tradition of Juvenal but denied that he would ever rival his original, however much he might "surpass it in grossness and obscenity."[41] One notable exception, however, was Lockhart's highly commendatory review of Cantos IX–XI in the September 1823 issue of *Blackwood's*. This review claimed that *Don Juan* embodies "the most powerful picture of that vein of thought . . . which distinguishes *a great portion of the thinking people of our time*" and "is destined to hold a permanent rank in the literature of our country."[42]

By that time, however, it was too late for reviews (either good or bad) to have any impact on Byron. From Greece he had Edward Trelawny write Leigh Hunt on 2 September urging that John Hunt publish Cantos XV and XVI without further delay.[43] The volume containing these cantos appeared on 26 March 1824, less than a month before Byron's death. The Dedication to *Don Juan*, which he had refused to publish anonymously because to do so would have been imitating the dastardly reviewers, was first published by Effingham Wilson in 1833.[44] The prose Preface, which he probably composed late in 1818 to explain his contempt for Southey and Wordsworth (more pointedly expressed in the Dedication) and which was originally designed to precede Cantos I and II, did not appear until Rowland E. Prothero published it in 1901. The fragmentary Canto XVII was introduced to the world by E. H. Coleridge in 1903.

The posterity on which Byron pinned his hopes has indeed vindicated his evaluation of *Don Juan*, and by the freer standards of our age the puritanical obstructions raised by his detractors strike the modern reader as either unnaturally prudish or hypocritical. In retrospect Byron appears justified in his conviction that a society so determined to erect barriers against his masterpiece deserved the satiric onslaughts he gave it.

THE NARRATOR AS SATIRIC
DEVICE IN *DON JUAN*

EARLY readers of *Don Juan* were at considerable disadvantage in having neither the Dedication nor the prose Preface to Cantos I and II, for in those two introductions the poet initially develops his satiric persona in the tradition of the *vir bonus* who sees the truth and is not afraid to express it. The Preface, cast in the form of a critical parody of Wordsworth's introduction to "The Thorn," is more than just a diatribe against Wordsworth and Southey. It is also an invocation of what Byron considered Dr. Johnson's common-sense approach to the illusions of literary fiction. Johnson, who in the Preface to his edition of Shakespeare (1765) defended the dramatist's neglect of temporal and locational unities, had argued that anyone who mistakes dramatic illusion for reality "may imagine more" and indeed must be considered "above the reach of reason or of truth."[1] In a parallel argument Byron maintains that anyone who can suppose Wordsworth's tale of an unnatural mother and her natural child to have been recounted by a retired sea captain "is requested to suppose by a like exertion of Imagination that the following epic Narrative is told by a Spanish Gentleman in a village in the Sierra Morena."

Certainly McGann is correct in asserting that this Preface initiates an "attack upon the Romantic exaltation of imagination as a divine poetic faculty," for as Byron conceived it, poetic imagining is not a reliable way of creating "truth" but rather a means of analyzing the world that literature ought to represent.[2] Hence the Preface mocks the creative imagination as essentially deceptive and, moreover, ridicules those so gullible as to believe,

through willing suspension of their rational powers, that the rav-
ings and absurdities in "The Thorn" can be attributed to Wordsworth's prosaic narrator. Such people, Byron implies, want to be
hoodwinked into believing that an imaginative fiction is prefer-
able to reality. Byron therefore invites them to indulge their
imaginations even further—to make fanciful conjectures not
only about his narrator's identity but also about a hypothetical
English editor who, because he has good reason to detest the laureate, has interpolated the attacks on that "Pantisocratic apostle
of Apostacy."

Having recently read the *Biographia Literaria*, Byron was aware
of Coleridge's opinion that "The Thorn" had failed as a ventrilo-
quistic experiment because the "dull and garrulous discourser"
could not avoid producing a stultifying effect (Chapter XVII).
To avoid that pitfall Byron was presumably determined to create
a stimulating narrator with whom his intellectually responsible
readers might identify—a level-headed, practical man of the
world who would render criticism with the incisiveness and conviction of Dr. Johnson. In conjunction with the Preface, the Dedication was designed to establish Byron's persona as a rational,
humorous, just, and humane sophisticate in the Augustan poetic
tradition. He is the honest realist who loathes the drivel of Wordsworth, the obfuscating metaphysics of Coleridge, the sterile in-
anity of Southey, the political tergiversation of all the Lakers, the
tyranny of Castlereagh, and the inherent pettiness of all who
lack truly commendable poetical and political principles. Nor is
it difficult to deduce the persona's positive values from what he
vehemently deplores.

Partly by means of style, as George M. Ridenour and McGann
have shown, Byron relates his Dedication to the classical theory
of rhetorical styles.[3] Byron's knowledge of classical critics may not
have been comprehensive enough to make him a staunch adherent of what Longinus, Quintilian, and Cicero had postulated
about the high, middle, and plain styles. Even so, Byron was well
versed in classical literature and was such a devoted student of
Pope that he assimilated much of his mentor's stylistic practice.
In the Dedication to *Don Juan* the narrator's assertion that he is
"wandering with pedestrian Muses" (st.8) certainly invokes the
tradition of Horatian satire; the allusion to Horace's *saturis Musa-
que pedestri* ("in the satires of my pedestrian muse"—II.6.17)

conjures up the image of good-humored raillery, unpretentious realism, and gentlemanly causerie that the more urbane neoclassicists tried to emulate. The offhand manner and colloquial language that Byron's narrator affects are usually in the rhetorical plain style of Horatian satire, recalling Horace's assertions that his verses were, except for meter, more like conversational prose than generally accepted poetry (Satire I.4.38–65). Yet that self-effacing humility does not prohibit Byron from rising to the tone of solemn Old Testament prophecy or the epic grandeur of Juvenalian satire as occasion demands. Hence, for example, Byron employs the appropriate high style when holding up Milton as a desirable model, in contradistinction to the Lakers. In Milton he finds a magnanimous, Promethean man who, because of his political and poetical integrity, was able to create sublime poetry. By contrast to Milton, the provincial Lakers are made to look doubly ridiculous, for their pretensions to soaring "on the winged steed" entail an imaginative flight that is nothing more than a fraudulent escape from reality. And when opposed to Milton's liberalism, Castlereagh's oppressiveness (seen as the perverted cerebral lust of a eunuch) is doubly reprehensible and deserves a style reminiscent of Juvenalian fulmination. After these bitter denunciations in the Dedication, the narrator's assertion that his effusions are "in honest simple verse" contributes an irony surpassing even that which Horace's ingratiating persona casts over his subtle jibes.

Yet the diversity of the narrator's styles deserves to be seen as more than Byron's amalgamated inheritance from the Roman satiric tradition. As A. B. England has observed, the two varieties of verbal structure employed in *Don Juan* can also be traced to two varieties of English satire that flourished in the late seventeenth and early eighteenth centuries. Those passages in which Byron has subjected his material to a formality of language and rhetorical thought—that is, those approximating the lofty Augustan manner of Pope—imply a world order that the poem as a whole does not reflect. The more frequent verbal structure in *Don Juan*, as England has shown, is characterized by a burlesque, almost Hudibrastic, style—one marked by "a high degree of tolerance for disorder, impurity, and discontinuity of rhetoric and diction."[4]

It needs to be pointed out, moreover, that this vacillation, to which many critics have demurred, is an appropriate reflection of the narrator's perspective. And the ottava rima, which allows the poet to build up tensions and then destroy them, is ideally suited to convey this pattern. Man, Byron implies, superimposes a temporary order on his chaotic world, only to find in time that the order has been shattered and that he must set about fashioning a new one. Thus the process from chaos to order to chaos is endless, as each newly imposed order is subject to critical analysis that, by exposing its flaws, effects its collapse. As part of this ineluctable paradigm of nature, man is obliged to resign himself to the comic absurdity of recurrent shambles until he can devise a new contruct.

The mask Byron employs for his narrator is in keeping with the tradition of satirists who want their speakers to be part of the scene and yet sufficiently independent of it to be objective. Attempts to detach *Don Juan's* narrator from its poet have not proved utterly successful because the former is neither a purely fictitious character nor a wholly separable mask but rather a calculated embodiment of selective Byronic features that the poet wished to project. Though as *Don Juan* proceeds the distinction between mask and poet tends increasingly to disappear, Byron tries early in the poem to distance himself from the persona just as he had previously detached himself from the title character in *Childe Harold I*. The narrator's claim that he is "a plain man, and in a single station" (I.22.6) is biographically as inaccurate as his assertion that he "never married" (I.53.7). In the traditional pose of the satirist, he calls himself a "moderate-minded bard" who is quite content with just "a little love"; and unlike voluptuaries, he is satisfied with tried and true pleasures (I.118). Thus he advertises himself as a generally conservative, honest man with middle-of-the-road views. To make the narrator appear to be part of the cast of characters, Byron at the beginning places him amidst the scene of action in Seville, thereby adding conviction to his on-the-spot reporting. Though he boasts not only of having unusual insight into character but also of knowing Don Jose well (I.51.3–4), he seems somewhat obtuse in failing to understand why his well-intentioned interference should be unappreciated. Indeed his meddling in the affairs of Jose and Inez is rewarded, when Juan inadvertently empties "housemaid's water" on the busybody's head (I.24), with ironic justice.

In other instances, however, the narrator is clearly meant to be an alter ego of Byron himself. When, for example, the narrator claims to be a superannuated, thirty-year-old man whose life is over (except, of course, for vicarious enjoyment), he expresses an idea often uttered, though rarely adhered to, by Byron. In fact, the narrator's aging from thirty to thirty-five is perfectly synchronized with the poet's (I.213; XII.2). Certainly the narrator represents his creator when he admits to having been "bred a moderate Presbyterian" (XV.91.8) and to being "half a Scot by birth" (X.17.7). When he concedes that he might have chosen Piccadilly as the site of London scandal but has reasons for leaving "that pure sanctuary alone" (XIII.27), there can be no question that the poet *in propria persona* is referring to his own marital residence. Even more compelling is the unequivocal identification of the narrator with Byron when the former describes himself as "the grand Napoleon of the realms of rhyme" and specifically names some of his works (XI.55–56).

Yet one must realize that the narrator is not Byron's only mask in the poem. From time to time other characters such as Don Juan, Don Jose, and John Johnson express their creator's partial views on reality, and the author's voice encompasses all of them. The dynamic thrust of the poem results primarily from an unresolvable dialectic in which the romantic Juan, who expresses Byron's sentiments more through actions than reflective thoughts, is ironically played off against the worldly narrator. Anne K. Mellor, in her analysis of the opposition between the naive Juan and the skeptical, cynical narrator, has noted that as the poem proceeds their antithetical views temper one another. As Juan grows older and more worldly through experience, he assumes more of the narrator's perspective despite his perennially "virgin face" (XVII.13.8). As the narrator, reliving his own life through Juan and recollections of past experience, is forced to reevaluate the world, he becomes increasingly aware of the self-imposed limitations of his own blasé detachment. The "constant alternation between these widely divergent characters or modes of consciousness," Mellor states, "is itself an analogue for the process of human growth, or self-creation and self-transcendence."[5]

Not only do the narrator's opinions change with the passage of time; at a given moment his views may stand in ironic opposition to one another. The effect of such apparent contradiction upon the reader is twofold. First, he realizes that he cannot whole-heartedly believe whatever the narrator says; and on a more so-phisticated level, he also becomes aware that life's problems, as seen from different stances, are incapable of clear-cut, facile so-lutions. The narrator's cynical comments on the love of Juan and Haidée, for example, may offend the reader who would prefer to empathize with the idyllic lovers. Yet it is the narrator who also conveys the highly romantic depiction of the lovers. Hence the reader must ultimately concede that each of the antithetical view-points, far from negating the other, contains partial elements of "truth" and that neither presents the whole picture. Unresolved ironies are the narrator's prime rhetorical means of compelling the reader to see reality from different perspectives and to acknowledge that conflicting ideas are tenable within a larger framework.

What especially endears Byron's jaunty narrator to his read-ers is that, like Horace, he is willing in his self-analysis to point out his own foibles, thereby strengthening his ties to fallible hu-manity. As Hazlitt described this propensity in *Don Juan*, "You laugh and are surprised that any one should turn round and *travestie* himself."[6] Only a poet with supreme self-assurance would dare assert that his second canto might suffer the fate of bad poetry in being used to line portmanteaus (II.16.6–8). And in acknowledging that the reader has recently been patient with him, he admits to having been as verbose as an auctioneer (XIII.74.1–4). In its simplest, most direct form such satire as-sumes the guise of winning self-deprecation ordinarily associ-ated with Socratic irony. The narrator becomes mockingly melo-dramatic when lamenting that at thirty, with gray hair and squan-dered heart, he is not what he was in youth; hence his need to take up with "a good old-gentlemanly vice" such as avarice (I.212–16). Furthermore, the foppish outlook he sometimes as-sumes virtually requires him to poke fun at his own snobbish, self-indulgent tastes, thereby becoming the butt of his own dis-dain. Yet one senses that he does not completely undermine his posturing but rather reveals its shortcomings. Closely related to such self-parody is his artistic diffidence, manifested through self-conscious commentary on his methodology. When he re-marks on the difficulties of selecting a hero or a rhyme, his self-consciousness undermines the superiority to which an artist ordinarily pretends in his final redaction. Admittedly, there may be partial truth in his assertion that "this last simile is trite and stupid" (I.55.8); yet if the narrator (or Byron) had fully believed that, the simile would have been canceled. The poem often conveys the sense of developing casually as it progresses, thus giving rise to Hazlitt's assertion that *Don Juan* is "a poem written about itself."[7] The poet, by allowing his semi-conscious thoughts to rise to the surface, often gives us insight into his own mental processes as he creates, revises, or de-creates.

One of the favorite forms of self-satire in *Don Juan* is that which undermines through contradiction, showing the discrepancy between good intention and actual behavior. This inconsistency indicates not a "seeming myriad of speakers," as Marshall suggested,[8] but a human tendency to vacillate—the *mobilité* to which we are all subject. Though the narrator claims to loathe "that low vice curiosity" (I.23.5), his interest in salacious gossip makes it clear that he is always ready to pry into others' affairs. Similarly, his praise of constancy as a virtue is overthrown at a masquerade by his own wandering fancies, which he ultimately justifies as the pattern of natural change (II.209–14). In a very human way he resolves every spring to reform, but unfortunately his "vestal vow takes wing," leaving him once more to be "reclaim'd" (I.119). Even while affirming that description is his forte he will not describe and then proceeds to do so (V.52.1); and later he insists: "I won't describe . . . I won't reflect, . . . I *won't* philosophize, and *will* be read" (X.28). His earlier assertion that "The regularity of [his] design / Forbids all wandering as the worst of sinning" (I.7.3–4) forms the ironic background for his constant digressions, on which he also comments disparagingly (III.96; XIII.12.1; XV.84.5). Yet these digressions, like learning through experience in the external world, are clearly a way of exploring the inner being through suppositions or the free play of associations; they therefore become a means to greater perception. Ultimately he defends even contradictions on the relativistic grounds that there is no absolute truth upon which all humanity can agree but only different perspectives on it (XV.87–90). As a philosophical skeptic, he must conclude that, like everyone else of intellectual integrity, he knows nothing of which he can be certain (XIV.3.1–4). Honest doubt he addresses as "sole Prism / Of the Truth's rays" (XI.2.6–

7). Consequently he builds up a succession of ironies based on the tension of apparent contradictions. In time his dialectic crumbles, only to reestablish itself in a new paradox that follows the same progression. To facilitate expression of such fluctuating views, Byron uses the ottava rima with even more versatility than in *Beppo*. Nowhere is its adaptability better suited than as the medium for such a variety of thoughts constantly being recombined and reshaped in new and unexpected ways.

The flexible poetic form also allows the poet to adroitly modulate the persona's involvement in the narrative in accord with artistic need. Especially in the later cantos there are moments when the narrator assumes a casual, self-assured detachment, boasting a Mephistophelean pose, declaring, "I am but a mere spectator" (XIII.7.6), and absolving himself of any responsibility. He claims to "perch upon an humbler promontory" than that of the great philosophers, casting his eye upon whatever suits his story, never straining at versification, but merely rattling on loquaciously like an improviser (XV.19–22). Occasionally, like most satirists, he fancies himself more sinned against than sinning. Although by his own proclamation he is the mildest, meekest, most forgiving man, he is attacked by those who unjustifiably hate him (IX.21). Yet despite his evident annoyance, he aspires to calm self-sufficiency:

> I say, in my slight way I may proceed
>   To play upon the surface of Humanity.
> I write the world, nor care if the world read,
>   At least for this I cannot spare its vanity.
> My Muse hath bred, and still perhaps may breed
>   More foes by this same scroll: when I began it, I
> Thought that it might turn out so—*now* I *know* it,
> But still I am, or was, a pretty poet. (XV.60)

This judicious distancing contributes to the vaunted control exerted by the poet over his narrator, and also by the narrator over his material. Throughout the poem it is the narrator's voice, however changeable, that serves as the chief organizational principle. Repeatedly the narrator utters something such as: "Here I must leave him, for I grow pathetic" (IV.52.1) to show how he completely manipulates his characters, withdrawing from them when their suffering or delight moves him excessively. He even admits to being a puppet master who controls Juan to suit his chaste publisher's whims (IV.97). Thus the poet, positioning himself at the best vantage point for whatever he wishes to communicate, makes his presence felt behind as well as within his story.

Much of the satire is handled with such a light touch that it is almost indistinguishable from comedy, and even when the subject matter is serious, it is often treated in a superficially flippant manner. Yet I cannot agree with Marshall's view that the poem is not satire at all because it provides "no suggestion of the ideal" or that *"Don Juan* should be regarded as a vast literary joke."[9] The narrator, even while conceding that the world will think him immoral, repeatedly insists that his object is morality (XII.39.2–3; XII.55.4; XII.86.3). In the opening canto he defiantly challenges anyone to assert "that this is not a moral tale, though gay" (I.207), and his protestations become more resolute as the poem continues. He certainly declares a sanative purpose—to do as much through poetry as Newton did to restore fallen man through knowledge (X.1–3). But he believes in achieving that goal by first showing what is wrong, introducing varied topics

> as subservient to a moral use;
> Because my business is to *dress* society,
> And stuff with *sage* that very verdant goose. (XV.93)

His method is "to show things really as they are, / Not as they ought to be" (XII.40.1–3). In an implied statement of the satirist's positive goal, he asserts that since "gentle readers" have a propensity to close their eyes to what they do not wish to see, it is his moral obligation to open their eyes to reality (VI.88.1–5). And this passage, significantly, occurs in the canto with which Byron, after having been persuaded to abandon *Don Juan,* resumed the poem with self-confident vigor. No doubt he exaggerates when he advertises that his fifth canto has "a moral to each error tacked" and when, with one eye upon the Horatian dictum, he asserts it is "formed rather for instructing than delighting" (V.2.4–6). But being deadly solemn, as pious critics would have him be, is not his characteristic approach to the world's evil.

When Madame de Staël accused Byron of abetting immorality, he replied, according to Lady Blessington's account, that he had "sometimes represented vice under alluring forms, but so it was generally in the world, therefore it was necessary to paint it so." [10] Moreover, in his own defense Byron told de Staël that, unlike her, he had never depicted virtue in the guise of dullness or shown vice to be productive of happiness. The narrator in *Don Juan* defends his candor by claiming that his muse is "the most sincere that ever dealt in fiction"; she "treats all things, and ne'er retreats / From any thing" (XVI.2−3). Yet, he insists, she never hurts anyone; her "worst reproof's a smile" (XI.63). To the charge of belittling the value of human life, he answers that his views are no more nihilistic than the pronouncements of many famous moralists (VII.3−6). If he laughs at life, he does so only to check his emotional involvement in the world's sorrows (IV.4.1−2).

Throughout the poem Byron's narrator declares that his determination to effect social reform is not only responsible but heroic since his role as satiric gadfly inevitably provokes antagonism. To bolster his righteous honesty against all detractors, he assumes, in the tradition of the Earl of Shaftesbury, that ridicule is the test of truth; in his opinion, the underlying objection lodged against the first two cantos was that they contained "too much truth" (IV.97.3−4). Unlike his "epic brethren gone before" (I.202), the poet refuses to deal in fabulation. The obligation "of a true poet," he insists, is "to escape from fiction" and present the unvarnished realities of our world (VIII.86,89). The narrator holds up *Don Quixote* as the prototype of the "real Epic" (XIII. 8−11), even while lamenting nostalgically that, "Of all tales . . . the saddest," it shattered the romantic illusions of chivalry. Accordingly, the descriptions in *Don Juan* are advertised as not only "accurate" but "*Epic*, if plain truth should prove no bar" (VIII. 138.4−5). The narrator claims inspiration not from the mendacious patroness of romance but from the "true Muse" (VIII. 1.5). In a similar vein Byron told Lady Blessington, "I always write best when truth inspires me, and my satires, which are founded on truth, have more spirit than all my other productions, for they were written *con amore*." [11]

Since the desired truth, as the narrator interprets it, is tested not by those nebulous assumptions according to which most people live but by concrete reality, he usually identifies it with "fact" (VII.81.2). After completing the first five cantos, Byron wrote Murray: "Almost all Don Juan is *real* life—either my own—or from people I knew" (*BLJ*, VIII, 186). Yet to substantiate claims to veracity, the narrator capriciously refers those who remain incredulous "To history, tradition, and to facts, / To newspapers, whose truth all know and feel, / To plays in five, and operas in three acts" (I.203.1–4). Because those sources are notoriously unreliable, he thereby undermines his own credibility, in effect admitting that his art strives for only an approximation to empirical data. Although he calls himself a "philosopher" (VI. 22.1) and a man "fond of true philosophy" (I.220), he means something quite different from what those terms ordinarily imply. His demeaning of Platonism, Stoicism, and Berkeleyan idealism constitutes a conspicuous thrust against systematized philosophy. And when he himself becomes too speculative, relapsing into the insoluble labyrinth of metaphysics, he tries to regain a solid physical basis or even dismisses the subject (I.133–34; VI.22). What he endeavors to be is a friendly sage, like Horace, offering practical, experiential wisdom that will improve human behavior by encouraging man to confront his own nature without illusion. He feels obliged to deal in applicable realities in order to strip the sham from theoretical philosophy, fanciful criticism, and pretenses about motivation.

Yet even the narrator, impelled as he is by the desire to please, sometimes cloaks his true feelings with avowals of good intentions. When the progress of Julia's love leads to adultery, he protests: "And then—God knows what next—I can't go on; / I'm almost sorry that I e'er begun" (I.115.7–8). To make the lubricious tolerable in polite society, he repeatedly proclaims an unwillingness to offend the refined reader. In so doing he reveals that the raw, animalistic impulses of humanity that civilization pretends to have subdued lurk just beneath the surface, waiting to be called forth. The moment he piously announces, after having already divulged highly derogatory information about his characters, that scandal is his aversion and that he detests "all evil speaking, even in jest" (I.51.7–8), the reader is alerted to the blatant discrepancy between assertion and actuality. And since the assumption underlying the narrator's belated self-righteous declarations is that in cultivated society one needs only to affirm his rectitude in order to be exonerated, Byron pokes fun at both the culture that encourages such hypocrisy and the individual who undermines his own integrity to gain social acceptance.

At other times the narrator resorts to clever subterfuge, detours, and double-entendres to circumvent the social barriers to plain speaking. If a suppressed feral nature obtrudes on his civility, he strives, in feline fashion, to cover up the ground as rapidly as he has manured it. After slyly hinting at the intimacy of Inez and Alfonso, he feebly tries to discredit such "lies" by attributing their origin to malicious fabrication (I.66). Sometimes he uses a seemingly innocent word that means something quite different to the worldly wise (e.g., *Phrygian* in the double sense in which Virgil used it), or he coins words like *Cazzani* and *Philo-genitiveness* to cloak his obscenity in esoteric drapery. Nor does the narrator have qualms about affecting a coy refinement, as when he relates that Julia, seeking revenge, denied her husband "several little things he wanted" (I.180.4). At other times his genteel vulgarity dissipates his love of specific detail into vague generality, as when he declares that the harem wondered why Gulbeyaz would buy an odalisque who might then share "her throne and power and every thing beside" (VI.36.8). No matter how risqué the underlying idea may be, he feels compelled in the fashion of a Regency Mr. Spectator to temper wit with veneered morality.

One of the narrator's shrewdest ploys is his asserted withholding of information that might have been brought forth, for when he pretends to gloss over the unspeakable, the reader inevitably assumes the worst. Exactly where or how Juan was concealed in Julia's bed or what happened to Juan and the Ghost at Norman Abbey the narrator positively declines to tell, and his refusal confirms our worst suspicions. As an amiable gossip the narrator is unrivaled in literature because his ruse of staunchly refusing to speculate without verifiable evidence makes his rhetoric overwhelming. Nothing is more convincing than his claim to be withholding information in the interest of fairness: "For my part I say nothing—nothing—but / *This* I will say—my reasons are my own" (I.52.1–2). A man whose conscience virtually forces him to continue, against the superficial rules of etiquette, must, one assumes, be driven by the desire to see justice prevail. From his vast stockpile of possible information the usually omniscient narrator can single out those details which point in the direction of his innuendoes and lead his readers down the path his selectivity has predicated. Through this system of eating his cake and having it too, the narrator unmistakably conveys the reality without ever having expressed it. Sometimes to avoid unsettling his gentler readers he prefers not to complete statements such as his recollections of college life: "For there one learns—'tis not for me to boast, / Though I acquired—but I pass over *that*" (I.53. 1-2). Or he tantalizes us by catching himself short: "I say no more—I've said too much" (XVI.77.2). Yet he knows that no perspicacious reader will take such disclaimers seriously. They are all part of the narrator's psychological technique, especially at a crucial moment, for heightening suspense and titillating the reader into demanding more.

It is when the narrator becomes most Olympian that his satire is most devastating, and this lofty condescension, which Hazlitt attributed to Byron's alleged spite and pride, has periodically offended some readers. There are times, to be sure, when the narrator, through the use of substandard language ("And now, my Epic Renegade! what are ye at?"—Dedication 1.5) or a sweeping condemnation of Wordsworth's style as his "aversion," appears to dismiss people and matters as though they were undeserving of consideration. And the obliteration of lawyer Brougham's identity through the assimilation of his name into a pun ("A legal broom's a moral chimney-sweeper"—X.15.1) is accompanied by an equally patronizing tone. Partisan critics ("Praetorian bands") who attempt to set up their candidates for poetical emperor receive the most contemptuous dismissal, for regarding them the narrator contends: "It is hardly worth my while / With such small gear to give myself concern" (XI.62.1-63.3). James R. Sutherland, who regarded Byron's "off-hand, contemptuous manner" as "the new note in English satire," observed: "We can put up with denunciation, for then we are at least being taken seriously; but to be dismissed as a sort of dull joke is highly insulting." [12] Inevitably this technique of brushing aside contemporaries as though they counted for nought proved stinging, even among those who should have recognized that anything truly beneath contempt deserved no comment.

Some of the narrator's oblique declarations of truth are achieved, paradoxically, through outright lying. Certainly no one who had actually bribed the editor of a contemporary review (not even his grandmother's) would advertise his malfeasance (I.209–10). His declaration that he has already bought "public approbation" could have come only from someone completely confident that his indirect attack on William Roberts of the *British Review* and the toadying habits of some writers would be seen as a complete hoax. Nor would many readers be misled by his feigned naïveté in claiming not to know why Lady Adeline takes such extraordinary interest in Juan, or by his more blatant pretense of ignorance about what houris of the Moslem heaven want to do with the young Khan. Sometimes the narrator indulges in specious reasoning so irrational for a man of sense that the reader is actually expected to conclude the opposite. When lust is attributed to the sun and the greater degree of propriety found in "nations of the moral north" is therefore connected with their inhibiting cold, the reader is supposed to understand that this facetious logician cannot possibly hold the premises on which he grounds his arguments. He fully intends his readers to see through such mendacity and tacitly acknowledge that small talk is often nothing more than polite lying.

Had the narrator not already established his character, according to the rules of social etiquette, as an essentially reliable critic of all he surveys, his occasional deceptions might ruin his credibility. One of Byron's supreme achievements as a satirist— one that points beyond the eighteenth-century mode to that flourishing today—is his creation of a complex narrator whose relationship to both reader and subject matter cannot be taken wholly at face value since it is ironic and frequently shifting. Though his complicated, intriguing personality is stained with the social corruption he derides, nevertheless his compassion for the fallen world compels the reader to identify with both the satirist and the satiric targets. Never does the narrator assume, except in jest, an impeccably moral attitude that might erect psychological barriers between reader and satiric object. Far from alienating his readers, his implicit awareness that to be human is to be flawed compels the reader to reexamine the degree to which each individual, through hypocrisy, contributes to the world's corruption. Never as a solemn preacher or a cynical scoffer but rather as a sophisticated observer, he lives among us, implying the ideals he intends but seldom stating them, instead leaving them for the reader to infer. Though his effusions rarely produce the "honest simple verse" to which he modestly pretends in the Dedication, it is hard not to admire him, even when he resorts to duplicity to express his involvement with erring humanity. Despite occasional self-pity and laments for the meaninglessness of life, the narrator does not appear to me to be a predominantly alienated or tragic figure.[13] In my opinion he has come to terms with the progressive disillusionment he calls life and with an inconsistent, ever-changing world that he understands only in part. Though scarred, he has not been overwhelmed, and he obligingly invites us to profit from his experience. However chaotic and unfathomable he finds the universe to be, Byron's narrator continues to expand his consciousness of life's abundance.

ᔐ CHAPTER 7 ᔑ

SATIRIC FORM IN *DON JUAN*

THE form of *Don Juan* is so indeterminate as virtually to defy categorization. Since the classical epic, Roman satire, Italian epic romance, mock-heroic poetry, the picaresque novel, Restoration comedy, the realistic novel, the novel of manners, the pantomime, Gothic romance, the ballad, the lyric, and neo-classical satire have all left their imprint on the poem, it is not surprising that the receptacle containing such varied ingredients should be amorphous. Critics who have felt uneasy about calling *Don Juan* a "hold-all" have resorted to designating it as a metrical novel, a mock-epic, an epic carnival, an epic of negation, epic satire, or merely satire. While excellent cases can be made for all these labels, none is utterly satisfactory for the poem as a whole. One of the few delineations with which no critics would cavil is James R. Thompson's description of *Don Juan* as "a kind of generic explosion produced by the nineteenth-century pressure to redefine form in highly personal terms."[1]

What is undeniable, in any case, is that the form, or formlessness, accurately reflects Byron's view of life and man's disordered, incongruous, and unpredictable world. His concept of artistic form, as McGann has maintained, is not concerned with internal unity but, in the Horatian tradition, with rhetoric and function.[2] Form, either in the classical sense of a preconceived mold or in the Romantic sense of a product of organic development, has little meaning for *Don Juan*. So long as a poetical work was "simple and entire," as Byron translated the Horatian dictum in *Hints from Horace*, and also was organized in such a way as to express most effectively what the poet had to say, form could take care of itself. Byron's repeated assertions that the cantos of *Don Juan*, whether organized around topics or episodic narrative, could go on almost indefinitely suggest a looseness of structure and an open-endedness that challenge conventional notions of form. The shapelessness of *Don Juan*, however, was not a serious problem with regard to satire. Since its Roman inception, satire has been thought of as a hodgepodge (*farrago*), a medley, or a miscellaneous collection. It has tended to be so unstructured that, as Northrop Frye affirmed, "a kind of parody of form seems to run all through its tradition."[3] Acquaintance with the tradition, which included many varieties of satire and different levels of style appropriate to them, had taught Byron that there was actually no prescribed form.

He was sufficiently skilled as a classicist to appreciate what the Romans called formal satire. In Latin *satura* designated only a particular literary genre—a seemingly unordered poem mixing unfavorable criticism with moral observations. In English, however, the term *satire* could be applied to any artistic composition in which the author's intention was to arouse contempt for his subject. More loosely, it might refer to isolated passages in compositions that were not predominantly derogatory, to the temper characterizing such works, or even to the techniques employed to degrade. It is revealing that in letters and conversations Byron most frequently referred to *Don Juan* as a satire. It is also significant that early reviewers saw the poem primarily as satire—on everything, including the epic. And whatever the generic modulations of the poem, its substance is undeniably permeated by the satiric spirit, even in instances when that spirit, as both Ernest J. Lovell and Alvin B. Kernan have observed, is so thoroughly blended with either comedy or tragedy that it can hardly be identified as "serious" satire.[4] Since there was no satiric form adequate to a large composition, a more comprehensive genre, such as the epic, was needed as a carrier—one in which a variety of intentions, including the satiric, could function. Within this matrix Byron was able to incorporate not only many kinds of satire but in one instance, the Constantinople episode, an illustration of *satura*.

His conscious adaptation of both the form and substance of Roman satire in Canto V suggests that he wished that portion to be seen in the light of a continuing tradition. This imitation was his way of announcing his genre and establishing his pedigree. His two introductory stanzas beginning that canto advertise his intention of forsaking "amorous writing" in favor of an edifying variety that attaches morals to every error and attacks all the passions. Properly interpreted, the narrator's role becomes that of the Roman satirist with Stoic inclinations. Moreover, the dialogue in which Johnson explains his Stoic philosophy to Juan (V.13–25) is an authentic replica of the dialogue form in which both Horace and Persius treated Stoic doctrines. Horace actually invented the satiric dialogue and used it with subtle irony to involve prolocutor and adversary in a dramatic skit. Persius, though strongly inclined toward dramatic conversations even when the presence of his opponent in a debate had to be imagined, used the Horatian innovation as framework for only two whole satires, while Juvenal was even less disposed toward dialogue form. It was Pope, in his *Imitations of Horace*, who proved to be most skillful of all in pitting speakers against one another in an evolving discussion.[5] Pope's example probably inspired Byron to attempt a similar feat.

The Stoic "paradox" enunciated by Johnson—that all those who have failed to liberate themselves from their passions are enslaved—was part of the Roman satiric tradition, having been used by Horace and Persius in dialogue form. In Horace's Satire II.3 Damasippus expounds the topos that all who are not wise enough to be masters of themselves are mad and thereupon accuses Horace, cast in this case as the adversary, of madness. Similarly in Satire II.7 Horace's slave Davus, in the role of prolocutor, tries to convince his "enslaved" master that only Stoic philosophers who have renounced all passions (men like Davus himself, of course) are free. Drawing on both of the foregoing Stoic dialogues of Horace, Persius's fifth satire employs toward its conclusion an imagined conversation between the satirist and a hypothetical freed slave to demonstrate that only philosophers are free.

In view of the popularity of Stoic discourses, Johnson's comments on universal slavery in Canto V of *Don Juan* might not be linked specifically to Persius's fifth satire were it not for Byron's unmistakable verbal borrowing from notes offered by Madan to his translation of Juvenal and Persius.[6] Drawing on Madan's explanation of Persius's farfetched metaphors, which are presumably based on the shedding of snakeskin, the fluttering of limed birds, and the struggling of beasts in nets, Byron clustered all three images in the following passage:

> some grand mistake
> Casts off its bright skin yearly like the snake.
>
> 'Tis true, it gets another bright and fresh,
>   Or fresher, brighter; but the year gone through,
> This skin must go the way too of all flesh,
>   Or sometimes only wear a week or two;—
> Love's the first net which spreads its deadly mesh;
>   Ambition, Avarice, Vengeance, Glory, glue
> The glittering lime-twigs of our latter days,
> Where still we flutter on for pence or praise. (V.21.7–22.8)

Three of man's ensnaring passions in life's progressive disillusionment—love, ambition, and avarice—are among the six deterrents to liberty discussed in Persius's fifth; and in Horace's two Stoic dialogues they are also attacked as prime obstacles to equanimity. Vengeance and glory, on the other hand, are strongly identified with Juvenal, particularly in Satire X, Byron's favorite.[7]

Byron also had precedents in Roman satire for his ironic presentation of Stoicism from several perspectives. Persius, who would have his readers believe that he never wavers from adherence to Stoic tenets, concedes at the close of his fifth satire that his philosophy is not for ignoramuses like the coarse centurion. Horace, in his two Stoic dialogues, presents the advocates of Stoicism as unreliable counselors—Damasippus, a social outcast as well as former madman, and Davus, an insolent slave; both fail to convert the satirist, whom they accuse of being enslaved by follies. But whereas Horace merely implies that the rigorous demands of Stoicism are more readily postulated than practiced, Byron's narrator makes that inference explicit: Juan's recent misfortunes are said to have been enough "to shake a stoic" (V.9.1), and later when Juan ceases weeping he is said to have "called back the stoic to his eyes" (V.121.5).

Yet Johnson, despite outward manifestations of English sang-froid, does not qualify as a true Stoic. Indeed his reliance on fate or *fortuna* as the ruling force in men's lives recalls Juvenal's association of fatalism with false Stoics who do not live by what they preach (Satires II.65; IX.32,35). Even while claiming to be inured to life through crushing adversities, Johnson is sufficiently moved to offer consolation to the tender-hearted Juan. What the former advocates is not so much true Stoicism as an attitude of resignation. Declaring that knowledge can be gained through viewing one's present state from the proper perspective, he argues that the experience of slavery will teach a man how better to behave when a master (V.23.5–8). His ironic undercutting of Stoicism, when he asserts that its requisite detachment from life is purchased at the exorbitant price of human feelings, has parallels in Horace, who concludes his Stoic dialogues with contrived jests or congés that question man's ability to abide by Stoic principles.

Byron's skill in combining various ingredients drawn from Roman satire into a traditional satiric form deserves special attention. Though the subject of Johnson's discourse derives primarily from Persius, the general tone of the dialogue more closely resembles the Horatian mixture of genial humor and wry cynicism than the earnest didacticism of Persius. Yet it was Byron's originality in readapting classical materials that earned him a place as a contributor to the tradition. His conversion of metaphorical enslavement into physical reality and his use of Constantinople's slave market as a microcosm of mercantile society, where everyone offers himself to the highest bidder, ingeniously and vastly enriched the possibilities for a thematic conflict between freedom and slavery in that episode. Even Stoic philosophy is so modernized as to be assimilable into Robert Walpole's truism on human venality ("all have prices, / . . . according to their vices"— V.27.7–8) and to be assailable ultimately as a philosophy of insensibility ("To feel for none is the true social art / Of the world's stoics—men without a heart"—V.25.7–8). And the dialogue between Johnson and Juan is more than an unresolved debate on Stoicism. As a dramatic mode of dialectic, it stimulates each speaker to a revelation of his own perspective, as well as to a deeper perception of the limitations inherent in his own outlook. Through his naive questioning of Johnson's cynical approach, Juan serves as friendly adversary or *provocateur* in evoking the differences between sentimental youth and disillusioned age. One of Byron's finest achievements in this *sermo* is the unexpected combination of a crescendo suggesting a modified Stoicism as the key to survival and an ironic coda questioning its validity as a guide to life.

Possibly because Byron saw a number of parallels between Constantinople, which he called "Rome transplanted" (V.86.8), and Rome under the early caesars, he drew many other suggestions for his fifth canto from Roman satire and thereby emphasized further his connection with that still vital tradition. The narrator's frequent references to the role of capricious fortune in that section are reminiscent of Juvenal and, to a lesser degree, Horace rather than of Moslem belief. It is likely that Byron had mentally assimilated the extensive commentary Madan wrote for Juvenal's tenth satire on the significance of Fortuna in pagan Rome. Certainly Byron was indebted to the substance of two Juvenalian satires (VI and X) for the encounter involving Juan and the lustful sultana Gulbeyaz. For ideas, phraseology, and analogies he also drew on Madan's notes about the nymphomaniac empress Messalina and her determination to force the handsome Gaius Silius to become her husband. Much of the broad sexual jesting in the fifth canto echoes that of Juvenal. Castration, for example, in addition to being an accepted Turkish practice, may have been suggested by hints in Juvenal's tenth that Madan had explicated. While circumcision remained a notable difference between Christian and Moslem in Byron's day, as his earlier letters observed, he would also have recalled the recurrent jests in Horace, Persius, and Juvenal about Jewish circumcision. Juan's transvestism, as well as its sexual overtones, had precedents in Juvenal and in Madan's notes to Satires II and X. But throughout that episode it is not so much the imitation of the model that deserves study as the ingenious transformation of Juvenalian materials in the alembic of Byron's imagination. Byron's achievement, in altering even the "tragic satire" of Juvenal into half-serious comedy dealing with feminine lust, masculine chastity, marital fidelity, and tyranny over all that should be free, shows how completely he could absorb the ingredients of Roman satire into his own creation.

While the imitation of *satura* is evident only in Canto V, the overall randomness of *Don Juan* suggests satiric content. It is pri-

marily through the satiric spirit, especially as it is assimilated into
epic form, that Byron's satire functions. Despite the poem's open
defiance of epic conventions, the narrator repeatedly claims that
Don Juan is an epic and that its contents (love, war, shipwreck,
and even a "view of hell") qualify it for that designation. There is
good reason, furthermore, to believe that Byron took those
claims seriously, that he intended something more than another
comic epic in the Italian tradition. It would be easy, especially in
the early cantos, to assert that *Don Juan* is a mock-epic since that
subgenre not only incorporates satire in its burlesque of epic
conventions but also uses the ideals of previous epics to illus-
trate, by allusion, the contrast between earlier greatness and
contemporary pettiness. But as Brian Wilkie has shown, *Don
Juan* is not just a mock-epic.[8] Byron was determined that, unlike
his "epic brethren gone before," he would write a *true* epic depicting man and his world realistically. On the assumption that
Don Juan in scope and purpose deserved to be compared to Homer's *Iliad*, Byron told Thomas Medwin in late 1821 or early
1822 that his poem was "an epic as much in the spirit of our day
as the Iliad was in Homer's."[9] Evidently he thought it mirrored
the religious, political, and social attitudes of his own era as com-
prehensively and accurately as Homer's epic had reflected his
age. Byron's invocation of Homer's aid before the siege of Ismail
(VII, 79–80), his use of language less formal and stylized than
Virgil's or Milton's, and his rejection of a providential or teleo-
logical design for background of the protagonist's "heroism" indicate that Byron in some ways felt a closer affinity with Homer
than with the later epic poets. But fundamental changes in the
inherited tradition were necessary to produce a modern epic depicting the ideals—or lack of them—in contemporary society,
and satire was essential in sharpening its negative features.

   When in 1823 Byron called *Don Juan* an "Epic Satire" (XIV.
99.6), he acknowledged its hybrid nature. His poetic commentary on *Don Quixote* (XIII.8–11)—upon which Ridenour has
elaborated [10]—suggests the relationship that Byron apparently
saw between satire and epic. Even though Cervantes may have
assumed that in our corrupt world only a fool or a madman
could champion chivalric values, he was not, in Byron's judgment,
ridiculing the noble idealism for which Quixote fights. Cervantes' "hero" is "right" in

Redressing injury, revenging wrong,
  To aid the damsel and destroy the caitiff;
Opposing singly the united strong,
  From foreign yoke to free the helpless native. (XIII.10.1−4)

Yet we smile at the spectacle the deluded knight makes of himself, and, reflecting on the folly of defending virtue, we realize
the melancholy plight in which Cervantes has involved us. Thus
what Cervantes may have begun as satire on the absurdities
of knight-errantry resulted in a "real Epic unto all who have
thought" (XIII.9.8). By demolishing the traditional concept of
heroism, he destroyed the old form of epic romance. In its place
he provided a genuine, realistic epic, the only kind viable in a
skeptical, disillusioned age.

This reading of *Don Quixote* has implications for Byron's interpretation of epic satire in *Don Juan*. Like Cervantes, Byron strove
through satire to banish a false vision of life. In the course of
achieving that goal he produced, like Cervantes, a literary form
that radically readapted epic traditions, the epic hero, and the
very idea of heroism—a form that could integrate other literary
genres into itself and accommodate satire as part of its realistic
approach. The union of such an epic and satire was more compatible than might have at first appeared, for the traditions of
the two genres already met on common ground. Love, war, shipwreck, banquets, and glimpses of Hades, essential ingredients in
the epic, were also standard fare in Roman *satura* and neoclassical adaptations. In *Don Juan* epic of a negative thrust could easily
exist in symbiotic relationship with satire. The epic element, impelled by narrative, was identifiable with the onward momentum
of life; the satiric, conversely, with whatever threatened man's
progress. True heroism and idealism, however rare, were not to
be scorned, though their goals were usually unattainable and
their adherents often appeared foolish to a cynical world. This
ironic situation, as Byron saw it, represented the dilemma of
modern man, and "Epic Satire" was his way of embodying it.

Quite likely the term *epic satire* also had another association for
Byron. Although he may have thought of *Don Juan* in its earliest
stages as primarily in the *genus tenue* and the casual Horatian
mode, as the poem developed more grandiose proportions he
acquired a loftier sense of its mission—one comparable to the

Juvenalian concept of satire in the *genus grande*. Particularly
from careful study of Juvenal's Satires I, VI, X, and XV, Byron
learned that true-to-life satire might be as edifying as tragedy or
epic. Even though Juvenal respected the great epics of the past,
he had the utmost contempt for poetasters of his day who
strained beyond their abilities to attempt the highest genres. Traditional epic and tragedy, with their artificial conventions, im-
practicable ideals, and hackneyed mythological subjects, seemed
no longer viable to Juvenal because they were irrelevant to contemporary life. What was needed, in view of the corruption per-
meating every stratum of Roman society, was a literature of
truth rather than of literary invention—in short, one that depicted reality as Juvenal saw it. If satire was to supersede the out-
worn genres in the old poetic hierarchy and assume their instructive functions, the satirist was obliged to aspire to a *genus
grande* that would approximate, even while radically readapting,
epic form. In practice Juvenal substantiated those assumptions
through elevated rhetoric, an impassioned style, and a heroic
determination to amend society through exposure of wrong-
doing.[11] A mock invocation to Calliope in his fourth satire (ll.
34–36) suggests that a satirist who records the truth has tran-
scended the need of epic inspiration, and he dismisses her as peremptorily as Byron would later with "Hail, Muse! *et cetera*" (*DJ*
III. 1.1). Juvenal's frequent imitation of epic, whether with serious intent or, when style was inappropriate to subject matter,
for humorous effect, further showed that he strove for a nobler
goal than that ordinarily associated with the satires of Horace
and Persius. It may well be that Juvenal's works, to which Byron
repeatedly returned over the years, deepened his concept of satire so that it evolved beyond a youthful lashing out at whatever
displeased him into a sophisticated view of life encompassing all
things human.

CHAPTER 8

THE SOCIAL ANIMAL AS THE BUTT OF SATIRE IN *DON JUAN*

I N RESPONSE to the first strictures on *Don Juan* in 1819, By-ron cavalierly defended his poem as only "a playful satire" that was "never intended to be serious."[1] As he continued its composition, however, he became increasingly insistent that it be taken in earnest. Admittedly, much of the poem is predicated on what Northrop Frye has called a *comic* acceptance of the world rather than a *satiric* rejection of it and therefore cannot be in-cluded in the category of savage indignation. Yet one cannot slight Byron's assertion, in a letter of 25 December 1822 to Mur-ray, that *Don Juan* would ultimately be recognized for what it was meant to be: "a *satire* on *abuses* of the present *states* of Society" (*BLJ*, X, 68). The focus of his satire is also enunciated unequivo-cally, in 1823, in his poetic statement that, despite the inclusion of subjects like politics, policy, and piety, his real business as sati-rist was "to *dress* society, . . . that very verdant goose" (*DJ* XV. 93.5–6). To achieve that end, Byron subjected to critical scrutiny both man and the social chains that warped his potential.

Except for the return to a Rousseauistic Eden in the Haidée episode, Byron did not ordinarily make a sharp distinction be-tween evil society and inherently good mankind. Nor did he, like William Godwin and his followers, believe that man's rationality could so overwhelm his bestial instincts as to make the perfect-ibilian state likely. The vestigial Calvinism in Byron's view of hu-man nature was evidently strong enough for him to regard man's proclivity to sin as the underlying cause of society's corruption. Any attempt to ameliorate the postlapsarian condition therefore had to begin by examining man himself. Yet since the individual does not exist in isolation, it was necessary to consider man as a social animal in his customary habitat.

What liberates Byron's satire on the human race in *Don Juan* from the thralldom of historical annotation is its portrayal of human nature so incisively and so accurately that the poetic depictions are applicable to mankind in all societies. Even the personal enemies whom Byron caricatured because of their idiosyncratic faults became epitomes of general types that we recognize among us today. Obviously he had learned that, to have an effective bite, satire had to rely on concrete, topical details. To have lasting applicability, however, it had to merge the particular with the universal. This goal he achieved by concentrating on that anomalous mixture of good and evil, weakness and strength, deity and dirt—humanity, as represented by a multifarious selection of specimens.

Juan is exceptional because he moves in debased societies without losing much of his inherent goodness—at least until the Empress Catherine spoils him into self-indulgence. Because he is willing to risk his life (whether on a sinking ship or a battlefield) in behalf of others, Juan alone retains a modicum of heroism in a world that has corrupted altruistic valor into the petty acquisitiveness of English highwaymen or the calculated opportunism of Lord Henry Amundeville. Whether Juan is interpreted as the natural man, as a burlesque of the natural man, or as the personification of comedy, he indisputably behaves according to impulse rather than externally imposed mores. Hence in every social setting he remains the outsider. However adaptable he may be, he retains his comparative innocence, his naïveté often serving as a shield. An excellent foil to society, he brings out the contrast between human and social values. As Lord Henry astutely observes, Juan is one who "would not see depravity / In faults which sometimes show the soil's fertility" (XIII.22.5–6). Such tolerance, in contrast to the satirical narrator's lack of forbearance, may indeed create an instability of tone. But it also adds another dimension to Byron's perspective on the fallen world with which all of us are obliged to become reconciled if we expect to endure. The satire takes on a tragic aspect when we perceive that the world Byron so accurately represents will corrupt and ultimately overwhelm all of us. As Kernan rightly maintains, Byron's satire is directed chiefly against those obstacles that man, usually in the name of society, sets up to impede the onward flow of life.[2] This is not to say that Byron's emphasis on the flaws, rather than the merits, suggests a hopeless depravity in man. His function, like that of Old Testament prophets, was to show thinking men some of the many injustices that cried out for amendment. The poet's method differed from that of the humorless prophet or preacher because the satirist could tell the truth with either the disarming smile recommended by Horace or a sardonic laugh.

As middle-class demand for propriety increased during the later years of the Regency era, writers and publishers were obliged to conform to at least the appearance of morality. This demand for verbal propriety, to which Byron refused to submit during the attempted censorship of *Don Juan*, he regarded as a sham that was symptomatic of a thoroughly corrupt society because the cover-up merely encouraged the crime. Remonstrating against such practice, he quoted Voltaire in his Preface to Cantos VI–VIII: "Plus les moeurs sont dépravés, plus les expressions deviennent mesurées; on croit regagner en langage ce qu'on a perdu en vertu." Such insincere lip service to morality, usually in terms of pious platitudes, was what Byron termed *cant*, and since he deemed it the chief obstacle to social reform, it often received in various guises the brunt of his satiric attack. In his first reply to Bowles (1821), he lamented that "in these days the grand '*primum mobile*' of England is *cant*; cant political, cant poetical, cant religious, cant moral; but always *cant*, multiplied through all the varieties of life" (*LJ*, V, 542). Indeed it might be concerned with virtually any subject, including sentiment, heroism, or the love of nature, but was always associated with an uncritical acceptance of clichés favored by esteemed social circles or coteries. As Byron defined *cant*, it was primarily "a thing of words, without the smallest influence upon human actions."[3] Unfortunately, he thought, the English felt free to act as they pleased so long as they honored "verbal decorum." He compared this detestable habit to "looking after the shadow" while losing "the substance of goodness" and expressed the view that only exposure to ridicule would conquer it.[4] He further voiced his disgust not only that cant had become such a "vile substitute" for morals but also that "the good-natured world" confused his attack on the one for disdain of the other.[5] Since parochial middle-class society had become so pleasantly deluded that it could not differentiate between the two, strong realism was needed to jolt it out of complacency.

Many situations in *Don Juan*, by portraying duplicity elevated to a fine art, expose the falseness of society's demand that, regardless of the consequences in human misery, acceptable exteriors be upheld. In keeping up the external appearances of their sham marriage, Jose and Inez show that socially encouraged lying has become virtually ingrained. To defend an honor that no one, not even she herself, believes in, Julia in her boudoir lies superbly, and we applaud the guilty adulteress. The simplistic belief that closing one's eyes to "the facts of life" will eliminate them, as in the case of Juan's puritanical education, has not only abetted deception but has also made the revelation more prurient. Self-delusion, to which Byron thought humanity highly prone, often produces consequences equally disruptive. Whereas Juan's self-mystification at the first experience of love may be glossed over as naive and natural, Julia's attempts to convince herself that her love for Juan can transcend the flesh constitute a self-delusion that invites catastrophe, for good intentions activated by deluding premises cannot produce good results. Lady Adeline's self-deception is far more innocent: she does not even understand her subconscious motive for saving Juan from the Duchess's "talisman" (XIV.62). Her rationalization is so convincing that she herself believes it to be true.

Too often, however, people deliberately misrepresent themselves in order to dupe others. In an effort to cloak her infidelity, Gulbeyaz showers unusual cordiality on her husband; and to discredit Julia in Alfonso's eyes, Inez feigns loving friendship to Julia only to tempt her with Juan. Sham is the very essence of Inez, whether in her intellectual accomplishments, her theoretical (but unapplied) goodness, or her so-called "magnanimity" in failing to defend a maligned husband. The narrator assures us that by popular estimate she possesses "virtues equall'd by her wit alone" (I.10.4) and proceeds ironically to show the validity of that statement, for she has neither virtue nor wisdom. When Inez praises Catherine for "maternal" interest in Juan, the narrator unequivocally declares this sanctimonious misconstruction to be nothing more than deliberate hypocrisy (X.31–34). By revealing such discrepancies between pretense and reality, Byron achieves some of his finest effects as an ironist.

At the core of human problems Byron places selfishness, manifested most often by the desire for personal gratification at others' expense. The lust for power, glory, and fame can be attributed to an eagerness to aggrandize the self, and men of power are, with rare exceptions, motivated primarily by self-love (XIV.102). In what may be a satirical jibe at Shelley's wish to make love the basis of an idealistic philosophy, the narrator declares love itself to be only vanity—"Selfish in its beginning as its end" (IX.73.1–2). In Audacia Shoestring's aspirations to winning a ducal husband, we see marriage as nothing but selfish ambition. Though Juan is not in love with Catherine, the attentions of a woman so far above him flatter his vanity such that he, like all her other favorites, feels himself a king. In Catherine, as well as the Sultan, self-love demands a succession of amatory conquests, though none satisfies for long, and this insatiable desire is clearly related to their ambitions in war. As the narrator observes, ambitions in love and war are usually rewarded in youth; in age, avarice, a redirection of the selfish pursuit, becomes a compensatory replacement (I.216; X.22). Ambitions of one sort or another drive all to magnify their egos, and Juan's Spanish cousins demonstrate their eagerness to use him for their own advancement in Russia. Even the humane Baba, after learning that his argument against the drowning of Juan displeases Gulbeyaz, relents and consoles himself with the realization that he prefers "his own neck to another's" (VI.116). In the most desperate circumstances man even resorts to cannibalism, killing and eating his fellow men to insure his own survival. "The gull and crow," we are told, "Flock o'er their carrion, just like men below" (IV. 28.7–8). Hence it is ironic that Lambro, in confiscating cargoes and selling the marketable plunder, should be condemned for lawless piracy, since in our materialistic civilization man's greedy, imperialistic aspirations follow much the same pattern and may even be extolled if they abide by authorized rules. Wealth, through which all ambitions may be gratified, thereby becomes the highest deity because it represents the ultimate power.

Instead of permitting human love to be the altruistic giving of oneself, as it can be with Haidée or with Juan's care for Leila, ac-

quisitive society has perverted it into a means of satisfying selfish desires even while averring its essentially spiritual nature.
Though Byron does not deny its spiritual element, especially
under the idyllic circumstances of a Cycladean island or in the
extraordinarily pure Aurora Raby, the ultramundane narrator
qualifies the sentimental ideal by emphasizing the brief duration
of passion, its intoxicating effect, its dependence upon physical
well-being, and man's natural inclination toward inconstancy. Society further aggravates man's inherent frailty by banning all love
that does not conform to categories known as Platonic, canoni-
cal, spiritual, or marital in a futile attempt to regulate what can
flourish only in a free and natural condition. The injustice of
such regulation is compounded by punishments such as that of
Julia for a sincere love and that of the pregnant country girl who
has poached on "Nature's manor." Without the spiritual leaven-
ing, love becomes just a brief gratification of corporeal need.
Thus Juan can physically evacuate his recollections of Julia as he
reads her sentimental letter and wretches with seasickness, and
Catherine after Juan's departure requires no more than twenty-
four hours to flush out her yearning for him. Our mercantile society, which squelches all spiritual concerns, forces men to be so
preoccupied with materialistic matters that they lack the necessary leisure on which love thrives. Women, on the other hand,
because they are denied opportunities outside the home, must
rely on it as their prime resource. Therefore among women,
whether they are "pedestrian Paphians" or honorable matrons
determined to marry their daughters to wealthy husbands, love
becomes a vendible commodity. As Juan discovers in the London
"marriage mart," young girls are exhibited and auctioned off
like Smithfield horses. The inevitable results of such sales are
possessiveness, infidelity, resentment, boredom, and misery.
Even the marriage of the Amundevilles, who once thought themselves in love, has become "Serene, and noble,—conjugal, but
cold" (XIV.86). As Byron depicts the world, true love is rare,
happiness in marriage at best evanescent.

Women are not exonerated from blame for the deplorable relations between the sexes, but "female errors," as Byron calls
them in allusion to Pope's *Rape of the Lock*, are usually seen as the
inevitable flaws forced upon "the weaker vessel" by a male-
dominated society. English bluestockings, for example, presume

to assert their dominion over the intellectual milieu despite, and partly because of, the inferior education accorded them. Women in general, because their roles have been restricted by society, tend to be envious of the more fortunate of their own kind, especially beautiful women, to whom greater opportunities are open. Byron also assumes that women, being sheltered, are more inclined than men to be deluded about reality. Moreover, since the feminine virtues extolled by society demand softness and compliance, few women are "very stable / In their resolves" (XV.6.3–4), and often a discrepancy exists between their intentions and their actions. And though some men, such as Southey ("that incarnate lie") and most politicians, make careers out of artful deception, women have been forced to become mendacious just to survive in their inferior position. As the narrator observes,

> Now what I love in women is, they won't
> Or can't do otherwise than lie, but do it
> So well, the very truth seems falsehood to it. (XI.36.6–8)

Like wine, women are often at variance with their labels and, once decanted, are likely to undergo adulteration. The embodiment of all these faults, though she admits to none, is Donna Inez, against whom the poet directs his most biting satire on womanhood. And since society approves the pharisaical pretenses of that malicious, superficial woman so egocentric as to believe herself virtuous, she is able to wreak great unhappiness.

Yet Byron's satire is not directed against women's sexuality, which he regards as natural, but rather against those who would deny or misuse it. While the promiscuous lust of Catherine serves as the butt of much sexual joking, her pleasure in lovers as sex objects is no more reprehensible than that traditionally accorded men and, furthermore, is asserted to be healthier than the sexual trickery of that stingy, half-chaste Elizabeth of England, who teasingly exploited sex for power (IX.81). Even if woman has been called "the worst Cause of war," the "gate of Life and Death," and the reason for man's fall, the narrator nevertheless deems her ample compensation for man's lapse since by her he rises and falls again (IX.55–56). When scorned, a woman such as Gulbeyaz can indeed become a ferocious animal; yet the eunuch

Baba's ensuing derision of feminine obstinacy, pride, indecision, changeability, and immorality is ironically undermined by his "neutrality," for his altered state compels an unmanly, unnatural perspective (VI.117).

The other topic banned from polite nineteenth-century conversation—religion—is subjected to equally candid scrutiny. The numerous slurs on both its doctrine and practice need not suggest agnosticism in Byron but rather a determination to assail the constraints, venalities, bigotries, and hypocrisies that, simply because of association with a sacrosanct topic, had often been immune to criticism.[6] Byron's most irreverent jibes appear in the first two cantos. His parody of the Decalogue for his own poetical commandments (I.204–6), the jest about Inez's fatuous correlation of the Hebrew concept of "God" and the English "damn" (I.14), the reference to "post-obits of theology" (I.103.8), and Julia's regret that her prayers to the Virgin may have been answered (I.75–76) transcend deistic rationalism and in Byron's day were enough to evoke the charge of blasphemy. Moreover, his statement that man's reward for giving pleasure or pain to the living is eternal damnation (II.192) and his discomfort at the implications of St. Luke's story of Abraham, Lazarus, and the rich man in the hereafter (II.86) seriously question divine justice and mercy. Nor were the pious pleased by his assertion that nothing calms the spirit so much as "rum and true religion" (II.34), his aspersions on the sins of St. Augustine and St. Anthony (I.47, 64), or his reminder that heretics have been burned in the name of Christianity (I.83). Especially offensive to Catholics were the reference to a priest taking one of Jose's mistresses (I.34), the suggestion that souls of the drowned would not be freed from "purgatorial coals" until their relatives were willing to pay for masses (II.55), and Pedrillo's scornful damning of a man who requested final absolution (II.44). Yet we must remember that iconoclastic satire, designed as it is to jolt the reader, cannot be a doxology in praise of the status quo.

After the violent public outcry against irreligion in the first installment of *Don Juan*, Byron was more careful to focus his attacks on the hypocrisy of the falsely religious, and in several instances he expressed his affirmation of genuine spiritual aspirations. The lyrical Ave Maria stanzas of Canto III (101–3) represent almost a hymn to the Virgin, although they may strike the reader as too obvious an advertisement of Christian devotion, especially when followed by the proclamation of a pantheistic worship of nature. To substantiate his lament that man misinterprets Christ's "pure creed," he declares his belief in Christ's divinity and swears that he "never arraigned his creed, but the use—or abuse—made of it" (XV.18 and n). This argument, echoing the satirist's usual justification for censure, is certainly valid for Byron's religious satire after Canto II. What he chose to assail would, in most cases, also incur disapproval from the majority of readers. His assertion that ardor of belief varies in accord with fear of death (XI.5–6), like his claim that monks ("Those vegetables of the Catholic creed"—XIV.81) find sloth an enemy to piety, embodies psychological truths that few would deny, though many might object to their flippant presentation. The deceit of clergy who do not live their religion continued to draw his ire—in references to "a *forty-parson-power* to chaunt" the praise of hypocrisy (X.34) and to the Rev. Rodomont Precisian, "Who did not hate so much the sin as sinner" (XIII.87). Byron directed his most devastating ridicule against Joanna Southcott, the prophetess who claimed that she was the vessel of another parthenogenetic miracle and that she could dispense sealed passports to heaven. In the poet's view she represented the epitome of fanaticism, mystical obfuscation, and presumptuous fraud.[7] Byron was certainly not unusual in objecting to the antinomian tenet that faith alone, irrespective of good works, should merit salvation or even in pointing to the injustice of sacrificing an innocent Savior to atone for humanity's guilt. Evidently unable to accept beliefs on demand (XVI.5.5–8), he clearly expressed the conviction, later reiterated by some Victorians, that since many traditional doctrines had grown archaic, religion needed a new impetus (XV.90). Yet Byron never quite resolved his ambivalence toward religion. His narrator reveals the dilemma by first addressing Doubt as Truth's prism, then pleading with Doubt: "Spoil not my draught of spirit" (XI.2.5–7).

Even though dogmatic Christianity may inadvertently mislead humanity about the realities of a fallen world, it is not the worst oppressor of liberty. Byron declares his opposition to "all who war / With Thought," and Thought's most threatening foe is the coalition of tyrants and sycophants that enables political tyranny to flourish (IX.24). As an implacable foe of despotism in any form (IX.23.7–8), he acknowledges revolution, however mixed its blessings, as the ultimate hope for achieving popular freedom (VIII.50–51). Yet Byron himself distrusted radical reformers like Henry Brougham, against whom he directed scathing stanzas (deleted before publication) and whom he described as an unscrupulous demagogue seeking to establish his own power structure.[8] While conceding a predisposition to oppose power and a proclivity to defend the underdog, the narrator admits that if those currently governing were toppled, he would become an ultra-royalist since he hates "even democratic royalty" (XV.23). He also fears the irrational, often despotic anarchy of mobs (IX.25) and satirizes the "illumination" produced by French mobs that misused lampposts as gallows (XI.26–27). Politics, since it depends upon the manipulation of power and wealth, is seen as inherently corrupt and corruptive. Byron declares the "double front" to be the essence of political life and describes politicians as men who "live by lies, yet dare not boldly lie" (XI. 36.5). Basically honorable though Lord Henry may be, he is nevertheless compelled to go "burrowing for boroughs," "buy" his constituents' favor, dispense "promises to all," mouth political platitudes, and follow no set principle except expedience (XVI.70–76).

In his most punitive denunciation of specific politicians, however, Byron focuses on two Tory ministers—Wellington and Castlereagh—whom he considers largely responsible for repressing liberal movements and restoring so-called "legitimate" dynasties. Wellington, whom Byron thought overrated and overpaid, is belittled for losing at Waterloo until the Prussians' arrival, for failing to liberate Europe, and for being a war profiteer at taxpayers' expense. Castlereagh, whose popularity had been declining since 1815 because of his association with arch-reactionary measures, is flailed even more severely as a cold-blooded eunuch whose sex drive has been perverted into lust for blood, especially in suppressing the Irish rebellion of 1798, and greed for power. In Byron's view Castlereagh's futile attempts to tyrannize over humanity are akin to his malapropian efforts to subdue the English language: both failures have revealed cerebral impotence. Hence the poet heaps ridicule upon Castlereagh's Parliamentary speeches ("Which none divine, and every one obeys"—IX.49.6), his appearance, his suicidal insanity, and the unjustified burial of this "Werther of Politics" in the Abbey.

But the worst use of coercive power to force one's will upon others is that of militarism, and in the two cantos depicting the siege of Ismail (VII and VIII) Byron employs his bitterest irony to deflate the Homeric concept of noble wars, heroism, and military glory. Indeed his undermining of ideational values, often through ironic allusions to Homer, is more damaging to the classical epic than his repeated burlesque of epic devices throughout *Don Juan*. Byron has heroic poetry, especially the *Iliad*, more clearly in mind here than in any other section, and in the battlefield accounts he fulfills his promise of a realistic epic. He dynamically brings his satire up to date in his sardonic jest on Wordsworth's pronouncement of "Carnage" as "God's daughter" (VIII.9).[9] Eager to strip aggressive wars of their glamor and show them in their true light, Byron informed Moore that the siege cantos contain "much of sarcasm on those butchers in large business, your mercenary soldiery" (*BLJ*, IX, 191). He clearly distinguishes between legitimate "Defence of freedom, country, or of laws," such as Leonidas and George Washington fought, and wars waged to gratify the "mere lust of power," such as the politician Grigory Potemkin ordered against the Turkish stronghold (VII.40). Unfortunately hypocritical propaganda, such as Alexander Souvarow's exhortation "to slay the Pagans" who oppose Christians (VII.64), often cloaks the baseness of aggressive wars. In the midst of the destruction he has wrought, Souvarow, who is likened to Nero singing over a burning Rome, composes a couplet declaring that his victory at Ismail adds glory to God as well as to the Christian Empress (VIII.133—34). On a humbler plane illusions of glory are challenged by questioning whether a man's "immortality" in a casualty bulletin compensates for his death, especially if his name there is rendered unintelligible (VII.20—21). Heroic fame, as Byron asserted earlier (I.2—5), is soon forgotten, and even when remembered it depends more on chance than just desert (III.90).

This is not to suggest, however, that Byron denigrates individual bravery in battle. Juan, whose "virgin valour never dreamt of flying" (VIII.36), fights more valiantly than Johnson, whose experience has taught him to retreat when the odds are unfavorable, and Juan is among the first over the wall. Moreover, Byron clearly admires Juan for wounding the two Cossacks threatening Leila (VIII.93–94), and the heroism of the Tartar Khan, who with his five sons fights bravely to the bitter end rather than surrender, wins the respect of even his Russian enemies. Nor is the satire on Souvarow devoid of some praise. Despite being a bloodthirsty, ruthless, and coldly calculating butcher, he has the charisma of a great leader so dedicated to his goal (admittedly, an ignoble one) that he works relentlessly to discipline his troops. But his use of civilization's worst abomination, war, to satisfy his megalomania makes him reprehensible while his antithesis, Daniel Boone, lives a happy life in accord with nature. War, in addition to bringing taxes, debt, and famine at home, reduces the combatants to barbarism, whether they are mercenaries fighting for fame or booty, noblemen demanding privileges of rank, or "military martyrs" ready to sacrifice themselves and their followers. Though Byron's humor verges at times on the sardonic, especially in his seemingly callous approach to butchery and ravishment, nevertheless his satire is highly effective in depicting the sheer hell resulting from human slaughter.

As Byron saw it, civilization could be threatened not only by such lapses into barbarism but by an undermining of intellectual values. In the attacks upon contemporary poets in *Don Juan*, most emphatically in his poetic decalogue (I.205–6), Byron returns to his vatic role as watcher over his country's poetry. The degeneracy of contemporary English literature is from his viewpoint symptomatic of social ills presaging further decline. If some of his stinging epithets, such as "that deep-mouthed Boeotian, 'Savage Landor'" and "That neutralised dull Dorus" for Henry Milman, show less social responsibility than spleen, we must remember that a satirist strives for cleverness rather than truly balanced evaluation. Among the most crushing jests is the patronizing slur on Keats, who allowed his mind to "be snuffed out by an Article" just when he "promised something great, / If not intelligible" (XI.60). In his private letters Byron derided him even more harshly for association with the Wordsworth-Hunt group, for aspersions on Pope, and for occasional bad taste in his juvenilia.

It was the Lakers whom Byron held up to unrelenting ridicule for their deliberate efforts to alter standards of literary taste as well as their desertion of the liberal cause. In his judgment they were renegades who, after having their aspirations dashed by the failures of the French Revolution, turned their rebellious inclinations against the established literary tradition and ultimately sold out their so-called principles for an easy, self-gratifying conservatism. Wordsworth in particular seemed to have retreated from the great world to deal with his own trivial responses to nature and rustic life, denying the realm of passion and significant action. The Lakers' poetry, especially that preoccupied with introspection and personal eccentricities, is therefore derided as smug, dull, petty, oversentimental, insular, and egocentric. Byron explains its insipidity by maintaining that its creators, because they denied their physical nature in favor of their spiritual, were only half-men. Of their behavior as spineless turncoats in politics, Byron asserts with biting irony:

> All are not moralists, like Southey, when
>   He prated to the world of "Pantisocrasy";
> Or Wordsworth unexcised, unhired, who then
>   Season'd his pedlar poems with democracy;
> Or Coleridge, long before his flighty pen
>   Let to the Morning Post its aristocracy. (III.93.1–6)

Instead of being humble about their shortcomings, they seemed extraordinarily arrogant—Wordsworth, with his apocalyptic visions, in assuming that like Joanna Southcott he has been divinely impregnated; Southey in aspiring to soar beyond his limited ability (hence the naughtiest of suggestions that, despite many attempts, he cannot "bring it off"—Dedication 3); and Coleridge in explaining his unintelligible metaphysics.

In letters and conversations Byron shows little admiration for either the integrity or the intellect of most writers. The trimmer poet at Haidée's banquet (itself a burlesque of epic feasts and the *cenae* of Roman satire) is ridiculed as the typical literary sycophant giving his public what it will pay to hear and finally withdrawing into ineffectual drunkenness. This Eastern anti-Jacobin, modeled primarily on Southey with possibly a sidelong glance at "Anacreon" Moore, serves as the vehicle for Byron's most telling satire on the insincerity and lack of steadfast principle in contemporary poetry (III.82–86). Yet even while branding the

Lakers as "shabby fellows," Byron concedes that because of their natural endowments, however misused, they are "poets still, / And duly seated on the immortal hill" (Dedication 6.7–8).

Other professions as well draw satiric fire in *Don Juan*. Lawyers, by whom Byron felt himself repeatedly fleeced in life, are consistently abused for their unscrupulousness, greed, and intellectual dishonesty. Those discussing the proposed divorce between Jose and Inez in language "obscure and circumspect" reveal their callousness by regretting only that his death has spoiled "a charming cause" (I.33), and the legal chicanery of Alfonso's divorce subsequently provides evidence of their preoccupation with technicalities rather than justice. The venal attorney who accompanies Alfonso into Julia's bedroom cares nothing about real justice and is visibly amused, even when no evidence is found, because he knows that a domestic quarrel will result in his financial advantage. Moreover, lawyers are said to be much like critics in concerning themselves with the baser aspects of life and literature; hence the devastating attack on Henry Brougham ("A legal broom") uses this analogy to show why he is "so dirty" in both roles (X.14–15). In particular, Sir Samuel Romilly, whom Byron often lambasted in letters, is singled out for crocodile tears after his suicide had been legally declared the result of insanity (I.15), since Byron could not forgive Romilly's desertion of him to aid Lady Byron in the separation proceedings. As a result of his own youthful tribulations, Byron also expresses contempt for moneylenders and declares two of the world's most influential bankers, Nathan Rothschild and Alexander Baring, to be the actual rulers of the world (XII.5).

But his most comprehensive satire on a social group concentrates on the governing classes of England. The fashionable society of that group offered an artificial, anachronistic world dominated by a hereditary aristocracy whose strains had often deteriorated. In fact, some noblemen, as Byron's dismal paradigm outlines (XI.74), merely wasted themselves in dissipation. Yet the British aristocracy still contained a vital oligarchy of talented, interesting people who had largely escaped the effeteness of other European aristocracies by keeping their doors open to rising achievers in politics, literature, and commerce. Middle-class aspirers on the fringes of power and peerage did not challenge the old aristocracy so long as a possibility existed that they might be assimilated into it; thus members of both classes maintained a symbiotic relationship based on reciprocal benefits. Climbers such as Audacia Shoestring and Mrs. Rabbi, "the rich banker's squaw," were labeled *parvenus* in snobbish circles, but the fact that ambitious people strove to be accepted in aristocratic society attested to its hegemony over the social, cultural, political, and even ecclesiastical life of the nation. Byron rightly called it a "heterogeneous mass" comprising an angelic innocent such as Aurora Raby, an uninhibited sensualist like the Duchess of Fitz-Fulke, a critic-writer-clergyman such as the Rev. Rowley Powley, a bloodthirsty military leader like General Fireface, and politicians like Longbow and Strongbow.

Byron, whom a series of fortunate deaths had elevated out of youthful poverty into aristocratic wealth, always felt that he was partly an outsider in the British aristocracy. Though inevitably dazzled by his introduction into "that microcosm on stilts" (XII. 56.1), he in time discovered that its superficial glitter was not sufficiently attractive to compensate for its interior hollowness. Consequently the "Great World" palled long before it ostracized him for breaking its cardinal tenet about transgression—"not to leave't undone, but keep't unknown." His bittersweet recollections of English society retain his early fascination, but mixed with strong repugnance.

The milieu of the "twice two thousand" who presumptuously assume the world was created for their benefit is seen in *Don Juan* through both Juan's external observation and the narrator's internal perspective as a society of inconsistencies, false standards, gorgeous spectacle, and empty ritual. Since polished exteriors are all-important, tact and superficial refinement are preferred to sincere morality. The narrator's advice to Juan for success in London is: "Be hypocritical, be cautious, be / Not what you *seem*, but always what you *see*" (XI.86.7–8). Quite understandably, therefore, contradictions abound. Although the English claim to be Christian, the only god they worship in deed is Mammon. While freedom is in theory highly touted, social practice and colonial aggression deny it. Newly arrived in a land cherishing respect for law, Juan is obliged to kill an assailant to protect his own life (XI.18). Merit is said to be the true measure of man, but meritorious achievement is in fact admired only when translatable into tangible reward. And despite England's boast of public and private respectability, prostitutes roam the streets of London while politicians, in a comparable way, offer their services for sale.

To a foreigner such as Juan the manners and customs of the British aristocracy seem very peculiar. Good society is so "smooth'd" that individuality has been eliminated from both manners and dress. As a result it is "one polish'd horde, / Form'd of two mighty tribes, the *Bores* and *Bored*" (XIII.95). In an environment infected by the endemic disease of *ennui*, the pursuit of pleasure is little more than an attempt to avoid the dull mediocrity that conformity has enforced and, as such, becomes a relief from rigidly prescribed patterns of behavior. Though English women appear on the surface to be like "Polar summers, *all* sun, and some ice" (XII.72.8), they often conceal a hidden fire that breaks out in a *grande passion*. Since scandal causes women to lose caste in a society that gladly sacrifices scapegoats to atone for transgressions of the whole group, English women must behave hypocritically. As an innocent outsider, Juan has no way of knowing how vindictive this society can be toward transgressors of its social codes. Inevitably he discovers many pitfalls for eligible bachelors—the marriage market, the half-prostitute, the seemingly cold coquette, the married woman who takes extramarital love seriously, and legal damages sought by wronged husbands. To him English passion seems "half commercial, half pedantic" (XII.68.5)—indeed anything but natural. Though men dominate most spheres of endeavor, bluestockings strive, rather unsuccessfully, to establish their own gynocracy as arbiters of taste in aesthetic matters. In the specialized coteries of the aristocracy Juan is recherché because he seems adaptable to all: his exterior is elegant, his mind active, and his wealth adequate.

To depict both the London social season, which coincides with the session of Parliament, and a country houseparty, Byron focuses on two landed aristocrats—Lord Henry and Lady Adeline Amundeville. Both characters embody his admiration and derision. Lord Henry, as the prototypical younger son with above-average abilities and a well-developed sense of social responsibilities, is imperturbable, sophisticated, and secure in his hauteur. Cool to the point of stuffiness and so self-satisfied as to be proud, he nevertheless lacks what sensitive women call "Soul." In his determination to be a successful politician he strives to be "all things to all men." Patriotism and public service evoke from him conventional platitudes, which he mouths without being conscious of their, or his own, emptiness:

> Heaven, and his friends, knew that a private life
> Had ever been his sole and whole ambition;
> But could he quit his king in times of strife
> Which threatened the whole country with perdition?
>
> (XVI.74.1–4)

As lord of the manor he performs his duties and is gracious to his constituency on "public days," dispensing promises and equivocations as generously as his food and drink. Even while doing all the proper things (often rather perfunctorily), he is too preoccupied with politics and too imperceptive of human feelings to be a satisfactory husband.

With equal grace and "calm Patrician polish" (XIII.34), his wife fulfills what is expected of her without having any genuine enthusiasm for anything. Never having allowed herself to stray from prescribed patterns, Lady Adeline fails to understand her own heart, and, as the narrator foretells, her self-deception will precipitate the impending catastrophe. In singing, as well as in criticizing and creating poetry, she studiously assumes the nonchalance of an aristocratic amateur with exceptional taste, thereby substituting one kind of pride for another. She plays her role as ingratiating hostess with such charming versatility and *mobilité* that her subsequent ridicule of country guests evokes the charge of duplicity from Juan and Aurora. Yet both Lady Adeline and Lord Henry represent the best of the English aristocracy—people who appear to be flourishing in their natal environment but actually are thwarted and crushed by it. The mellowing of Byron's satiric tone in the English cantos, to which Steffan has correctly pointed,[10] may well be attributable to the poet's empathy with gifted people who have been prevented from fulfilling their capabilities and from achieving happiness because they have yielded to the snares of a repressive, stultifying society. Thus the final episode, insofar as the powers capable of effecting good are subverted, moves into a more somber vein.

If *Don Juan* was involuntarily halted before solving (or even attempting to solve) the enigmatic riddles of life, Byron nevertheless brought his readers closer to an understanding of human problems through his forthright scrutiny. Though scattered examples of "philosophic nihilism" and "despair" certainly exist in the poem, I cannot agree with Wilkie and Gleckner that they represent the dominant mood of the poem as a whole.[11] Moreover, I vehemently reject Fuess's assertion that Byron's "broader philosophical satire on humanity . . . is essentially shallow and cynical."[12] On the contrary, I believe that *Don Juan*, despite occasional lapses into despondency and spleen, reflects a deep conviction that life and the spectacle it affords are endlessly fascinating even though life's plan is incomprehensible and ultimately unknowable. It reminds us of one of the greatest stimuli to the onward thrust of life, the awareness of man's obligation to improve his lot. The paradox with which Byron confronts us is that the man who ardently tries to rid society of its moral confusions and unnecessary shackles also realizes that an ideal condition is unlikely to come about. Reconstructions of Eden, though they provide the goals toward which man must strive, are at best only temporary exceptions to the rule. Society, however, is not to be rejected or wholly condemned for its shortcomings any more than is man for his predisposition to sin. As Byron comments in his peculiar dialectic of giving with one hand and taking with the other, "The world upon the whole is worth the assertion / (If but for comfort) that all things are kind" (*DJ* XIII.41.3–4). However skeptical he may have been of establishing categorical truths and philosophical systems, his determination to understand mankind in a social setting not only counterbalances the negative thrusts but also affirms that humanity deserves amelioration.

↶ CHAPTER 9 ↷

FOUR LATE SATIRES

THE LAST satiric works to be dealt with—*The Vision of Judgment*, *The Blues*, *The Irish Avatar*, and *The Age of Bronze*—form a varied menu of styles and subjects, much as Byron's early satiric works did. The first three were composed during a five-month period of 1821 as relief from his dramas, on which he had been engaged after the hiatus in *Don Juan*'s progress following Canto V. *The Age of Bronze* was written in late 1822 and early 1823 between Cantos XII and XIII of *Don Juan*. Unfortunately these four satires, composed after the mode of *Don Juan* had been clearly determined, do not show a further advancement in his art. In fact, all except *The Vision* are definitely regressive.

Even after Byron in the first five cantos of *Don Juan* had proved himself a master satirist (to his own satisfaction if not that of his critics), he continued to experiment. It was as though, once having hit his mature stride, he hoped to repeat his recent ottava rima successes in a return to his earlier poetic forms. *The Irish Avatar* is in anapestic quatrains, *The Age of Bronze* in Popean couplets, and *The Blues* in freer tetrameter couplets predominantly anapestic. Only *The Vision of Judgment* is in ottava rima. The poems also differ markedly from each other in theme and approach. Though the basic topic in both *The Irish Avatar* and *The Age of Bronze* is political, the former is impelled by intense personal animus whereas the latter is predominantly didactic. *The Blues*, in dialogue form, is an inept attack on a diffuse target of which Byron was contemptuous—a bluestocking coterie. As one of his worst poems, it resembles a crude, undeveloped outline abandoned ultimately without resolution. *The Vision of Judg-*

ment, on the other hand, is one of Byron's best works, offering a unity of concept and concentration of power that none of his other satires possesses.

DISGRUNTLED with the poetical productions of his own countrymen, Byron on 12 September 1821 informed Murray that should he ever return to England he would write a satire far more stringent than *English Bards* because the contemporary "literary world" stood "in need of such an Avatar" (*BLJ*, VIII, 206–7). Four days later, infuriated by news of the enthusiastic Irish welcome of George IV on a state visit, he composed a poem entitled *The Irish Avatar*, presumably because he felt the Irish were in dire need of such reproof. In anapestic quatrains reminiscent of Tom Moore's, Byron denounced the people of Ireland for receiving their tyrannizer as though he were indeed the incarnation of a divinity ("the Messiah of Royalty"). From Ravenna on the following day he sent the poem, with an appended note, to Moore, then living in exile in Paris. He assumed that his friend would be highly receptive, for Moore himself had often satirized the enemies of Ireland, though Moore's style inclined toward raillery rather than mordant wit. But knowing that Moore might be sensitive about criticism of his countrymen, Byron added: "Can you forgive this? It is only a reply to your lines against my Italians. Of course I will *stand* by my lines against all men; but it is heart-breaking to see such things in a people as the reception of that unredeemed ******* in an oppressed country. *Your* apotheosis is now reduced to a level with his welcome, and their gratitude to Grattan is cancelled by their atrocious adulation of this, &c., &c., &c." Subsequently conceding that the poem had been written "in the greatest hurry and fury," Byron sent Moore some additions and urged him to make emendations (*BLJ*, VIII, 213–15, 219).

Since Byron knew that no British journal would be bold enough to issue this defamation of the crown, he directed Moore on 20 September to have twenty copies privately printed and to send him six in Pisa (*BLJ*, VIII, 219). Therefore *The Irish Avatar* was first printed anonymously in Paris by Galignani in 1821.[1] On 9 October Byron, assuming that the poem had not reached Moore in Paris, sent a copy to Murray with the request that it be relayed to Moore upon the latter's impending incognito visit to England (*BLJ*, VIII, 236). With consummate irony about two poets low in his esteem, Byron facetiously added: "It is doubtful whether the poem was written by Felicia Hemans for the prize of the Dartmoor Academy—or by the Revd. W. L. Bowles with a view to a bishopric—your own great discernment will decide between them." Byron also alerted Kinnaird and Hobhouse to this new production, which he called a poem "upon the late Irishisms of the Blarney people in Dublin," because he knew it would delight their radical natures (*BLJ*, VIII, 238, 240).

The underlying impulse for writing *The Irish Avatar* was clearly his smoldering antipathy toward the king, which flamed so vividly in this poem as to cause Goethe to pronounce the verses on George IV "the sublime of hatred."[2] The king's state visit to Ireland in August 1821 had been planned before the queen's final illness, and evidently the king saw no reason to let her death stand in his way. Indeed her demise must have come as welcome relief to him after the failure of his divorce proceedings against her. Earlier in 1821, when news of Napoleon's death reached England and the king was informed, rather ambiguously, that his "greatest enemy" was dead, he had calmly replied, "Is she, by God!" Inevitably the Whigs had rallied round "England's injured Queen" in her domestic battles, and at her death Whig newspapers reported events from a viewpoint antagonistic to the king. *The Times*, which like the Hunts' *Examiner* had staunchly defended the queen's integrity, deliberately juxtaposed accounts of the king's joyous festivities in Dublin and reports on the progress of the queen's body en route to her native Brunswick. The Whig *Morning Chronicle* ironically recorded that during his triumphal entry into Dublin on 17 August the king, waving the Order of St. Patrick, not only bowed to the cheering crowds but often removed his hat adorned with a large bunch of shamrock, pointed to it, and then placed his hand over his heart.

Factual accounts of these events reached Byron in Italy and served as the underlying stratum of *The Irish Avatar*. Not surprisingly, the opening volley against George IV derides the impropriety of the king's jubilation while the queen's remains were as yet unburied. Byron's comment on His Majesty's "shamrock histrionics" is:

> long live the Shamrock, which shadows him o'er!
> Could the Green in his *hat* be transferred to his *heart*! (6.3−4)

It obviously seemed to Byron, as well as Whig reporters, that in Ireland the monarch had become a hypocritical demagogue "working the crowd" to gratify his own ego. The satiric attacks are exceptionally bitter because the king and Castlereagh (who was part of the royal entourage on this visit) had hitherto ruthlessly oppressed the Irish politically, economically, and religiously. The sincerity of George IV, who publicly declared he had loved Ireland since "the day [his heart] first beat," is undermined by Byron's reference to "the long-cherished Isle which he loved like his—bride." Nor does the king's corpulence escape ridicule, for the poetical comparison of him to "a goodly Leviathan rolled from the waves" recalls the epithet Whigs had long applied to George, the "Prince of Whales."

Yet if the king, who was famous for turning his charm on (or off) as occasion demanded, deserved condemnation for impropriety and duplicity, it was his Irish subjects, deceived by royal amiability, who evoked Byron's utmost contempt. As early as the first installment of *Childe Harold's Pilgrimage* (1812), he had commented on the tendency of enslaved peoples to "lick yet loath the hand that waves the sword" (I.16.8), and evidently he thought the Irish too degraded to act rationally or responsibly. Recalling the king's visit to Ireland, Byron in the spring of 1823 told Lady Blessington: "Your countrymen behaved dreadfully on that occasion; despair may support the chains of tyranny, but it is only baseness that can sing and dance in them, as did the Irish on the [King]'s visit."[3] A natural instability in the Irish temperament, he felt, would "leave them long what centuries have found them—slaves." Their servile behavior, manifested in a wild display of joy, is interpreted in *The Irish Avatar* as not only a reprehensible groveling before their tyrant but as a betrayal of distinguished Irish leaders such as Henry Grattan, John P. Curran, and R. B. Sheridan, who had championed Irish rights in Parliament. Contemporary Irish leaders such as the Earl of Fingall and Daniel O'Connell were being "bought" with royal favors, but it was incomprehensible to Byron that the *profanum vulgus* should willingly express adulation of a monarch who had hitherto denied them his blessing. Nor did it seem logical that the

Irish should welcome Castlereagh (called "a Sejanus" and a "cold-blooded Serpent"), who had cruelly suppressed rebellion in his native land. The warm Irish reception thus brought Byron's wrath down upon an entire nation:

> Till now I had envied thy sons and their shore,
>   Though their virtues were hunted, their liberties fled;
> There was something so warm and sublime in the core
>   Of an Irishman's heart, that I envy—thy *dead*. (st. 31)

Moore was no doubt pleased with the final tribute of the poem to "the glory of Grattan, and genius of Moore," mitigating, as it does, any blanket condemnation of all Irishmen. Actually *The Irish Avatar* was one of Byron's ways, in addition to his gift of the memoirs, of rehabilitating his friend in "fortune and men's eyes." Moore had become liable for a debt of £6,000 as the result of his Bermuda deputy's embezzlement; and since he could not reimburse it, he was obliged to live abroad. Moreover, the Bermuda defalcation and Moore's earlier attacks on the Prince Regent had led to frequent slurs on him in the Tory press. His enemies were especially quick to pounce after *The Times* on 1 August 1821 noted that the Irish poet had been referred to in French newspapers as *Sir* Thomas Moore and commented that, even though he was better entitled to knighthood than many who had received it, his staunch principles would likely cause him to reject such an honor. On 5 August the newspaper *John Bull*, in rebuttal to *The Times*, pointed out that Moore was absent from England because he was a "public defaulter" in his "sinecure office" and was unlikely ever to be offered knighthood. After a letter to the *Morning Chronicle* defended Moore, *John Bull* further defamed him on 12 August by admitting that it could not, "from principle, esteem" anyone who had written political satires and profligate love poetry as Moore had done. Thereupon the *Examiner*, in its lead article for 26 August, rose to Moore's defense even while condemning his fellow countrymen for their reception of the king.

Moore's repeated ridicule of the Prince Regent—notably in *Parody of a Celebrated Letter* (1812), in squibs in the *Morning Chronicle*, and in the enormously popular *Intercepted Letters, or the Twopenny Post-Bag* (1813)—made him persona non grata not only with the king and his Tory cohorts but also, as he discovered, with Irishmen trying to curry royal favor. Moore recorded in his diary that at a dinner honoring the king in Trinity College, Dublin, "some Sir Noodle" had boasted of Ireland's "poetical talent" but had studiously avoided mentioning Moore; subsequently a toast was drunk to "*Maturin* and the *rising* Poets of Erin."[4] Byron probably knew of this slight to the friend who proudly viewed himself as Ireland's national poet, for on 28 October he wrote Moore: "Let me hear from you on your return from Ireland, which ought to be ashamed to see you, after her Brunswick blarney" (*BLJ*, VIII, 251). Moore's reactions to *The Irish Avatar*, nevertheless, were quite contrary to Byron's expectations. Upon receipt of the poem on 3 November he noted in his diary that the servile Irish "richly deserved" Byron's condemnation but that the king had "acted well and wisely."[5] Moore was evidently able to look beyond the immediate humiliation and hypocrisy of the king's state visit with a hope that royal conciliation would ultimately benefit his oppressed country. Such an attitude was typical of a man who had always tried to stay on the safe side of the libel laws.

Byron's Promethean nature, however, could not sanction the truce between tyrant and slaves. Unfortunately his rage against both the king and the Irish was too bitter to permit the detachment necessary for the best satire, and the poem marks the nadir of Byron's pessimism about the relationship between a monarch and his subjects. One of the satire's major strengths derives from a skillful exploitation of paradoxes—Ireland providing "Feasts furnished by Famine," a king publicly celebrating during official mourning, an opponent of Catholic emancipation welcomed by Irishmen as a triumphant savior, and Irish traitors being rewarded for their treachery while Irish patriots sleep in "cold English graves." What appears to be an inconsistent satiric stance on these disparities is actually part of the poem's rhetoric. The poet seems to vacillate between pity for an impoverished, starving nation and absolute contempt for a servile people, between ironic praise of the king and outright condemnation of him as fool and oppressor. By implication Byron's ironic urging that the Irish follow in their conqueror's train must be counterbalanced by an unstated exhortation to rebel. *The Irish Avatar* is intended to show its readers the need for incisive action if the wrongs it describes are to be redressed.

B YRON's disgust with the political implications of the Congress of Verona prompted *The Age of Bronze*. The coalition of major powers that had redrawn the map of Europe after Napoleon's fall, and had thereafter tried to settle common problems in conference, met for the last time in Verona from 20 October to 14 December 1822. Comprised of representatives from Great Britain, Russia, Austria, Prussia, France, and a few other countries, this Congress was convened primarily because the French wanted the consent of their European allies to intervene militarily in Spain in order to overthrow a constitutional regime there and reestablish the autocratic rule of the Bourbon monarch Ferdinand VII. Since King Ferdinand had expressed the hope of regaining Spain's lost American colonies, possibly with French aid, the French proposal in Verona assumed global significance. Leaders of Russia, Austria, and Prussia staunchly opposed the spread of revolutionary principles anywhere; in the preceding year, at the Laibach conference, they had commissioned Austria to suppress Italian revolutions in the interest of European peace. Hence the three members of this "Holy Alliance" readily sanctioned France's plans. It was contrary to Britain's interest, however, to have its growing trade with independent American republics stifled by their return to Spain or to encourage Russia's designs for intervening in the Turkish Empire. Therefore Britain's envoy, Wellington, was instructed by Foreign Minister Canning to take a strong stand against French intervention in Spain.

Both in England and on the Continent newspapers gave the Congress wide coverage, particularly as it drew to a close. In December Byron began his *Age of Bronze* to deride the entire European Concert, its repressive policies, and the recent conference designed to enforce them. To him it seemed that this meeting of reactionary political leaders in Verona, then under Austrian rule, was only another futile attempt to turn back the clock. Though Prince Metternich and his cohorts were determined to shore up the old dynastic tyrannies that had prevailed before the Napoleonic era, their efforts could do little to stem the growing tide of popular freedom. The supreme irony, in Byron's opinion, was that the monarchs of Russia, Austria, and Prussia (all newly liberated from Napoleonic rule) should try to "be *their* Tyrant's ape" (ll. 97–98) in deciding the world's fate. Hobhouse went to Verona specifically to see the august gathering in session and was apparently hopeful concerning its results,[6] but Byron, far less sanguine about the outcome, wrote him from Genoa on 14 December: "I doubt if the Congressors will be so pacific as you anticipate" (*BLJ*, X, 57). On 28 January the French king announced his country's readiness to restore Ferdinand VII to the Spanish throne, and in the following months French forces overran Spain.

On 10 January 1823 Byron wrote Leigh Hunt in Genoa that he had sent off his manuscript of *The Age of Bronze* to Mary Shelley for copying (*BLJ*, X, 81). As he described the poem, it was "calculated for the reading part of the Million—being all on politics &c. &c. &c. and a review of the day in general—in my early English Bards style—but a little more stilted and somewhat too full of 'epithets of war' and classical & historical allusions." Six days later he sent the copied poem, by then consisting of some 740 lines, to Kinnaird; and on 1 February he sent 18 additional lines for insertion (*BLJ*, X, 94). Though the poem had originally been intended for the third number of the *Liberal*, Byron concluded that since it was "a *temporary* hit at Congress" it ought to be published "*now alone.*" He was willing to have Kinnaird entrust it to any publisher he pleased so long as it was published separately and immediately (*BLJ*, X, 110). On 1 April 1823 it was issued by John Hunt in an ambitious edition of 2,000 copies (*BLJ*, X, 133). Though the poet's name did not appear on the title page, Byron was determined that if it were pirated he would claim his rights in court. Contrary to his fears that Hunt had overprinted, almost all the copies of this first edition were sold during the week after publication (*BLJ*, X, 154).

Critical reception of this political satire was inevitably mixed. John Wilson, who wrote a smart-alecky review of it for the April issue of *Blackwood's*, found its Opposition bias so offensive that he suggested, perhaps ironically, that its author was less likely Byron than a cockney imitator, though certainly "an Ass."[7] The *Literary Gazette* attributed the poem to "the Pisan Junta," granting that it contained "less rancour and inhumanity than we are accustomed to from that venomous den."[8] On the other hand, the Hunts' *Examiner* claimed that *The Age of Bronze* had for the first time "given full scope to the satirical talent with which [Byron] is unquestionably gifted in a high degree, by including in one poem all the most *piquant* topics of present interest."[9] The *Monthly Magazine* for May averred that, in spite of technical blemishes, *The Age of Bronze* contained "some of the most masterly strokes of keen sarcasm that have ever proceeded even from [Byron's] pen."[10] The *Edinburgh* [*Scots*] *Magazine* for April, even while acknowledging some flawed versification, granted Byron's poem its most eloquent praise by declaring: "The sentiments are occasionally lofty and magnificent; the thoughts vigorous and impressive; the language condensed and energetic; the satire generally keen, sometimes terrible."[11]

Apparently critics in 1823 were not puzzled by the topical allusions that trouble most twentieth-century readers. The cryptic information on the title page, like much else in this neoclassical satire, depends on an identification of its source for basic meaning and on an ironic application to the contemporary scene for its satire. The title, in conjunction with the poem itself, suggests that the present is a decided falling off from the preceding age of silver, when great men like Napoleon, William Pitt, and Charles James Fox dominated the world arena. The subtitle, "Carmen seculare et annus haud mirabilis," narrows the temporal focus to the year 1822, which Byron considered a time of no miraculous occurrences, and ironically evokes the associations of Horace's odal hymn entitled *Carmen saeculare*.[12] Whereas Horace had been called upon, at the revival of the *ludi saeculares*, to commemorate a new era of imperial glory, Byron announced that he had assumed a similar vatic role in ironically celebrating a new age of tyranny inaugurated by the "secular games" in Verona. The epigraph "Impar *Congressus* Achilli" makes it perfectly clear that he felt the conference would have no lasting impact, for the entire Congress was in his estimation not equal to a single Achilles. Though Byron's Latin quotation from the *Aeneid* I.475 is compelled to assume a meaning it could never have had in its original context, one must remember that from Virgil's viewpoint Achilles, though an enemy of Troy, was the greatest warrior of his time. From Byron's viewpoint Napoleon, and not Wellington, was the contemporary Achilles.[13] The main thrust of Byron's poem is that the Congress of Verona will have less success in reestablishing the tyrannical powers of "legitimacy" than Napoleon had in establishing his and, moreover, that Napoleon's revolutionary doctrines will ultimately spell doom for all monarchies.

The desultory thoughts of this poem are unified largely by the section on Napoleon. As Byron's final commentary on the fallen giant who died a prisoner on St. Helena in 1821, it constitutes, like Johnson's portrait of Charles XII in *The Vanity of Human Wishes*,[14] more than just an object lesson on the fate of vaulting ambition and the evanescence of earthly power. In Byron's most mature evaluation, Napoleon's outstanding contribution was the liberation of humanity from the old feudal order, for he demonstrated that thrones were maintained not by divine or hereditary sanction but by military force. Yet when Napoleon was himself in a position to contribute peacefully to civilization's advance, as Washington, Franklin, and Bolivar had done, he proved to be only a flawed Prometheus because he lacked the selfless magnanimity of the greatest heroes:

> A single step into the right had made
> This man the Washington of worlds betrayed:
> A single step into the wrong has given
> His name a doubt to all the winds of heaven. (ll. 233–36)

By establishing his own brand of absolutism and indulging his lust for imperial glory, he betrayed his early ideals, his people, and himself as well:

> Alas! why passed he too the Rubicon—
> The Rubicon of Man's awakened rights,
> To herd with vulgar kings and parasites? (ll. 138–40)

His downfall is therefore interpreted as a consequence of his greatest achievement, for once he had "burst the chains of millions" and shown the oppressed what freedom was, he could not reestablish those fetters. The spark he kindled continues to inspire subjugated peoples to revolt—in Greece, in the Spanish colonies, and in Spain itself.

The royal personages assembled at Verona have apparently not learned the lessons of Napoleon's rise and fall, and it is against them that Byron directs the poem's cleverest satire. In his usual way of pouring contemporary material into an inherited mold and then reshaping it to suit his purpose, he draws an incongruous analogy between the three Holy Alliance monarchs and the Trinity:

> The blest Alliance, which says three are all!
> An earthly Trinity! which wears the shape
> Of Heaven's, as man is mimicked by the ape.
> A pious Unity! in purpose one—
> To melt three fools to a Napoleon. (ll. 395–99)

From among the three, Byron singles out for additional scorn the Czar of Russia, a theoretical liberal but actual tyrant. Comparing Czar Alexander with his classical namesake and projecting himself into the role of the Cynic Diogenes, Byron readapts legendary anecdotes that cast aspersions on the Czar's integrity:

> I am Diogenes, though Russ and Hun
> Stand between mine and many a myriad's sun;
> But were I not Diogenes, I'd wander
> Rather a worm than *such* an Alexander!
> Be slaves who will, the cynic shall be free;
> His tub hath tougher walls than Sinopè:
> Still will he hold his lantern up to scan
> The face of monarchs for an "honest man." (ll. 476–83)

In a similar way he condemns Napoleon's second wife, Marie Louise, seen leaning on the arm of Wellington, as a burlesque of Andromache, who became the captive of her husband's vanquisher. She is ridiculed not only for having forsaken her exiled husband but also for having formed a liaison with her one-eyed chamberlain, whom Byron in deliberate misapplication of mythology calls "The martial Argus, whose not hundred eyes / Must watch her through these paltry pageantries" (ll. 741–42).

"Legitimate" royalty, though it symbolizes the old feudal order, is not, in Byron's view, the chief obstacle to liberty. Some of the most vitriolic satire is directed against the reactionary ministers gathered at Verona—Metternich, Montmorenci, Chateaubriand, and Wellington; for they are the real manipulators, "who sway the puppets, pull the strings" (l. 708). Yet such power brokers would be unable to function without the support of self-seeking interests in their own countries. In England their strong-est backers, and consequently the recipients of Byron's censure, are the landowners; greedy for profit, they would even have pro-longed the war to keep grain prices and rents inflated. (In a technical *tour de force* Byron makes *rent* one of the rhyme words in seven successive couplets to emphasize its importance to the landed interest.) He sees as equally reprehensible the Jewish in-ternational bankers such as the Rothschilds, whose loans finance the imperialistic pursuits of "bankrupt tyrants." Not until this coalition of royalty, myopic politicians, profiteers, and money-lenders is broken can the liberals' hopes for peace and liberty be fulfilled.

The Age of Bronze, written while Byron was smarting from criti-cal strictures on his supposedly flippant jesting in *Don Juan*, re-flects a determination to return to his earlier adaptations of se-rious, if not tragic, Juvenalian satire. Therefore it relies for much of its punch on invective and declamatory style rather than hu-mor. As though to recapture some of the lost popularity of *Childe Harold's Pilgrimage*, it also returns to that earlier poem's rhetorical manner in juxtaposing a glorious past beside a fallen present. To achieve succinct comparisons and contrasts, how-ever, Byron resorts to an extraordinary number of literary, his-torical, biblical, and mythological allusions that result in cryptic condensations of thought. Much of the ironic satire depends upon a reader's comprehension of the clever incongruity of care-fully wrought epithets—e.g., "power's foremost parasite" for Metternich, "inglorious Cincinnati" for English landowners dur-ing wartime. Yet as the modern reader wrestles with footnote erudition in order to understand Byron's poetically compressed knowledge, he would be wise to consider what Carl Woodring has astutely termed "Byron's sense of history as palimpsest,"[15] for that concept explains much about the substance and the style of *The Age of Bronze*.

History as Byron conceived it is a continuum guiding both present and future—a lesson that humanity must learn or be doomed to repeat the errors of the past. Not all of history, how-ever, is to be read as "the Devil's scripture," as it is called in *The Vision of Judgment*. The fact that greatness has existed in the past and been duly recorded is the strongest indication that it is likely to recur. Wisdom deduced from humanity's collective experience is therefore highly appropriate for Byron's final return to the Augustan mode in *The Age of Bronze*; it justifies didacticism and provides the positive norm against which contemporary deviation can be compared. As the opening lines assert, the present can be better if men actively will it to be so. Thus the poem is not only a graphic account of declination in 1822 but also an impassioned exhortation to all peoples to free themselves from tyranny. In denouncing what is wrong, the satirist as prophet assumes unequivocally that right will ultimately triumph, for despite a dismal present the awakening of liberty heralds a brighter future.

A MUSING recollections rather than indignation apparently sparked one of Byron's mildest satires, *The Blues*, in the summer of 1821. From Ravenna on 7 August he sent Murray the work he modestly claimed to have "scratched off lately—a mere buffoonery—to quiz 'the Blues' in two literary eclogues" (*BLJ*, VIII, 172). Since it was too short for separate publication and since Murray sponsored no miscellany, Byron was uncertain of how or even whether it should be published but requested a proof if it were thought "worth the trouble." He was definite about not wanting his name attached, knowing that the poem would "have all the old women in London" down upon him "since it sneers at the solace of their antient Spinsterstry." About two weeks later he rescinded his request for a proof, claiming the composition was "buffoonery never meant for publication" (*BLJ*, VIII, 216). It was apparently among those unpublished works that Byron on 2 November 1822 directed Kinnaird to retrieve from Murray (*BLJ*, X, 26).[16]

Having changed his mind about publication, Byron on 24 February 1823 requested that Leigh Hunt return *The Blues* to him because he wished to make some emendations (*BLJ*, X, 108). About three weeks later he informed John Hunt in London that he had forwarded through Leigh "a corrected proof of *The Blues* for some ensuing number" of the *Liberal* (*BLJ*, X, 122). Although Byron expressly recommended the Pulci translation for the third issue and *The Blues* for later since he knew the satire would

alienate some readers, John Hunt saved the Pulci for the fourth
and on 26 April 1823 published *The Blues* anonymously in the
third number of the *Liberal*.

Byron must have been additionally galled, in view of his growing disenchantment with both Leigh Hunt and the *Liberal*, by
the failure of reviewers to distinguish his work from that of a poetaster such as Hunt. The *Literary Chronicle* of 26 April asserted
that the third issue contained "not a line . . . worthy of Lord Byron, and not much worthy of Leigh Hunt."[17] It dismissed *The
Blues* as a "silly production" in which the author apparently
aimed at wit but missed his mark. The *Literary Register* of 3 May
maintained that the cockney author of *The Blues* (i.e., Leigh
Hunt) had revealed his ignorance of polite society in that vapid,
pointless composition.[18] The *Edinburgh [Scots] Magazine* for May
termed *The Blues* "very smooth, current, harmless drivelling"
and assumed that Byron had had nothing to do with that issue.[19]
Moreover, *Blackwood's* for May had Odoherty declare that the
third issue contained "*not one line* of Byron's."[20]

What prompted Byron to write *The Blues* in the summer of
1821 is unknown. Possibly, as an escape from the composition of
serious plays and the disintegration of his domestic situation in
Ravenna, he conjured up recollections of earlier days when he
had been lionized in London's literary circles. Perhaps Peacock's
novels *Melincourt* (1817) and *Nightmare Abbey* (1818) showed him
how inviting the affected conversations of litterateurs were to
satire, and he may have recalled Moore's farcical operetta *M. P.,
or the Blue-stocking* (1811). Byron's memory may also have harked
back to Christopher Anstey's *New Bath Guide* (1766), which
(though cast predominantly in epistolary mold) relied heavily on
dialogue in anapestic tetrameter couplets to satirize the artificial
life of Bath.[21] Despite the fact that he seemed magnetically drawn
to bluestockings all his life, Byron constantly advertised his aversion to "ladies intellectual," who were a popular object of masculine raillery in England. Keats, for example, berated "a set of
Devils, . . . Women, who having taken a snack or Luncheon of
Literary scraps," presumed to expertise beyond their knowledge.[22] Hazlitt, fearful that bluestockings might neutralize the
virility of English literature, asserted that feminine influence was
encouraging artificial literary refinement, introspective writing,
and public reliance on critics.[23]

The poem's subtitle, *A Literary Eclogue*, and its Virgilian epigraph, which Byron translates loosely to force application to cerulean ladies, immediately suggest a burlesque of Virgilian bucolics.[24] But instead of having artless shepherds converse about their preoccupations in the pastoral world, Byron presents two dramatic "idylls" in which pseudo-intellectuals of Regency London expose their shallowness in anapestic couplets. In the first skit two urban shepherds—Inkel, an ambitious poet, and Tracy, a fashionable man about town—discuss their involvement in the literary landscape. The second skit, essentially a comedy of manners, satirizes a bluestocking coterie in session, partaking of "a luncheon and learn'd conversation." For his characters Byron drew upon firsthand experience, since he himself had attended bluestocking salons (*BLJ*, III, 214, 228). Many of the people he caricatured had already been sketched in his London journal (1813–14), in letters, and in earlier satires; moreover, in the ensuing months they would be recalled for his "Detached Thoughts" (1821–22) and, later, for the English cantos. For *The Blues* he created a group of backbiting wits, scribblers, and would-be literati who are reluctantly patronized by Sir Richard Bluebottle (Lord Holland) only to please his literary wife. Among the assemblage are Lady Bluebottle, Lady Bluemount (Lady Beaumont), and Miss Lilac (Annabella Milbanke), a prim young lady "as blue as the ether," as well as the bore Botherby (Sotheby) and the lecturer Scamp (probably Hazlitt), a charlatan obsessed with literary "schools."

Through their repartee Byron presents his own assessment of the literary scene. Unfortunately the old charges regarding Lakers Wordswords and Mouthey (Southey), that they lack integrity and insist upon writing poetry according to absurd systems, are threadbare. Equally stale by 1821 is the derision of Wordswords not only as a poet of leech-gatherers, peddlers, and asses but as a pensioner rewarded for turning his coat. Far more incisive are Byron's attacks on malicious reviewers who take pleasure in "cutting up" authors, on writers who abet the reviewers by reveling in the destruction of their rivals, and on bluestockings who parrot reviewers. Byron also holds up to ridicule popular theories that he repeatedly opposed—that posterity would rehabilitate Wordswords and Mouthey, that nature (as Bowles had argued) is poetically superior to art, that enthusiasm ("the gas of the soul") is the stimulus of creative imagination, and that feeling is the essential ingredient of poetry.

Though Byron cleverly deflates these poses and solemn pontifications with artificial language, preposterous rhetoric, and fantastic multiple rhymes, *The Blues* lacks both the original wit and substance of his better satires. Trapped in dramatic form and in a determination to realistically portray a salon atmosphere, Byron was limited to the dull, affected conversation of tedious personalities. His disdainful attitude toward his characters further precluded successful delineation.

I F A bluestocking coterie represented the debasement of taste in a limited circle of high society, then Robert Southey, as poet laureate, symbolized for Byron the corruption of literature on a national scale. Had Southey been humble and unassuming about his mediocre talents, he might not have incurred Byron's wrath. But there was something priggish, pompous, and presumptuous about the man, as well as his writing, and Byron determined to launch one last overwhelming assault on him. The resulting *Vision of Judgment* shows that an honest hatred, if properly controlled and distanced, can be turned into an artistic triumph.

Southey's vanity as a poet and self-righteousness as a moralist were alone sufficient to draw Byron's satiric fire. But it was the contradictions in Southey's utterances (and therefore, presumably, in his character) that made him most vulnerable to attack. Though Byron could forgive a man for altering his opinions, he thought it intolerable that the author of the revolutionary drama *Wat Tyler* (printed surreptitiously in 1817, twenty-three years after composition) should advocate Tory measures for the suppression of seditious literature (*BLJ*, V, 220–21). Moreover, a writer who had labeled reviewing as "the ungentle craft" in his biography of Henry Kirke White had no business writing vitriolic reviews such as Southey produced for the *Quarterly* and other Tory journals (*BLJ*, VIII, 163). What could one conclude of a man who in his jacobinical youth had composed a poem praising the regicide Henry Marten and later, when paid to do so, ground out sycophantic tributes to the royal family? What were the sincere sentiments of a poet who pacifistically denounced war in "The Battle of Blenheim" and subsequently wrote *The Poet's Pilgrimage to Waterloo* extolling the British victory? Such inconsistencies, Byron felt, not only canceled out the laureate's credibility but suggested that Southey, who would apparently alter his opinions whenever it was advantageous to do so, was spinelessly devoid of principle.

For over a decade after the drubbing Byron gave him in *English Bards*, Southey forbore making any public response to Byron's published taunts, but ultimately he was provoked to retaliate in print.[25] Though the laureate certainly had not read the vitriolic attacks on him in Byron's unpublished "Reply to *Blackwood's*" and the unpublished Preface to *Don Juan*, he had soon after the publication of *Don Juan* read excerpts from it in which he had been skewered; moreover, he had been told that its suppressed Dedication was mockingly addressed to him.[26] To his friend C. H. Townshend, Southey declared that he would not go out of his "course to break a spear with" Byron but might inflict a scarring wound if the opportunity arose. Such an occasion presented itself when he wrote his Preface to *A Vision of Judgement* (published on 11 April 1821), for after defending his English hexameters, he could not resist denouncing what he called the "Satanic school" of contemporary poetry.[27] He lamented that readers were so critical of formal innovations and so tolerant of "those monstrous combinations of horrors and mockery, lewdness and impiety" then polluting English poetry. Without naming any of the offenders or their works, he unmistakably attacked Byron as the leader of that heinous school, whose evil he declared to be political as well as moral, and exhorted the "rulers of the state" to take notice.

In response Byron jested, in the Appendix to *The Two Foscari* (published on 11 December 1821), about Southey's "pious preface," declaring the blasphemy of *A Vision* to be "as harmless as the sedition of Wat Tyler, because it is equally absurd." Byron denied that he himself had ever written anything as conducive to revolution as Southey had or as subversive of the established church as Southey's life of John Wesley. After drawing attention to the laureate's "shifting and turncoat existence" and calling him "a hireling," Byron asserted: "There is something at once ludicrous and blasphemous in this arrogant scribbler of all works sitting down to deal damnation and destruction upon his fellow creatures." Before encountering Byron's reply, Southey had be-

come aware of the satiric portrait of himself as the trimmer poet
at Haidée's feast (Canto III, published on 8 August 1821), but
acknowledgment of that irrefutable fact would have been more
damaging than his silence. The *Foscari* note, on the other hand,
provided just the kind of proud audacity he had already labeled
diabolic. As the self-appointed champion of public morality, he
addressed a smug rejoinder to the editor of the *Courier* on 5
January 1822, boasting that he had given the Satanic school "a
designation *to which their founder and leader answers*."[28] He further
congratulated himself on his just denunciation of "men who, not
content with indulging their own vices, labour to make others
the slaves of sensuality like themselves" and of "public panders,
who, mingling impiety with lewdness, seek at once to destroy the
cement of social order, and to carry profanation and pollution
into private families, and into the hearts of individuals." In a
condescending afterthought he even recommended that if Byron were to attack him again it ought to be in rhyme, because
meter would oblige someone lacking self-control to "*keep tune*"
and also diminish the vulgarity of his insult.

    After reading a reprint of Southey's uppity rejoinder in Pisa,
Byron became so enraged that he wrote a detailed reply to the
editor of the *Courier* and also challenged Southey to a duel.[29] Byron never actually sent the letter to the *Courier*, and Kinnaird, to
whom the challenge was entrusted, prudently decided not to deliver it. The poetical attack invited by the laureate, however, had
already been composed and sent to England without any definite plans for publication. It was begun as a travesty of Southey's
Vision in Ravenna on 7 May 1821 and put aside until "about the
20th of September." Byron informed Moore on 1 October that
he had completed about sixty stanzas of a poem designed "to put
the said George's Apotheosis in a Whig point of view, not forget-
ting the Poet Laureate for his preface and his other demerits"
(*BLJ*, VIII, 229–30). While contemplating a tactful way of engaging a new publisher, Byron on 4 October sent the 106 stanzas
of his completed *Vision* to Murray for preliminary printing,
adding that if the latter were "afraid to publish it," he might turn
it over to another publisher, who would be assured "that if he
gets into a scrape I will give up *my name* or person" (*BLJ*, VIII,
232–33). Knowing that his poem contained matter that would
delight Whigs, Byron urged Kinnaird, Hobhouse, and Moore to

look it over and described his *Vision* as a "reversing [of] Rogue Southey's—in my finest ferocious Caravaggio style" (*BLJ*, VIII, 233, 235–36, 240). The poem had also circulated outside his immediate circle of friends, as attested by the assertion in the *European Magazine* for January 1822 that Byron's *Vision* was "*unfit for publication*" (81 [1822], 71). But after reading Southey's attack on him in the *Courier*, Byron on 6 February 1822 expressed to Kinnaird his absolute determination that the poem would be published (*BLJ*, IX, 100).

On 15 November 1821 Byron had asked Kinnaird what he thought of finding a publisher other than Murray for *The Vision*, since Murray's appointment as Admiralty publisher might be jeopardized and his prestige among friends of the *Quarterly* diminished if he issued such an attack on monarchy and Tory policies (*BLJ*, IX, 61). As for the combination of "serious and ludicrous" at which Kinnaird had apparently caviled, Byron referred him to Fielding's *Journey from this World to the Next* and Francisco de Quevedo's *Visions* to judge whether he had "infringed upon the permitted facetiousness upon such topics as means of Satire" (*BLJ*, IX, 62). Similarly he protested that he had carefully avoided "*all profane* allusion to *the Deity*" and pointed to satirists of bygone ages who had offered cavalier depictions of angels and demons. If no prestigious London publisher was willing to accept the poem, he wanted Kinnaird to have fifty copies printed privately on the assumption that then, despite Murray's difficulties over the issuance of *Cain*, some bookseller would assent to sponsor it (*BLJ*, IX, 100). To Moore, however, Byron conceded on 4 March that his *Vision*, though "one of [his] best in that line," had already "appalled the Row" and presumably would have to "take its chance" with Galignani in Paris (*BLJ*, IX, 118). Yet when a reconciliation with Murray was effected, Byron renewed his earlier hopes and on 15 March wrote Murray about his plan to publish *The Vision* "anonymously and *secretly*—as *it* will be *pirated* of course & remedy refused" (*BLJ*, IX, 125). Having mollified the text, Byron on 13 April pointedly asked Murray whether he intended to publish *The Vision* (*BLJ*, IX, 142). Despite continued prodding (*BLJ*, IX, 146, 168), Murray did not respond, and Byron wearied of his evasiveness. On 3 July and again on 6 July he instructed Murray to turn over to John Hunt the corrected (i.e., mitigated) copy of the poem and its Preface for publication in the first number of the *Liberal*, the periodical Byron, Shelley, and the Hunts planned to produce (*BLJ*, IX, 179, 181–82). Of John Hunt, Byron added: "He must publish it at his *own* risk—as it is at his own desire." The obvious though unuttered truth was that Byron was delighted to have found someone intrepid enough to take that risk.

In the ensuing transfer of manuscripts, Murray not only failed to deliver the Preface to Hunt but also turned over the text of *The Vision* that Byron called "it's most republican and uncorrected state" (*BLJ*, X, 26). Just as he had once deemed the Preface to *Don Juan* necessary for readers' comprehension of his aversion to Southey and the other Lakers, so too Byron laid great store by the Preface to *The Vision* because it explained that his animosity was directed not toward George III but toward the laureate and his absurd panegyric. Especially since Murray felt insulted by John Hunt's behavior and then passed along indiscretions Byron had privately written about the Hunts, Byron came to suspect that Murray had acted out of malice.[30] Though the publisher claimed the mishap was inadvertent, the Hunts were absolutely convinced that it was deliberate, for there had been hostility between Leigh Hunt and Murray ever since 1816, when the latter published *The Story of Rimini* and then refused to buy its copyright.[31] To what extent Murray's antipathy influenced other Tory publishers is problematic, but for months before the *Liberal* made its initial appearance on 15 October 1822, conservative journals were attacking it and its iconoclastic sponsors.[32]

The first number of the *Liberal* contained, among other items, three sardonic epigrams by Byron on Castlereagh's suicide, his reductive *Letter to My Grandmother's Review* demeaning William Roberts of the *British Review*, and the text of *The Vision of Judgment* relinquished by Murray. Except for notices in the *British Luminary* and the Hunts' *Examiner*, reviews of the first issue of the *Liberal* were extraordinarily savage.[33] Defending Byron's *Vision* in advance of publication, the reviewer for the *Examiner* on 13 October argued that if Southey had the right to penetrate heaven and presume to utter final judgment on human character, "the same liberty" should be accorded others. While most of the hostile critics granted the absurdity of Southey's poem, they felt that it did not contain the blasphemy, lewdness, profaneness, obscenity, vulgarity, irreligion, or depravity of Byron's. Taking virtually no notice of *The Vision*'s poetic merit, they concentrated on it as the product of what they termed "the Pisan Conspiracy." Byron's levity about religious topics heightened the moral outcry, and his jests about a recent sovereign who had suffered blindness and insanity in his last years were considered to be in bad taste. It is doubtful that Byron read any of the condemnations, but Murray, exulting over the fallen author and the detested Hunts, could not resist writing Byron on 29 October 1822 about the public reaction to the first installment of the *Liberal*: "Never since I have been a publisher did I ever observe such a universal outcry as this work has occasioned and it is deemed to be no less dull than wickedly intended. . . . You see the result of being forced into contact w[it]h wretches who take for granted that every one must be as infamous as themselves."[34]

Since John Hunt was the only member of the *Liberal* "conspiracy" then in England, he was forced to bear the brunt of legal action. Charles Murray, attorney for the vigilante group known as the Constitutional Association of Bridge Street, brought a charge of libel against John Hunt for publishing Byron's *Vision*, and during the December sessions in Middlesex Hunt was indicted not only for defaming the character of George III but also for attempting to disgrace George IV in such a way as to discredit the monarchy.[35] Upon learning of Hunt's prosecution, Byron offered to stand trial in his place but was informed that such a substitution would be inadmissible (*BLJ*, X, 47). Though Byron paid for Hunt's legal counsel, he was not pleased with the way the Hunts had managed the matter, and he accused John Murray of partial responsibility for the legal difficulties (*BLJ*, X, 66–68, 72). In a letter of 23 December 1822 to Kinnaird Byron exonerated himself perhaps more than was warranted by asserting that he had only reluctantly acceded to Leigh Hunt's request for the manuscript of *The Vision*, "cautioning them *to omit* any *actionable* passages" and later advising John Hunt to consult a lawyer "before he published the vision." A week later he wrote Kinnaird: "I am willing to be *both ostensible* and *responsible* for the poem—and to come home and face the consequences on the Author—though I did *not* wish the publication of the V. and indeed particularly warned him to pause—or erase passages likely to be obnoxious" (*BLJ*, X, 72). Hunt's case did not come to trial until 15 January 1824, at which time the jury found him guilty. Sentence was delayed until 19 June 1824, when John Hunt was fined £100 for damages (paid to the crown, according to Marchand, by the executors of Byron's estate) and forced to enter into securities for five years against any other seditious act.[36]

While one can admire the clever satire and irony of Byron's *Vision* without prior knowledge of the circumstances that prompted its composition and publication, one cannot fully appreciate it as a travesty without some recourse to Southey's funeral ode. Both poems use the same basic fable—that of George III being brought before the bar of heaven, confronting his accusers, and gaining admittance despite Satan's opposition. But whereas Southey treated it with extraordinary solemnity, Byron reduced the event to a mundane legal procedure. Southey had employed language so formal as to suggest a religious epic, often underscoring his pious sentiments with echoes of the Anglican prayer book. Byron, on the other hand, even when alluding to scripture, employed the technique of low burlesque in resorting to language so colloquial as to deflate the situation and undermine Southey's cant. Whereas the laureate had invested his characters with either angelic goodness or diabolical evil suggestive of absolute standards, Byron endowed his characters with practical, realistic ethics that at best implied moral relativism. And because Southey claimed to have been chosen to experience an apocalyptic vision, which he strove to convey through ethereal imagery, Byron insisted that his "true narrative" would recognize human limitations and draw "comparisons from clay."[37]

To achieve his satiric purpose Byron needed to make some crucial alterations in Southey's ready-made myth. The splendor of the royal funeral, which Byron termed "a sepulchral melodrame," is dismissed with the remark that "It seemed the mockery of hell to fold / The rottenness of eighty years in gold" (X.7–8). Similarly, the pomp attending George III's arrival at heaven's gate, the momentous significance attached to the judgment of his soul, and his triumphant entry into heaven required deflation in order to counter Southey's overblown ceremonies. The consignment of George III to a suitable place in the afterworld posed a formidable problem, as Rutherford has observed,[38] since Byron could not, after condemning Southey for having presumptuously rendered last judgments, send him to hell. To prevent the trial from proceeding to a negative conclusion, Byron had to create some diversionary tactic that would permit the king to enter heaven unnoticed. The necessary distraction is Southey himself, hauled into court for unjustly doing what only the celestial session ought to do. To dispose of the living Southey, Byron then resorted to an ingenious adaptation of the Phaëthon myth, which since late antiquity had been interpreted as an allegory on the man who refuses to recognize his own limitations. Whereas Zeus fatally struck Phaëthon, the reckless driver of the sun's chariot, with a thunderbolt, causing him to plunge into the river Eridanus, Saint Peter knocks Southey down with his keys so that he falls into an English lake.

> He first sank to the bottom—like his works,
>   But soon rose to the surface—like himself;
> For all corrupted things are buoyed like corks,
>   By their own rottenness. (105.1−4)

Unlike Phaëthon, Southey survives, unrepentant, to scribble again.

Another basic difference between Southey's and Byron's versions is the latter's reliance less upon narrative and more upon dramatic technique. While *Don Juan* was held in abeyance, Byron had obviously developed considerable skill in writing dramatically, and that skill shows to excellent advantage in the presentation of *The Vision* as essentially a one-act play with unbroken unity of time, place, and action.[39] Indeed several sections—the barristers' speeches, the testimony offered by witnesses for the prosecution, and the exchanges between Southey and his adversaries—could be successfully staged with minimal alteration of the text. This is not to suggest that the narrator is superfluous, but inevitably his role differs from that of his counterparts in *Beppo* and *Don Juan*. He does not preempt center stage or indulge in long-winded digressions but acts rather as a chorus filling in necessary background and commenting on action. Even when events are presented solely through his account, as in the silent confrontation of Michael and Satan, they have an extraordinarily dramatic quality:

> He and the sombre, silent Spirit met—
>   They knew each other both for good and ill;

Such was their power, that neither could forget
  His former friend and future foe; but still
There was a high, immortal, proud regret
  In either's eye, as if 'twere less their will
Than destiny to make the eternal years
Their date of war, and their "Champ Clos" the spheres. (st. 32)

Often more is revealed about the characters through what they say than through what the narrator asserts about them. The political opportunism of Wilkes, for example, is superbly epitomized in just a few lines of his electioneering rhetoric: "'Behold a candidate with unturned coat! / Saint Peter, may I count upon your vote?'" (67.7–8). And pointed speech performs another important function: once the inciting action begins with the king's arrival, it is the dialogue, through which the characters interact, that propels the plot to its hilarious climax (the judgment passed on Southey) and its ludicrous anticlimax (the judgment eluded by George III). Dramatization of the conflicts, resulting in heightened tensions, sharpens the satiric focus, provides a matrix for poignant language, and helps fuse serious thought to comic effects.

The dramatic mode of presentation also enabled Byron to shift the harsher satire on George III away from his narrator and into the mouths of his dramatic characters. That arrangement was more suitable because his principal target was not the blind, insane monarch whom death had relieved of his misery but instead the living Southey. Upon learning of the king's death, Byron in fact had shown considerable sympathy in writing Murray: "I see the good old King is gone to his place—one can't help being sorry."[40] Indeed Byron might have addressed George III as Michael greets Satan in *The Vision*: "I ne'er mistake you for a *personal* foe; / Our difference is *political*" (62.4–5). But since Byron was determined to view Southey's apotheosis of the king from a distinctively liberal perspective, he was virtually forced into a political attack on the monarch who had consistently opposed Whig principles. Byron saw the day of monarchy coming to an end, and his republican inclinations were further roused by Southey's preposterous flattery of the British royal family and the fawning dedication of his *Vision* to George IV. Countering such views, Byron's Satan asserts condescendingly that kings are generally so bad and so mad that neither heaven nor hell can do much with them (st. 41). And Byron's Saint Peter provides a ludicrous, almost jacobinical, recollection of another monarch, Louis XVI, who arrived at heaven's gate carrying his severed head and demanding, with royal presumption, the status of a martyr.

The worst condemnation of George III is reserved for his arraignment by Satan, who charges that, despite a perverse abstinence from wine and women, the king had actually furthered the devil's cause. Though not deliberately bad, he had stupidly encouraged evil, thereby serving as a "tool" for the devil's henchmen. Albeit with a host of good intentions, he had sanctioned policies that had made his reign one of the bloodiest in history. The Whiggish Satan above all accuses the king of having been a despot, of having ruthlessly repressed "home subjects" or "foreign foes" who dared to utter "the word 'Liberty'" (st. 45). Over religion as well as politics he had refused to relax his tyranny and had adamantly opposed Catholic emancipation, which Byron himself had championed.[41] No wonder that Saint Peter vows to be damned himself before seeing "this royal Bedlam-bigot range / The azure fields of Heaven" (50.3–4). The witnesses for the prosecution (the same two who in Southey's *Vision* refuse to speak because they regret the lies they uttered against the king on earth) decline in Byron's version to bring further charges— John Wilkes, because having beaten the king politically he is now willing to "vote his *habeas corpus* into Heaven," and Junius, because his earlier charges will stand. But since admission to Byron's heaven depends more on good works than on faith (69.1–2),[42] there really is no appropriate place for the soul of George III, his earthly deeds having been not bad enough for hell and not good enough for heaven. His failure to accomplish anything significant in the world is brilliantly pointed up by Saint Peter, who asks, when the king is announced at the gate: "*What George? what Third?*" (18.3).

Whereas the king offers nothing in his own defense, Byron's Southey, when brought for judgment, inadvertently convicts himself by pleading "his own bad cause." Too obtuse to comprehend the underlying significance of his own words or deeds, he reveals himself to be an absolute fool, arrogantly trying to take over the whole show. His "gouty" hexameters, forced upon an unwilling audience, prove to all but himself what a wretched poet he is. The shrouded king, assuming that the previous laureate, Henry James Pye, has returned, utters his only words—to protest; and Saint Peter calls for prose. By identifying "scribbling" with "his bread, / Of which he buttered both sides" (96.3–4), Southey unintentionally admits his lack of principles. Blind to the implications of his own career, he boasts:

> He had written praises of a Regicide;
>   He had written praises of all kings whatever;
> He had written for republics far and wide,
>   And then against them bitterer than ever;
> For pantisocracy he once had cried
>   Aloud, a scheme less moral than 'twas clever;
> Then grew a hearty anti-jacobin—
> Had turned his coat—and would have turned his skin.
>
> He had sung against all battles, and again
>   In their high praise and glory; he had called
> Reviewing "the ungentle craft," and then
>   Became as base a critic as e'er crawled—
> Fed, paid, and pampered by the very men
>   By whom his muse and morals had been mauled:
> He had written much blank verse, and blanker prose,
> And more of both than any body knows. (sts. 97–98)

His proposal to turn a biography of either Satan or Michael into a vendible saint's life proves his willingness to prostitute the truth for gain. Indeed he unwittingly accedes to Asmodeus's charge— that the laureate has blasphemously libeled both history and the Bible—when he presumptuously advertises his *Vision* as the latest commandment:

>   yes—you shall
> Judge with my judgment! and by my decision
>   Be guided who shall enter heaven or fall. (101.2–4)

What he intends as a complete self-exoneration serves ironically to expose him as a pompous ass. His prototype could not possibly have imagined that, through a further irony wrought by time, posterity would remember him less for his own works than as the butt of Byron's satire.

What aroused Byron's ire far more than the repressive political situation under the monarchy was Southey's glowing representation of it in his *Vision*. In Byron's view it was bad enough that the laureate should have endorsed an unjust social order with divine sanction, but it was preposterous that he should have projected that political scheme upon heaven. Not only did Southey declare in his Dedication that "the happiest form of government" exists in Britain "under the favour of Divine Providence" and George IV's "protection." For his *Vision* he created a Celestial City where the "Ineffable Presence" and a hierarchy of angels govern through a pyramidal power structure and where privileges, as on earth, are commensurate with rank. Admission to his heaven evidently depended on abidance by orthodox social and religious tenets. In his Preface Southey characterized members of the "Satanic school" as those who "have rebelled against the holiest ordinances of human society," and in his funeral ode he cast the unregenerate Wilkes and Junius among the damned while portraying Washington and Milton, purged of their rebellious inclinations, among the saved.

With a clever twist of irony, Byron in his *Vision* carried out the assumptions of Southey's implied theology—that to question and rebel is diabolical[43]—and therefore relegated to hell all those who had taken action in behalf of freedom. Conversely, in a heaven where "the Angels all are Tories," those who have submitted to mundane and divine authority are accepted or, like George III, at least excused. In Byron's rendition, when the old king arrives at heaven's gate, an angel informs Saint Peter:

> He did as doth the puppet—by its wire,
> And will be judged like all the rest, no doubt:
> My business and your own is not to inquire
> Into such matters, but to mind our cue—
> Which is to act as we are bid to do. (22.4–8)

The injustice that Byron attacks both in Southey's Tory heaven and on earth is that those who wield political power arbitrarily establish a moral code endorsing their own behavior in the name of God. Might establishes right, and nonconformists are punished.

Byron's own theological skepticism is presented throughout

his *Vision* on two planes—his essentially comic, usually light-hearted, depiction of the inhabitants of heaven and hell, and his somber, sardonic commentary on divine justice and the afterlife. Despite his prefatory assertion that he had treated his "supernatural personages" more "tolerantly" than Southey and had not represented "the person of the Deity," as his precursor had done, there remains something irreverent about making angels so undignified and humanly fallible that they provoke smiles. At times Byron's casual language, incongruous rhymes, and jaunty tone suggest disrespect; moreover, the narrator's egalitarian assumptions challenge the very idea of heavenly superiority. The angels are singing out of tune, "hoarse with having little else to do" except to manage the astronomical machinery and record human woes. Now that few souls are admitted into Tory heaven, Saint Peter's job is a mere sinecure for a crotchety old gatekeeper, whom a cherub impudently addresses as "Saint porter." Peter gossips about acquaintances and refers snobbishly to Saint Paul as a "parvenu." His remarks concerning heaven's customary overthrow of "Whatever has been wisely done below" (st. 21) disparage celestial justice. Even Michael and Satan are reduced from the role of cosmic Manichaean duelists to the level of lawyers quibbling over their case, and the trial itself is tinged with hypocrisy. Ultimately Byron's irony becomes double-edged, for despite Michael's explanation that the king's "doom / Depends upon his deeds" (69.1–2), inadvertent mercy rather than legal justice is allowed to prevail as George III slips ignominiously into heaven.

Not until one recognizes the interrelation of sacred and profane in this witty burlesque on monarchy, politics, and theology do its disturbing implications become clear. Byron's anthropomorphic view of supernatural beings in *The Vision* suggests that heaven may be governed as capriciously and arbitrarily as earth; and the emergence of Michael—that urbane gentleman who compromises differences and avoids confrontations—as the most powerful figure in Byron's heaven reveals that temporizing is rewarded there also. Heavenly justice, which seems to be determined more by the ability to wield power than by objective criteria, may be as prone to miscarriage as that of human tribunals. The satire darkens even further in comments on the orthodox concepts of salvation and damnation. Byron seriously questions, on the one hand, the rectitude of granting divine grace to undeserving sinners and, on the other hand, the eternity of hell's punishment.[44] As he observed in his "Ravenna Journal" on 25 January 1821, salvation is something of which not even the most righteous man can be sure "since a single slip of faith may throw him on his back" (*BLJ*, VIII, 35). The narrator's comments in *The Vision* suggest, through the imagery of the "late-hooked fish" and the fish fry (st. 15), that eternal damnation is incompatible with the concept of a benevolent deity. His reference to the butchery of an innocent lamb (15.5) even strikes at the doctrine of the Atonement. Believing that Christ's sacrifice no more did "away with *man's* guilt than a schoolboy's volunteering to be flogged for another would exculpate the dunce from negligence," Byron declared to his morally earnest friend Francis Hodgson: "The basis of your religion is *injustice*" (*BLJ*, II, 97). Although Byron wanted to believe in a cosmic order that was moral, impartially just, and rationally explicable, *The Vision of Judgment*, like *Cain*, expresses his fear that it might not exist in heaven any more than on earth.

But since, according to the narrator, *The Vision* "is not a theologic tract," Byron was free to touch upon even profound thought flippantly. In this poem, more than in any other of his works, he has achieved sustained brilliance of language—racy, economical, and sufficiently flexible to pass without any tonal wrenching from the serious to the frivolous as subject or situation requires. As is common in burlesque, inappropriate diction and piquant metaphors are often used for satiric purposes: Michael is overblown as "the Viceroy of the sky" while the doctrine of damnation is deflated as "Hell's hot jurisdiction." Yet the poem, while its phraseology is consistently clever, does not strain conspicuously after pyrotechnical effect. It all appears completely natural, and the reader feels he is listening to a scintillating conversationalist speaking with ease. Even when the narrator waxes poetical, as in his description of Southey's dispersal of the heavenly throng, he represents the evanescence through an appeal to sensory perceptions:

> the whole spiritual show
> Had vanished, with variety of scents,
> Ambrosial and sulphureous, as they sprang,
> Like lightning, off from his "melodious twang." (102.5–8)

The ethereal splendor of heaven is thus reduced, by means of concrete diction and tangible imagery, to the mundanity of everyday life.

All the major characters employ distinctive modes of expression. Saint Peter's bumbling petulance can be seen in his query: "Well, what's the matter? / Is Lucifer come back with all this clatter?" (17.7−8). The solemn grandeur of Satan is conveyed in Miltonic cadence: "I triumph not / In this poor planet's conquest; nor, alas! / Need he thou servest envy me my lot" (40.2− 4). Michael reveals his forthright, obliging nature in a conversational style: "Let's hear . . . what he has to say: / You know we're bound to that in every way" (89.7−8). The repetitive stammer that marred George III's elocution in life is accurately represented by: "What! what! . . . / No more—no more" (92.7−8). And even the various nationalities among the prosecution witnesses employ their idiosyncratic speech: the Irishman brogues, "By Jasus!" and the American surmises, "*Our* President is going to war, I guess" (st. 59).

Most of *The Vision* is handled in such an airy manner that one might be tempted to think it more comic than satiric. Charles Lamb concluded that Southey's *Vision*, imbued as it was with "an arrogance beyond endurance," deserved prosecution more than Byron's, which he considered "most good-natured" and devoid of "malevolence."[45] Such a reaction, which applauds the travesty as an antidote to its original, was apparently what Byron wanted from his readers. The favorable response that *The Vision* has received is due partly to the extraordinary cleverness with which Byron overcomes the reader's built-in objection to attacks on what society has conditioned him to respect. Byron's wit in this poem is rapier-sharp and does not bludgeon satiric victims or shatter the predominantly jolly mood. Furthermore, the narrator is clearly established as a sensible, unpretentious man tolerant enough of others' transgressions to find them extremely amusing. Hence the reader laughs along with him on the assumption that it is all good fun. Indeed if one did not delve beneath the jesting, *The Vision* might be interpreted as an ingenious comedy.

But the incongruities between surface buffoonery and underlying seriousness make this work one of the finest examples of English Romantic irony, at the heart of which lies paradox. Even

though Byron's intense personal distaste for Southey provided
the impetus for the poem, hatred was never permitted to exert
control over art. Byron's subjective attitudes are so perfectly sub-
limated to the creation of what is to be the colossal joke that he
appears to be detached from his own subject. If he seems to allow his mind the free play associated with artistic creativity, he is
also dallying with his subject as a cat plays with a captive mouse,
daring his victim to escape. The extraordinary freedom with
which Byron appears to let his fable run its own course conceals
the superb control he exerts over narration, drama, and language. He himself hints at the paradoxical nature of the poem
by comparing it to Caravaggio's paintings, in which light and
dark, sacred and profane, solemn and ludicrous are held in a
dramatic tension or dialectic that is never resolved. Highly imaginative, even fantastic, events occur against a background of
stark realism, producing incongruities that dissolve in laughter.
Everything in the cosmos appears to be in a state of indeter-
minacy or inconclusiveness—an eternal confrontation of "his
Darkness and his Brightness"—that is characteristic of Romantic
irony. The narrator, when he speculates on theology, indulges in
self-parody on his own tentativeness, for the justice of heaven is
seen to be as uncertain as that of earth. Ultimately *The Vision*
suggests that the religious, political, and legal order man tries to
superimpose on his world is at best temporary, at worst illusory.
Yet even amidst the contradictions and uncertainties of an ironic
universe, where the realms of seeming, being, and becoming are
often blurred, Byron evidently felt obliged to oppose injustice
wherever he found it.

∾ CHAPTER 10 ∾

BYRON'S SATIRIC ACHIEVEMENT

SINCE much that Byron fought for in his day has already been accepted, one can easily fail to appreciate the intrepid nature of his satire. It is necessary to remember that in the early nineteenth century Byron achieved international distinction not just as a poet but as his epoch's most eloquent champion of freedom. His earliest formal satire reveals a desire to break the power that Scottish critics had arrogated to themselves, and today one can still admire the forceful wit with which he impaled both the presumption of the Scottish usurpers and the literary weaknesses of his compatriots. By proving that none could attack him with impunity, he indeed became what Shelley termed him—the "Pythian of the age"—and served as a model, even with his death in behalf of Greek independence, for those who refused to be oppressed by any form of tyranny. Whether the offenders were demagogues such as Henry Brougham seeking political power, lords such as Elgin exploiting the treasures of a downtrodden people, or kings such as George III and George IV trampling on the rights of subjects, Byron fearlessly attacked their wrongdoings in satire. Throughout *Don Juan* he reiterated the need for individual liberty, and in the anti-war cantos he cogently argued the right of countries to control their own destiny without foreign intervention. In the last of his completed satires, *The Age of Bronze*, he dared to challenge powerful world leaders who, for purely selfish reasons, were engaged in an international conspiracy to stem the rising tide of political freedom throughout the world.

Akin to Byron's resistance of tyranny in the external world was his assault on errors of the mind—particularly man's penchant for self-delusion. This willful blindness to truth, resulting from the acceptance in early youth of entrenched social and religious beliefs, could turn out comically, as with Horace Hornem, or tragically, as with Donna Julia. But in every instance it posed the major obstacle to enlightenment. With his usual temerity, therefore, Byron boldly took on human nature as the object of his satire. Particularly in the ottava rima satires, which offer a relatively tolerant, ironical view of man's flawed nature, he showed how man hides behind the cant of religion and custom rather than confront the harsher realities, and the reader is often struck by the perceptiveness of Byron's psychological insights. Long before Freud taught our age to delve beneath the conscious level, Byron demonstrated how Laura in *Beppo* conceals her real motives even from herself and substitutes socially acceptable ones. So incisive is Byron's exposure of universal types—hypocrites such as Donna Inez, literary pretenders such as Botherby, or opportunists such as Lord Henry Amundeville—that one admires not just his cleverness but his shrewd probing into the depths of the human mind.

Byron was intent upon leading his contemporaries away from an illusory view of life, one associated with Romanticism and metaphysical speculation. In his opinion the satirist's discerning eye afforded a more edifying (because ultimately more practical) vision than the fictions of his idealistic, parochial contemporaries, whose grasp of reality he questioned. Whether he ironically contrasted the merits of marital customs in Venice with those in England and Moslem countries, ridiculed the social hypocrisies of European countries, or unflatteringly portrayed the British aristocracy as he had intimately known it, he presented man and his world as he honestly believed them to be. In so doing, he confronted man's innate tendency to view himself idealistically. Both in personal letters and in the text of *Don Juan* he repeatedly emphasized the realism of his satire, based as its situations are on real life and drawn by a man who had intensely experienced the world. His success as a satirist, therefore, may be said to rest partly on his essentially accurate representation of reality. Though for the sake of rhetoric certain features were exaggerated and others repressed, most of his satiric depictions are effective because of their close resemblance to life.

Since Byron's goal was the revelation of truth that would set men free, he may be regarded as an ethical teacher in the sense in which he defended his persona's role in *Don Juan*. Believing that erroneous modes of thought had to be eliminated before valid ones could be instituted, he strove sincerely and candidly to expose the sham ideals that his contemporaries mouthed but did not live by. The first step toward moral betterment, he assumed, was recognition of human frailty, and in defense of his satire he asked the evangelistic Dr. Kennedy: "Am I not doing an essential service to your cause, by first convincing [people] of their sins, and thus enable you to throw in your doctrine with more effect?"[1] Unlike conventional satirists before him, however, Byron did not take a holier-than-thou attitude but readily admitted to being a fellow sinner well acquainted with the sins against which he inveighed. Moreover, his personae, conscious of a lack of universally accepted ethics, were obliged to set their own moral standards, usually on the basis of wisdom drawn from personal experience. In removing the foundation of moral absolutes from his characters, Byron broke with Augustan satire and its confident dogmatizing to establish a new satiric stance applicable to his own age. And it is his variety of satire—with its individualized norms, a more tentative approach, emphasis on application rather than theory, and predominantly ironic perspective—that has survived in modern poetry and prose fiction.

Byron's three ottava rima satires remain the most highly esteemed of his productions for reasons not difficult to discover. Despite their amalgamation of older traditions, they are unique and distinctly Byronic. It is not surprising therefore that the hybrid English tradition he enriched with the Italian should have culminated with him. In *Beppo* he defied the accepted standards of ethics, narrative, and satire in order to provide an ironic, pragmatic perspective on man and society—one requiring a relativistic morality and a novel approach. *The Vision of Judgment*, though it appears to be merely rollicking fun bringing George III to trial and Southey to utter disgrace, reveals that beneath the superficial insouciance of Byron's satire there lurk serious thoughts about both celestial and mundane justice. For its pungency of phrase, sparkling wit, and sheer ebullience, as well as its conceptual unity, this satire is often regarded as Byron's most perfect. Yet *Don Juan* must be considered his crowning achievement and one of the most original poems in our language. Its epic scope permitted him a panoramic survey not only of human nature but also of European society as he had experienced it. In spite of occasional lapses into despair, the narrator in *Don Juan* shows himself to be one who considers man and the world to be worthy of amelioration, and he assumes that his offhand, uninhibited criticism will be of assistance. He celebrates the power of love and the indomitable human spirit even while conceding that both are constantly threatened by the world's corruption.

The truly unique achievement of the ottava rima satires—one that prevents them from being imitated successfully—rests largely on the personality of the poet who holds us captive while he continues his performance. The supple stanza encouraged Byron, eager to spellbind his audience with his wit and vibrant personality, to be a fascinating conversationalist ready to project whatever thoughts came to mind. Whereas other stanzaic forms, especially the closed couplet, had constrained his exuberance, the ottava rima allowed him to be himself, to reveal the many sides of his nature that had previously been suppressed in his poetic art. Hence he intrigues us with an intellectual curiosity and openmindedness that, in playing with any subject, accept nothing as fixed or certain. He wins us over through his willingness to face up to the harsh facts of life and to insist, even while admitting that humanity's goals may never be attained, that it is man's obligation to attack injustice. Even if one does not agree with Byron's personal values or with his assessments of humanity, it is hard to deny that his satires compel readers to take a fresh look at perennial problems. Such was his aim in shattering complacency and thereby achieving what, in a letter to John Murray, he called "that influence over men's minds—which is power in itself & in it's consequences."[2] He undoubtedly succeeded. Not only do his satires continue to offer amusement and delight: they still jolt us out of our accession to habituated wrongs.

NOTES

CHAPTER 1

1. Although touches of satire exist in Byron's plays, poetical narratives, and other writings, this study focuses, with the exception of some juvenilia and *Childe Harold's Pilgrimage I* and *II*, on works that are predominantly satiric.

2. The distinction between *comic* and *satiric* is often semantic. George Meredith, in *The Idea of Comedy and the Uses of the Comic Spirit* (1877), claimed that Byron had excellent powers of humor and of satire but was deficient in the comic. G. R. Elliott, in "Byron and the Comic Spirit," *PMLA*, 39 (1924), 897–907, argued that Byron was a highly successful writer of comedy (particularly of the stoically detached kind later attempted by Meredith) but not of satire. Sigmund Freud, in *Jokes and Their Relation to the Unconscious* (1905), explained the comic, the humorous, and the satiric psychologically, associating satire with the hostile, degradational mode of the comic spirit. For a perceptive discussion of Byron's humor (and to a lesser degree his comedy and satire), see Robert Escarpit's chapter entitled "L'Humour" in *Lord Byron: un tempérament littéraire* (Paris: Le Cercle du Livre, 1955–57), II, 85–116.

3. Lord Byron, *Byron's Letters and Journals*, ed. Leslie A. Marchand (Cambridge, Mass.: Harvard Univ. Press, 1973–82), VI, 189—hereafter cited as *BLJ*.

4. Marguerite, Countess of Blessington, *Conversations of Lord Byron*, ed. Ernest J. Lovell, Jr. (Princeton, N.J.: Princeton Univ. Press, 1969), p. 195.

5. Blessington, *Conversations*, p. 205.

6. Byron canceled these lines, 114a–b, in proof in 1821. See Lord Byron, *The Complete Poetical Works*, ed. Jerome J. McGann (Oxford: Clarendon Press, 1980–81), I, 293n—hereafter cited as *CPW*. Quotations

from *Don Juan* in my text are from the Variorum Edition of T. G. Steffan and W. W. Pratt (Austin: Univ. of Texas Press, 1971). Other Byron poems that have not yet appeared in McGann's *CPW* are quoted from *The Works of Lord Byron: Poetry*, ed. E. H. Coleridge (London: John Murray, 1898–1904)—hereafter cited as *Poetry.*

7. Letter of 5 Oct. 1821 to Augusta Leigh. *BLJ*, VIII, 235.

8. Blessington, *Conversations*, p. 179.

9. Blessington, *Conversations*, p. 217.

10. Blessington, *Conversations*, pp. 156–57.

11. Blessington, *Conversations*, pp. 195–96.

12. Letter of 25 Nov. 1762 to Lord Bute. *Letters from George III to Lord Bute 1756–66*, ed. Romney Sedgwick (London: Macmillan, 1939), pp. 167–68.

13. Thomas Medwin, *Conversations of Lord Byron*, ed. Ernest J. Lovell, Jr. (Princeton, N.J.: Princeton Univ. Press, 1966), p. 69.

14. James Kennedy, *Conversations on Religion, with Lord Byron* . . . (London: John Murray, 1830), pp. 163–64.

15. Lord Byron, *The Works of Lord Byron: Letters and Journals*, ed. Rowland E. Prothero (London: John Murray, 1898–1901), IV, 485—hereafter cited as *LJ.*

16. See *BLJ*, VIII, 12, 19, 109.

17. In *English Bards*, where Pope is called "The first of poets" (l. 370), Byron laments that "Milton, Dryden, Pope, alike forgot, / Resign their hallow'd Bays to Walter Scott" (ll. 187–88). In *Don Juan* Byron asserts: "Thou shalt believe in Milton, Dryden, Pope" (I.205.1).

18. Subsequently Byron mentioned Churchill three times in letters and journals, wrote a poem about his visit to Churchill's grave in 1816, and referred to him briefly in his "Reply to *Blackwood's*" (1820). See *BLJ*, II, 206–7; IX, 11; "Churchill's Grave," *Poetry*, IV, 45–48; and *LJ*, IV, 485.

19. See *LJ*, IV, 485; and Churchill's poem "The Apology," ll. 376–87.

CHAPTER 2

1. Thomas Moore, *Letters and Journals of Lord Byron: With Notices of His Life* (London: John Murray, 1830), I, 28–29.

2. Letter of 9 June 1820 to Thomas Moore. *BLJ*, VII, 117.

3. Robert F. Gleckner, "From Selfish Spleen to Equanimity: Byron's Satires," *Studies in Romanticism*, 18 (1979), 173–205. See also Michael G. Cooke, *The Blind Man Traces the Circle* (Princeton, N.J.: Princeton Univ. Press, 1969), pp. 91–93; and George M. Ridenour, *The Style of "Don Juan"* (New Haven, Conn.: Yale Univ. Press, 1960), pp. 92–93.

4. Jerome J. McGann, *Fiery Dust: Byron's Poetic Development* (Chicago: Univ. of Chicago Press, 1968), p. 75.

5. Blessington, *Conversations*, p. 152.

6. William Hazlitt, *The Complete Works of William Hazlitt*, ed. P. P. Howe (London: J. M. Dent, 1930–34), VI, 24.

7. In a letter of 18 Mar. 1809 to his old friend William Harness, Byron complained that Cambridge had been not his alma mater but rather his "injusta Noverca." *BLJ*, I, 197.

8. For denials that Byron was a neoclassicist, see F. R. Leavis, "Byron's Satire," in *Revaluation: Tradition and Development in English Poetry* (New York: Norton, 1936), pp. 148–53; Nathan R. E. Carb, Jr., "Byron as Critic: Not a Neo-classicist," *West Virginia University Philological Papers*, 11 (1958), 16–21; Robert D. Hume, "The Non-Augustan Nature of Byron's Early 'Satires,'" *Revue des Langues Vivantes*, 34 (1968), 495–503; and C. Darrell Sheraw, "*Don Juan*: Byron as Un-Augustan Satirist," *Satire Newsletter*, 10 (1972–73), ii, 25–33.

9. The 1816 sale catalogue of Byron's library lists Pope's *Works*, the *Edinburgh Review* (from its founding), the *Critical Review* from 1795 to 1807, Churchill's *Poetical Works*, the *Rolliad*, *Pursuits of Literature*, Gifford's *Baviad* (two editions) and *Maeviad*, and *Poetry of the Anti-Jacobin* (two copies). Some of the other brief satires listed above may have been auctioned off in packages of booklets for which titles were not recorded. See William H. Marshall, "The Catalogue for the Sale of Byron's Books," *Library Chronicle*, 34 (1968), 24–50.

10. *BLJ*, I, 136. For manuscript and publication history, see *CPW*, I, 393–99.

11. "D," "'English Bards and Scotch Reviewers': Byron and Ridge, His First Printer," *Notes and Queries*, 2d ser., 6 (1858), 302–3.

12. Byron wrote that the poem contained 624 lines (*BLJ*, I, 188), but McGann argues convincingly that he meant 524 (*CPW*, I, 396). Marchand's accurate dating of Byron's misdated letters corrects the previously assumed chronology of E. H. Coleridge's introduction and Andrew Rutherford's "An Early MS of *English Bards and Scotch Reviewers*," *Keats-Shelley Memorial Bulletin*, 7 (1956), 11–13.

13. Leslie A. Marchand, *Byron: A Biography* (New York: Knopf, 1957), I, 166–69, 176–77; Robert Charles Dallas, *Recollections of the Life of Lord Byron* (London: C. Knight, 1824), pp. 15–47, 50–61.

14. See Marchand, *Byron*, I, 324; Thomas J. Wise, *A Bibliography of the Writings in Verse and Prose of George Gordon Noel, Baron Byron . . .* (London: Privately printed, 1932–33), I, 19–46.

15. Marchand, *Byron*, I, 148.

16. Medwin, *Conversations*, p. 142.

17. Letters of 26 Apr. 1821 to John Murray and Percy Bysshe Shelley. *BLJ*, VIII, 102–3.

18. Byron was proud that *English Bards* had won the friendship of R. B.

Sheridan, who did not care for his other poetry ("Detached Thoughts," *BLJ*, IX, 16).

19. John Gibson Lockhart, *Peter's Letters to His Kinsfolk* (Edinburgh: William Blackwood, 1819), II, 8.

20. *Edinburgh Review*, 12 (1808), 13 (hereafter *ER*).

21. *ER*, 28 (1818), 198.

22. William Wordsworth, *A Letter to a Friend of Robert Burns* (1816), *The Prose Works of William Wordsworth*, ed. W. J. B. Owen and Jane Worthington Smyser (Oxford: Clarendon Press, 1974), III, 126–28; letter of 18 Jan. 1808 to Walter Scott, *The Letters of William and Dorothy Wordsworth: The Middle Years*, ed. Ernest de Selincourt, rev. Mary Moorman, 2d ed. (Oxford: Clarendon Press, 1969), I, 191–92.

23. Note to l. 1070. *CPW*, I, 418.

24. Marchand, *Byron*, I, 346.

25. *ER*, 1 (1802), 64.

26. Letter of 3 Aug. 1814 to Thomas Moore. *BLJ*, IV, 152.

27. Blessington, *Conversations*, p. 172.

28. Moore, *Notices of His Life*, I, 157.

29. A. B. England, *Byron's "Don Juan" and Eighteenth-Century Literature: A Study of Some Rhetorical Continuities and Discontinuities* (Lewisburg, Pa.: Bucknell Univ. Press, 1975), pp. 48–49.

30. James T. Hodgson, *Memoir of the Rev. Francis Hodgson* (London: Macmillan, 1878), I, 98.

31. Byron's library auctioned in 1816 contained Madan's 1807 edition.

32. Citations are from the text of Madan's 1789 London edition. For a comprehensive discussion of Byron's use of Madan, see my "Byron's Imitations of Juvenal and Persius," *Studies in Romanticism*, 15 (1976), 333–55.

33. In *Lord Byron as a Satirist in Verse* (1912; reprint, New York: Haskell House, 1973), p. 51, Fuess theorized that Byron had originally "intended to follow the general plan" of Juvenal's poem but had abandoned that model after the first hundred lines. In "A Blueprint for *English Bards and Scotch Reviewers*: The First Satire of Juvenal," *Keats-Shelley Journal*, 19 (1970), 87–99, Clearman noted convincing parallels in subject, techniques, and organization between the two poems.

34. The poem, "A Bit of an Ode to Mr. Fox," advertises itself as an imitation of a Horatian ode (II.20).

35. Clearman, "A Blueprint for *English Bards*," pp. 89–90.

36. Moore, *Notices of His Life*, I, 101.

37. Byron's note to l. 211.

38. This review is reprinted in *LJ*, I, 341–43.

39. *ER*, 1 (1802), 63–83.

40. William H. Marshall, *The Structure of Byron's Major Poems* (Philadelphia: Univ. of Pennsylvania Press, 1962), pp. 27–36.

41. *Gentleman's Magazine*, 105 (1809), 248.

CHAPTER 3

1. Pope wrote Swift: "You call your satires, libels: I would rather call my satires, epistles. They will consist more of morality than of wit." For the neoclassical distinction between *satire* and *satura*, see Ian Jack, *Augustan Satire: Intention and Idiom in English Poetry 1660–1750* (Oxford: Clarendon Press, 1952), pp. 97–100.

2. See *CPW*, I, 425–26.

3. Marchand, *Byron*, I, 278–79, 293, 303; Dallas, *Recollections*, pp. 103–16.

4. For other accounts of the interplay (or lack of interplay) between Harold and the narrator-poet, see McGann, *Fiery Dust*, pp. 67–78; Robert F. Gleckner, *Byron and the Ruins of Paradise* (Baltimore, Md.: Johns Hopkins Press, 1967), pp. 39–90; Andrew Rutherford, *Byron: A Critical Study* (Edinburgh: Oliver and Boyd, 1961), pp. 26–35.

5. See *CPW*, II, 265–71; also McGann, *Fiery Dust*, pp. 94–111 for accounts of the composition, successive revisions, and publication history of the first two cantos. McGann has correctly asserted that "the poem in its original form was predominantly melancholic in its tonal quality" (p. 105).

6. *BLJ*, II, 81, 83, 90, 112–13.

7. Facetiously he added: "Nobody keeps their piece nine years now a days—except Douglas K[innaird]—he kept his nine years and then restored her to the public."

8. *BLJ*, VII, 229, 238; VIII, 21, 59–61.

9. Harold's stanzas on Horace were of sufficient interest to Hobhouse to inspire him to write a commentary on them in his *Historical Illustrations of the Fourth Canto of Childe Harold* (London: John Murray, 1818), pp. 42–46.

10. John Oldham, *The Works of Mr. John Oldham* (London: D. Brown et al., 1722), I, sig. G4ʳ.

11. My quotations from this work cite the two-volume London edition of 1753 published by W. Thurlbourne.

12. Leslie A. Marchand, *Byron's Poetry: A Critical Introduction* (Boston: Houghton Mifflin, 1965), p. 31.

13. See especially William St. Clair, *Lord Elgin and the Marbles* (London: Oxford Univ. Press, 1967), pp. 166–79.

14. Medwin, *Conversations*, p. 211.

15. *CPW*, I, #151a.

16. For Hazlitt's contrary opinion—that the Turks, like Napoleon, did have the right to appropriate art works in conquered territory—see his essay "The Elgin Marbles," *Examiner*, 16 June 1816; reprint, *Works*, XVIII, 100–103.

17. John Cam Hobhouse, *A Journey through Albania and Other Provinces of Turkey . . . during the Years 1809 and 1810* (London: J. Cawthorn, 1813), I, 347n.

18. See Hobhouse, *Journey*, I, 292; and St. Clair, *Lord Elgin*, pp. 187–202.

19. John Galt, *Autobiography* (Philadelphia: Key and Biddle, 1833), I, 107–18. Galt's "Atheniad" was first published in the *Monthly Magazine* for February 1820 and later, in ameliorated form, in his *Autobiography* (1833).

20. Publication in 1815 of the *Remains of John Tweddell* revived specific charges about Elgin's dereliction of duties and abuse of ambassadorial power to steal whatever he wanted. See St. Clair, *Lord Elgin*, pp. 230–41; for a review of Tweddell's *Remains*, see *ER*, 25 (1815), 285–315.

21. St. Clair, *Lord Elgin*, p. 199n.

22. Moore, *Notices of His Life*, I, 352.

23. St. Clair, *Lord Elgin*, p. 194 and n.

24. *BLJ*, II, 228, 234.

25. Letter of 6 Mar. 1816 to John Murray. *BLJ*, V, 42.

26. Gleckner, *Byron and the Ruins of Paradise*, p. 33.

27. See *Emma*, chaps. 8 and 10 of Vol. II. R. W. Chapman, in his edition of *The Novels of Jane Austen* (Oxford: Clarendon Press, 1923), IV, 507–8 and inserts after 510, cites Thomas Wilson's *Companion to the Ball Room* (London: Button, Whittaker, 1816) as authority on this English hybrid.

28. Letter of Lady Caroline Lamb to T. Medwin, November (?), 1824. *LJ*, II, 453.

29. Marchand, *Byron's Poetry*, p. 33.

30. Letter of 26–27 Sept. 1812 to Lord Holland. *BLJ*, II, 210.

31. David V. Erdman, in "Byron's Mock Review of Rosa Matilda's Epic on the Prince Regent—A New Attribution," *Keats-Shelley Journal*, 19 (1970), 101–17, has suggested that a letter headed "The Waltz Dance," published in the *Courier* for 24 July 1811, may have served as the prototype for Horace Hornem's letter to the publisher.

32. Hume, "The Non-Augustan Nature of Byron's Early 'Satires,'" p. 500.

33. William Childers, "Byron's *Waltz*: The Germans and their Georges," *Keats-Shelley Journal*, 18 (1969), 81–95.

34. For an account of Byron's career as a Parliamentary Whig, see David V. Erdman, "Lord Byron and the Genteel Reformers," *PMLA*, 56 (1941), 1065–94; Erdman, "Lord Byron as Rinaldo," *PMLA*, 57 (1942), 189–

231; and Peter J. Manning, "Tales and Politics: *The Corsair, Lara*, and *The White Doe of Rylstone*," in *Byron: Poetry and Politics: Seventh International Byron Symposium, Salzburg 1980*, ed Erwin A. Stürzl and James Hogg (Salzburg: Univ. of Salzburg, 1981), pp. 204–30.

35. Lady Anne Hamilton's *Epics of the Ton* ridiculed Prinney's fondness for "a fat old woman" (l. 76), and Thomas Moore's *Intercepted Letters* also jested about his preference for elderly women.

36. Whiskers had recently become fashionable. Thomas Moore referred in "The Insurrection of the Papers" to "the Pr—e, in whisker'd state" and in "Parody of a Celebrated Letter" to Yarmouth's "red whiskers."

37. Samuel Smiles, *A Publisher and His Friends: Memoir and Correspondence of the Late John Murray* (London: John Murray, 1891), I, 217.

38. Wise, *Bibliography of Byron*, I, 71–72.

39. Both Smiles and the *British Critic*'s monthly list of publications give the publication date as February 1813.

40. *Satirist*, 13 (Apr. 1813), 385–87.

41. *British Critic*, 41 (Mar. 1813), 301–2.

42. See Childers, "Byron's *Waltz*," pp. 94–95; Erdman, "Byron's Mock Review," pp. 102–3. Erdman has convincingly argued that an anonymous "Regent-baiting" review of Rosa Matilda's "New Epic" in the *Morning Chronicle* for 2, 12 Sept. 1812 was Byron's and has suggested that *Waltz*, before it grew too long, may have been intended to follow that review in the newspaper.

43. See Fuess, *Lord Byron as a Satirist*, pp. 97–98; Marchand, *Byron*, I, 353–54. Erdman has defended Byron by maintaining that, since the Regent had been flirting with the Whigs again after Perceval's assassination in May, Byron may have been uncertain about his party's alignment for several weeks ("Byron's Mock Epic," p. 105n).

44. For an accurate account of the publishing history of the early issues of *The Corsair*—one that corrects T. J. Wise's—see William H. McCarthy, Jr., "The First Edition of Byron's 'Corsair,'" *The Colophon*, n.s., Vol. 2, No. 1 (Autumn 1936), 51–59.

45. For some of the attacks on Byron in the Tory press, especially in the *Courier* and the *Morning Post*, see *LJ*, II, 463–92. For Byron's reactions to them see his letters of 9, 10 Feb. 1814 to Leigh Hunt and Thomas Moore (*BLJ*, IV, 50–51).

46. See *BLJ*, IV, 37, 45–46, 49, 52; Smiles, *A Publisher*, I, 223–26.

47. *BLJ*, III, 38. Another version of the poem was first published in Galignani's 1818 Paris edition of Byron's poetry with the title "Windsor Poetics." Still another version, close to that which Byron sent Lady Melbourne and entitled "On a Royal Visit to the Vaults," was first published in E. H. Coleridge's edition (1904).

48. Smiles, *A Publisher*, I, 362.

49. *BLJ*, III, 240. Eleven stanzas of the poem appeared in Moore's *Notices of His Life* (1830); the complete text of this fragment was not published until 1904. The poem to which Byron pointed as the germ of his idea for the devil's peregrinations on earth, "The Devil's Walk," had been attributed to Richard Porson, though actually as "The Devil's Thoughts" (1799) it had been the collaborative product of Coleridge and Southey. It was later enlarged by Southey and published as "The Devil's Walk."

CHAPTER 4

1. See *BLJ*, II, 34, 63; *CPW*, II, 5.

2. *Poetry*, IV, 155–56; Marchand, *Byron*, II, 708–9 and n.

3. *BLJ*, V, 267. The reviewer of Whistlecraft's *Prospectus* in the *British Critic* (Oct. 1817) surmised that its author was the translator of Aristophanes—i.e., Frere.

4. Hobhouse recorded in his diary the story and the comments it elicited. See Marchand, *Byron*, II, 708 and n.

5. *BLJ*, VI, 24. For Byron's debt to Italian, as well as English, precursors in his new style, see Elizabeth French Boyd, *Byron's "Don Juan": A Critical Study* (1945; reprint, New York: Humanities Press, 1958), pp. 45–57; and Peter Vassallo, *Byron: The Italian Literary Influence* (New York: St. Martin's Press, 1984), pp. 43–165.

6. *BLJ*, V, 119, 124–25. For a later conversation of Byron and Shelley on Sgricci's powers, see Medwin's *Conversations*, pp. 137–38.

7. Both Ridenour, in *The Style of "Don Juan,"* p. 166, and McGann, in *Fiery Dust*, p. 281, cite this passage from *Corinne* (Bk. III, ch. 3).

8. John Chetwode Eustace, *A Classical Tour through Italy* (London: J. Mawman, 1813), I, 80.

9. That many readers were tired of his old strain is clear. The reviewer of Byron's *Manfred* for the *British Critic* referred to the play as "the effect of Don Bilioso in buskins, or of the dumps dramatized" (2d ser., 8 [July 1817], 38). The reviewer of *Beppo* for the *Edinburgh [Scots] Magazine* asserted that "the popular rage for the strange, the gloomy, and the terrible in poetry" had run its course (2d ser., 2 [Apr. 1818], 351).

10. Smiles, *A Publisher*, I, 372.

11. *BLJ*, VI, 15, 16, 21.

12. Smiles, *A Publisher*, I, 393.

13. Smiles, *A Publisher*, I, 394.

14. The stanzas developing Botherby (73–77), as Truman Guy Steffan has shown, were not part of the original matrix of 84 stanzas completed by 10 October 1817 but were probably the first five to be added by 23 October. See Steffan's "The Devil a Bit of Our Beppo," *Philological*

Quarterly, 32 (1953), 154–71. For other poetical attacks on Sotheby, see Byron's letters to Murray (*BLJ*, V, 252, 259; VI, 3–4, 27).

15. It has not been observed that Byron cleverly altered this quotation by adding a comma before *Apollo* in Horace's *Sic me servavit Apollo*. He thereby identified his friend as the rescuer whereas Horace had credited Apollo (god of justice, as well as poetry) after a friend had failed to rescue him.

16. Smiles, *A Publisher*, I, 394.

17. Johann Peter Eckermann, *Conversations with Goethe*, trans. John Oxenford (London: Dent, 1930), pp. 133–34.

18. *British Critic*, 2d ser., 9 (1818), 301–5.

19. Rutherford, *Byron*, p. 122.

20. Marchand, *Byron's Poetry*, p. 151; Marchand, *Byron*, II, 725–26.

21. *ER*, 29 (1818), 302–10.

22. For instructive discussion of allusion in *Don Juan*, see Peter J. Manning, *Byron and His Fictions* (Detroit: Wayne State Univ. Press, 1978), pp. 200–19.

23. Rutherford, *Byron*, p. 119n.

24. In this letter Byron included two satiric ballads ridiculing Knight's mediocrity and one poking fun at Murray's publishing practices. Knight, whom Byron had known at Cambridge and in Athens, was frequently the butt of jokes in Byron's letters to Murray.

25. Letters of 25 Mar. and 23 Apr. to John Murray. *BLJ*, VI, 24, 36.

26. Smiles, *A Publisher*, I, 396.

CHAPTER 5

1. E. D. H. Johnson, in "*Don Juan* in England," *ELH*, 11 (1944), 135–53, probably exaggerates the Methodist and Evangelical impact, but there can be no doubt that reviewers of *Don Juan* expressed the dominant middle-class sentiment.

2. In concentrating on the satiric aspects, my perspective differs from the account of composition and reception provided by Truman Guy Steffan in *The Making of a Masterpiece, Byron's "Don Juan"* (2d ed., Austin: Univ. of Texas Press, 1971), I, 3–60; from Willis W. Pratt's "A Survey of Commentary on *Don Juan*," *Byron's "Don Juan*," IV, 293–309; from Paul G. Trueblood's resume of reviewer opinion in *The Flowering of Byron's Genius* (Palo Alto, Calif.: Stanford Univ. Press, 1945), pp. 26–96; from Samuel C. Chew's account of pamphlets, sequels, and imitations spawned by *Don Juan* in *Byron in England: His Fame and After-Fame* (New York: Scribner's, 1924), pp. 27–75; from Theodore Redpath's *The Young Romantics and Critical Opinion 1807–1824* (New York: St. Martin's Press, 1973), esp. pp. 248–92; and from Herman M. Ward's *Byron and the*

Magazines, 1806–1824 (Salzburg: Institut für englische Sprache und Literatur, Univ. of Salzburg, 1973), esp. pp. 109–25.

3. See Hobhouse's entry for 4 Jan. 1818 in *Recollections of a Long Life*, ed. Lady Dorchester (London: John Murray, 1909–11), II, 88.

4. Hobhouse, *Recollections*, II, 107.

5. Marchand, *Byron*, II, 763–65.

6. Thomas Moore, *The Journal of Thomas Moore*, ed. Wilfred S. Dowden (Newark: Univ. of Delaware Press, 1983–   ), I, 137.

7. Moore, *Journal*, I, 141–42.

8. Hobhouse, *Recollections*, II, 111–12.

9. Smiles, *A Publisher*, I, 402–3.

10. John Keats, *The Letters of John Keats*, ed. Hyder E. Rollins (Cambridge, Mass.: Harvard Univ. Press, 1958), II, 59.

11. *Blackwood's*, 5 (1819), 286.

12. Smiles, *A Publisher*, I, 404–5; *Blackwood's*, 5 (1819), 483.

13. *Blackwood's*, 5 (Aug. 1819), 512–18.

14. *Examiner*, 31 Oct. 1819, pp. 700–702.

15. *British Critic*, 2d ser., 12 (Aug. 1819), 195–205.

16. *Edinburgh Monthly Review*, 2 (Oct. 1819), 468–86.

17. *Monthly Magazine*, 48 (Aug. 1819), 56.

18. *New Monthly Magazine*, 12 (Aug. 1819), 75–78.

19. Smiles, *A Publisher*, I, 405–8.

20. Steffan, *Making of a Masterpiece*, pp. 35–36.

21. Shelley's letter of 8–10 Aug. 1821 to Mary Shelley. *The Letters of Percy Bysshe Shelley*, ed. Frederick L. Jones (Oxford: Clarendon Press, 1964), II, 323.

22. Smiles, *A Publisher*, I, 413.

23. *BLJ*, VIII, 145, 147–48, 198, 235.

24. *BLJ*, VIII, 192–93; IX, 54.

25. *Examiner*, 26 Aug. 1821, p. 538.

26. *Blackwood's*, 10 (Aug. 1821), 107–15.

27. *British Critic*, 2d ser., 16 (Sept. 1821), 251–56.

28. *British Review*, 18 (Dec. 1821), 245–65.

29. *European Magazine*, 80 (Aug. 1821), 181–85.

30. *Gentleman's Magazine*, 92, i (Jan. 1822), 48–50.

31. *Edinburgh [Scots] Magazine*, 2d ser., 9 (Aug. 1821), 105–8.

32. Marchand, *Byron*, III, 988. In *Byron's Poetry*, p. 194n, Marchand has speculated that Canto VI may have been written even before V was sent off.

33. On 29 June 1821 Byron informed Murray that he had just read "John Bull's letter" and asked Murray to find out its author (*BLJ*, VIII, 145).

34. Marchand, *Byron*, III, 1039–40.

35. *BLJ*, VIII, 114; IX, 52, 55, 92–93, 162–65, 171; X, 36, 146.

36. For details see Leslie A. Marchand, "John Hunt as Byron's Publisher," *Keats-Shelley Journal*, 8 (1959), 119–32; and Steffan, *Making of a Masterpiece*, pp. 49–50.

37. *BLJ*, X, 62, 66, 72–73.

38. See the *Examiner*, 10, 17 August 1823, pp. 521–24, 529–31.

39. *Literary Examiner*, 5 July 1823.

40. *Gentleman's Magazine*, 93, ii (Sept. 1823), 250–52.

41. *Edinburgh [Scots] Magazine*, 2d ser., 13 (Sept. 1823), 357–60.

42. *Blackwood's*, 14 (1823), 282–93. This review was previously ascribed to William Maginn, but Donald H. Reiman, in *The Romantics Reviewed: Contemporary Reviews of British Romantic Writers* (New York: Garland, 1972), Pt. B, I, 210, is certainly right in attributing it to Lockhart.

43. Marchand, *Byron*, III, 1118.

44. Moore claimed that after Byron's death the Dedication was sold in the streets as a broadside (Lord Byron, *The Works of Lord Byron*, ed. Thomas Moore [London: John Murray, 1832–33], XV, 101n). But since no copy or trustworthy evidence of a piracy has ever appeared, T. J. Wise's designation of that hypothetical broadside as a "myth" (*Bibliography*, II, 13) has generally been accepted.

CHAPTER 6

1. Byron told George Bancroft in 1822 that Johnson's Preface "contained the most correct judgment of Shakespeare"; both Leigh Hunt and Lady Blessington claimed that Byron at times affected a Johnsonian manner. See *His Very Self and Voice: Collected Conversations of Lord Byron*, ed. Ernest J. Lovell, Jr. (New York: Macmillan, 1954), pp. 293, 328; and Blessington, *Conversations*, p. 20.

2. Jerome J. McGann, *"Don Juan" in Context* (Chicago: Univ. of Chicago Press, 1976), pp. 161–65.

3. George M. Ridenour, *The Style of "Don Juan,"* pp. 1–18; McGann, *"Don Juan" in Context*, pp. 68–69.

4. England, *Byron's "Don Juan" and Eighteenth-Century Literature*, pp. 15–22.

5. Anne K. Mellor, *English Romantic Irony* (Cambridge, Mass.: Harvard Univ. Press, 1980), pp. 49–50.

6. William Hazlitt, "Lord Byron," in *The Spirit of the Age, Works*, XI, 75.

7. Hazlitt, "Lord Byron," *Works*, XI, 75n.

8. Marshall, *The Structure of Byron's Major Poems*, p. 176. For the contrary view that the narrator is "a self-consistent speaker" whose many voices are the "manifestations of one voice," see George M. Ridenour, "The Mode of Byron's *Don Juan*," *PMLA*, 79 (1964), 442–46.

9. Marshall, *Structure*, p. 177.

10. Blessington, *Conversations*, p. 26. On 25 Dec. 1822 Byron wrote

Murray: "No Girl will ever be seduced by reading D[on] J[uan]—no—no—she will go to Little's poems—& Rousseau's romans—for that—or even to the immaculate De Stael— —they will encourage her—& not the Don—who laughs at that—and—and—most other things" (*BLJ*, X, 68).

11. Blessington, *Conversations*, p. 155.

12. James R. Sutherland, *English Satire* (Cambridge: Cambridge Univ. Press, 1958), p. 76.

13. See Alvin B. Kernan, *The Plot of Satire* (New Haven, Conn.: Yale Univ. Press, 1965), pp. 212-22, for a description that characterizes the narrator as estranged, rejected, and tragic. By emphasizing the comic, the tragic, or the satiric elements in *Don Juan*, critics have inevitably arrived at widely disparate views on what they consider the dominant tone of the poem.

CHAPTER 7

1. James R. Thompson, "Byron's Plays and *Don Juan*: Genre and Myth," *Bucknell Review*, 15, No. 3 (1967), 26.

2. McGann, *"Don Juan" in Context*, pp. 109-10.

3. Northrop Frye, *Anatomy of Criticism: Four Essays* (Princeton, N.J.: Princeton Univ. Press, 1957), pp. 233-34.

4. Ernest J. Lovell, Jr., "Irony and Image in *Don Juan*," in *The Major English Romantic Poets: A Symposium in Reappraisal*, ed. Clarence D. Thorpe, Carlos Baker, and Bennett Weaver (Carbondale: Southern Illinois Univ. Press, 1957), p. 138; Kernan, *The Plot of Satire*, p. 175n.

5. See John M. Aden, *Something Like Horace: Studies in the Art and Allusion of Pope's Horatian Satires* (Kingsport, Tenn.: Vanderbilt Univ. Press, 1969), pp. 3-46.

6. See my "Byron's Imitations of Juvenal and Persius," *Studies in Romanticism*, 15 (1976), 333-55.

7. For glory and vengeance in Juvenal X, see especially ll. 84-85, 104-7, 114-17, 133-62, 163-66. See Juvenal VII also for glory.

8. In "Byron and the Epic of Negation," *Romantic Poets and Epic Tradition* (Madison: Univ. of Wisconsin Press, 1965), pp. 188-226, Wilkie distinguishes four attitudes Byron takes toward epic. See also Ridenour, *The Style of "Don Juan,"* pp. 89-123; and Donald H. Reiman, *"Don Juan* in Epic Context," *Studies in Romanticism*, 16 (1977), 587-94.

9. Medwin, *Conversations*, p. 164.

10. Ridenour, *The Style of "Don Juan,"* pp. 98-100, 122-23.

11. For discussion of Juvenal's epic aspirations in satire, see Gilbert Highet, *Juvenal the Satirist: A Study* (Oxford: Clarendon Press, 1954), pp. 48-49, 152, 170; Inez G. Scott [Ryberg], *The Grand Style in the Satires of Juvenal* (Northampton, Mass.: Banta, 1927); and Edwin S. Ram-

age, David L. Sigsbee, and Sigmund C. Fredericks, *Roman Satirists and Their Satire: The Fine Art of Criticism in Ancient Rome* (Park Ridge, N.J.: Noyes Press, 1974), pp. 142–68.

CHAPTER 8

1. Letter of 12 Aug. 1819 to John Murray. *BLJ*, VI, 208.
2. Kernan, *The Plot of Satire*, p. 205.
3. *Letter to* **** ****** [John Murray], dated 7 Feb. 1821. *LJ*,V, 542.
4. Blessington, *Conversations*, p. 13.
5. Blessington, *Conversations*, p. 172.
6. C. N. Stavrou, in "Religion in Byron's *Don Juan*," *Studies in English Literature*, 3 (1963), 567–94, makes a strong case for religious skepticism but, in view of Byron's pronouncements here and elsewhere in favor of religion, probably exaggerates Byron's antagonism. For Byron's inconsistent religious opinions see Edward W. Marjarum, *Byron as Skeptic and Believer* (Princeton, N.J.: Princeton Univ. Press, 1938); and Marchand, *Byron*, III, 1104–5.
7. For more on Byron's derision of her, see my "Byron on Joanna Southcott and Undeserved Salvation," *Keats-Shelley Journal*, 26 (1977), 34–38.
8. For the stanzas on Brougham, toward whom Byron also cherished personal animus, see the Variorum Edition, II, 150–55. His scorn for any politician trying to lead the mob is clear in the satiric ballad deriding even his friend Hobhouse—"How came you in Hob's pound to cool" (1820).
9. Wordsworth, in "Thanksgiving Ode" (18 Jan. 1816), appears to have been unconsciously Malthusian in his desire to interpret the outcome of Waterloo as the fulfillment of divine will.
10. Steffan, *Making of a Masterpiece*, pp. 249–50.
11. Wilkie, *Romantic Poets*, p. 189; Gleckner, *Byron and the Ruins of Paradise*, pp. 329–32.
12. Fuess, *Lord Byron as a Satirist*, p. 215.

CHAPTER 9

1. On 21 Apr. 1822 the *Examiner* printed sts. 17–19, 21–32 without title, poet's name, and Castlereagh's name in st. 22. On 28 July 1822 the *Examiner* printed all 32 quatrains with the poem's title, omitting the poet's name and libelous words. Medwin, in three 1824 editions of his *Conversations*, printed expurgated versions of Byron's poem. Not until 1831, the year after George IV's death, did Murray include it among Byron's collected works.

2. Henry Crabb Robinson, *Diary, Reminiscences, and Correspondence,* ed. Thomas Sadler (London: Macmillan, 1869), II, 437.

3. Blessington, *Conversations,* pp. 142–43.

4. Thomas Moore, *Memoirs, Journal, and Correspondence of Thomas Moore,* ed. Lord John Russell (London: Longman, Brown, Green, and Longmans, 1853–56), III, 275–76.

5. Moore, *Memoirs,* III, 297–98.

6. Hobhouse, *Recollections,* III, 9.

7. *Blackwood's* 13 (1823), 457–60.

8. *Literary Gazette,* 5 Apr. 1823, pp. 211–13.

9. *Examiner,* 30 Mar. 1823, pp. 217–18.

10. *Monthly Magazine,* 55 (1823), 322–25.

11. *Edinburgh [Scots] Magazine,* 2d ser., 12 (1823), 483–88.

12. Byron was also probably acquainted with Prior's *Carmen Seculare,* which celebrates England and William III in place of Rome and Augustus Caesar.

13. Richard Garnett's suggestion that Achilles in Byron's quotation refers to a London statue of Achilles inscribed to Wellington is farfetched; to identify Wellington with the Greek Achilles is to elevate to heroic stature a man whom Byron detested. See *Poetry,* V, 535; *BLJ,* IX, 48–49; and Carl Woodring, *Politics in English Romantic Poetry* (Cambridge, Mass.: Harvard Univ. Press, 1970), pp. 218–19.

14. This similarity has been noted by M. K. Joseph, *Byron the Poet* (London: Victor Gollancz, 1964), p. 134.

15. Woodring, *Politics,* p. 221.

16. William H. Marshall speculated that Leigh Hunt's letter of 6 July 1822 to his brother John forwarding something "from Ld. Byron for *The Examiner*" contained *The Blues.* See Marshall's *Byron, Shelley, Hunt, and "The Liberal"* (Philadelphia: Univ. of Pennsylvania Press, 1960), pp. 54–56; also Luther A. Brewer, *My Leigh Hunt Library* (Iowa City: Univ. of Iowa Press, 1932–38), II, 154. But since Leigh Hunt in that letter refers to "whole stanzas" to be omitted from the unnamed work and claims its "libellousness is abundant," the poem in question was probably *The Irish Avatar* rather than *The Blues* or *The Vision,* as Prothero had assumed (*LJ,* VI, 123n).

17. *Literary Chronicle,* No. 206, pp. 257–59.

18. *Literary Register,* No. 44, pp. 273–75.

19. *Edinburgh [Scots] Magazine,* n.s. 12 (1823), 614–16.

20. *Blackwood's,* 13 (1823), 607.

21. The name Inkel in *The Blues* may derive from Anstey's *An Election Ball, in Poetical Letters from Mr. Inkle . . . to His Wife* (1776). According to Anstey's preface, Inkle's letters, which are in anapestic couplets, "made their first Appearance at Mrs. Miller's POETICAL COTERIE."

22. For Keats's ridicule of the bluestockings, see his *Letters*, I, 163, 252; II, 19, 139.

23. Hazlitt, *Works*, IV, 132–33; VIII, 236; XII, 364–65; XVI, 20–21, 213, 218; XVIII, 46, 308.

24. The opening dialogue between poet and opportunist, as well as the Horatian quotation announcing escape from a bore, suggests that Horace's Satire I.9 also contributed. For a real-life episode offering an even closer parallel to Horace's I.9, see #50 of "Detached Thoughts," *BLJ*, IX, 29.

25. For an account of the long quarrel between Byron and Southey, see Prothero's Appendix I, *LJ*, VI, 377–99 and Byron's unsent letter of 5 Feb. 1822 to the editor of the *Courier* (*BLJ*, IX, 95–100).

26. See Southey's letters of 20 July 1819 to C. H. Townshend, 31 July 1819 to G. C. Bedford, and 13 Aug. 1819 to H. Hill—*Life and Correspondence of Robert Southey*, ed. Charles Cuthbert Southey (London: Longman, Brown, Green, and Longmans, 1849–50), IV, 352–53; *Selections from the Letters of Robert Southey*, ed. John Wood Warter (London: Longman, Brown, Green, Longmans, & Roberts, 1856), III, 137, 142.

27. In a letter of 5 Jan. 1821 to G. C. Bedford, Southey claimed that the Preface had enabled him "to pay off a part of [his] obligations to Lord Byron and——, by some observations upon the tendency of their poems (especially Don Juan)"—*Life and Correspondence*, V, 55–56. See also Southey, *Selections*, III, 225.

28. *LJ*, VI, 391–92.

29. Medwin, *Conversations*, pp. 148–50; *BLJ*, IX, 95–102, 114–15; Marchand, *Byron*, III, 967–69.

30. *BLJ*, X, 13, 16–17, 21–23, 26.

31. Smiles, *A Publisher*, I, 308–13.

32. Marshall, *Byron, Shelley, Hunt, and "The Liberal,"* pp. 44–49.

33. *British Luminary*, 20 Oct. 1822, p. 754; *Examiner*, 13 Oct., 3, 10 Nov. 1822, pp. 648–52, 689–91, 705–7. For a resume of its reception by newspapers and journals, as well as in pamphlets, see Marshall, *Byron, Shelley, Hunt, and "The Liberal,"* pp. 97–126.

34. Marchand, *Byron*, III, 1040. Hobhouse and Moore, though politically liberal, had also tried to persuade Byron to sever the Hunt connections.

35. For accounts of the legal processes, see the *Examiner*, 5 Jan. 1823, pp. 13–14; Marshall, *Byron, Shelley, Hunt, and "The Liberal,"* pp. 126–34, 205–9; Marchand, "John Hunt as Byron's Publisher," pp. 129–32.

36. See the *Examiner*, 20 June 1824, p. 392.

37. See 28.5–8; 34; 54.5–6; 106.2.

38. Rutherford, *Byron*, pp. 235–36.

39. Bernard Blackstone, in *Byron: A Survey* (London: Longman,

1975), pp. 281–82, comments on the dramatic unities. Joseph, in *Byron the Poet*, pp. 138–40, sees *The Vision* as high comedy.

40. Letter of 21 Feb. 1820 to John Murray. *BLJ*, VII, 41.

41. For Byron's speech in the House of Lords on 21 Apr. 1812 in favor of Catholic emancipation, see *LJ*, II, 431–43.

42. In a footnote to *The Giaour* Byron condemned both Christians and Moslems who assumed that faith ought "to supersede the necessity of good works" (*CPW*, III, 418), and he expressed a similar view to James Kennedy (*Conversations on Religion*, pp. 135–36).

43. For elaboration of this point, especially as it applies to *Cain*, see Edward E. Bostetter, "Byron and the Politics of Paradise," *PMLA*, 75 (1960), 571–76. For an identification of Satan with Byron, Michael with Eldon, and Peter with Harrowby, see Stuart Peterfreund, "The Politics of 'Neutral Space' in Byron's *Vision of Judgment*," *Modern Language Quarterly*, 40 (1979), 275–91.

44. For Byron's refusal to believe in "eternal tortures," see #96 of "Detached Thoughts" (*BLJ*, IX, 45–46; his letter of 13 Sept. 1811 to Hodgson (*BLJ*, II, 98); and Kennedy, *Conversations on Religion*, pp. 227–28.

45. Robinson, *Diary*, II, 240. Entry for 8 Jan. 1823.

CHAPTER 10

1. Kennedy, *Conversations on Religion*, p. 167.

2. Letter of 17 July 1818 to John Murray. *BLJ*, VI, 61.

Aden, John M. *Something Like Horace: Studies in the Art and Allusion of Pope's Horatian Satires*. Kingsport, Tenn.: Vanderbilt Univ. Press, 1969.

Anderson, William S. *Essays on Roman Satire*. Princeton, N.J.: Princeton Univ. Press, 1982.

Beaty, Frederick L. "Byron on Joanna Southcott and Undeserved Salvation." *Keats-Shelley Journal*, 26 (1977), 34–38.

————. "Byron's Imitations of Juvenal and Persius." *Studies in Romanticism*, 15 (1976), 333–55.

Blackstone, Bernard. *Byron: A Survey*. London: Longman, 1975.

Blessington, Marguerite, Countess of. *Conversations of Lord Byron*. Ed. Ernest J. Lovell, Jr. Princeton, N.J.: Princeton Univ. Press, 1969.

Bostetter, Edward E. "Byron and the Politics of Paradise." *PMLA*, 75 (1960), 571–76.

————. *The Romantic Ventriloquists*. Seattle: Univ. of Washington Press, 1963.

Boyd, Elizabeth French. *Byron's "Don Juan": A Critical Study*. 1945. Reprint. New York: Humanities Press, 1958.

Brower, Reuben A. *Alexander Pope: The Poetry of Allusion*. Oxford: Clarendon Press, 1959.

Byron, George Gordon, Lord. *Byron's "Don Juan."* Vol. I: *The Making of a Masterpiece*, by Truman Guy Steffan. Vols. II–III: *A Variorum Edition*, ed. T. G. Steffan and Willis W. Pratt. Vol. IV: *Notes on the Variorum Edition*, by W. W. Pratt. 2d ed. Austin: Univ. of Texas Press, 1971.

————. *Byron's Letters and Journals*. Ed. Leslie A. Marchand. 12 vols. Cambridge, Mass.: Harvard Univ. Press, 1973–82.

————. *The Complete Poetical Works*. Ed. Jerome J. McGann. 3 vols. Oxford: Clarendon Press, 1980–81.

————. *The Works of Lord Byron: Letters and Journals*. Ed. Rowland E. Prothero. 6 vols. London: John Murray, 1898–1901.

————. *The Works of Lord Byron: Poetry.* Ed. E. H. Coleridge. 7 vols. London: John Murray, 1898–1904.

Calvert, William J. *Byron: Romantic Paradox.* 1935. Reprint. New York: Russell & Russell, 1962.

Chew, Samuel C. *Byron in England: His Fame and After-Fame.* New York: Scribner's, 1924.

Childers, William. "Byron's *Waltz*: The Germans and their Georges." *Keats-Shelley Journal,* 18 (1969), 81–95.

Clearman, Mary. "A Blueprint for *English Bards and Scotch Reviewers*: The First Satire of Juvenal." *Keats-Shelley Journal,* 19 (1970), 87–99.

Cooke, Michael G. *The Blind Man Traces the Circle: On the Patterns and Philosophy of Byron's Poetry.* Princeton, N.J.: Princeton Univ. Press, 1969.

Dallas, Robert Charles. *Recollections of the Life of Lord Byron.* London: C. Knight, 1824.

Dixon, Peter. *The World of Pope's Satires: An Introduction to the "Epistles" and "Imitations of Horace."* London: Methuen, 1968.

England, A. B. *Byron's "Don Juan" and Eighteenth-Century Literature: A Study of Some Rhetorical Continuities and Discontinuities.* Lewisburg, Pa.: Bucknell Univ. Press, 1975.

Erdman, David V. "Byron's Mock Review of Rosa Matilda's Epic on the Prince Regent—A New Attribution." *Keats-Shelley Journal,* 19 (1970), 101–17.

————. "Lord Byron and the Genteel Reformers." *PMLA,* 56 (1941), 1065–94.

————. "Lord Byron as Rinaldo." *PMLA,* 57 (1942), 189–231.

Escarpit, Robert. *Lord Byron: un tempérament littéraire.* 2 vols. Paris: Le Cercle du Livre, 1955–57.

Frye, Northrop. *Anatomy of Criticism: Four Essays.* Princeton, N.J.: Princeton Univ. Press, 1957.

Fuess, Claude M. *Lord Byron as a Satirist in Verse.* 1912. Reprint. New York: Haskell House, 1973.

Gleckner, Robert F. *Byron and the Ruins of Paradise.* Baltimore, Md.: Johns Hopkins Press, 1967.

————. "From Selfish Spleen to Equanimity: Byron's Satires." *Studies in Romanticism,* 18 (1979), 173–205.

Highet, Gilbert. *The Anatomy of Satire.* Princeton, N.J.: Princeton Univ. Press, 1962.

————. *Juvenal the Satirist: A Study.* Oxford: Clarendon Press, 1954.

Hobhouse, John Cam [Lord Broughton]. *Recollections of a Long Life.* Ed. Lady Dorchester. 6 vols. London: John Murray, 1910–11.

Hume, Robert D. "The Non-Augustan Nature of Byron's Early 'Satires.'" *Revue des Langues Vivantes,* 34 (1968), 495–503.

Jack, Ian. *Augustan Satire: Intention and Idiom in English Poetry 1660–1750*. Oxford: Clarendon Press, 1952.

Johnson, E. D. H. "*Don Juan* in England." *ELH*, 11 (1944), 135–53.

Jones, Emrys. "Byron's Visions of Judgment." *Modern Language Review*, 76 (1981), 1–19.

Joseph, M. K. *Byron the Poet*. London: Victor Gollancz, 1964.

Jump, John D. *Byron*. London: Routledge & Kegan Paul, 1972.

Kennedy, James. *Conversations on Religion, with Lord Byron*. . . . London: John Murray, 1830.

Kernan, Alvin B. *The Cankered Muse: Satire of the English Renaissance*. Yale Studies in English, No. 142. New Haven, Conn.: Yale Univ. Press, 1959.

———. *The Plot of Satire*. New Haven, Conn.: Yale Univ. Press, 1965.

Knoche, Ulrich. *Roman Satire*. Trans. Edwin S. Ramage. Bloomington: Indiana Univ. Press, 1975.

Leavis, F. R. "Byron's Satire." *Revaluation: Tradition and Development in English Poetry*. New York: Norton, 1936. Pp. 148–53.

Lovell, Ernest J., Jr. "Irony and Image in *Don Juan*." *The Major English Romantic Poets: A Symposium in Reappraisal*. Ed. Clarence D. Thorpe, Carlos Baker, and Bennett Weaver. Carbondale: Southern Illinois Univ. Press, 1957. Pp. 129–48.

McGann, Jerome J. *"Don Juan" in Context*. Chicago: Univ. of Chicago Press, 1976.

———. *Fiery Dust: Byron's Poetic Development*. Chicago: Univ. of Chicago Press, 1968.

Manning, Peter J. *Byron and His Fictions*. Detroit, Mich.: Wayne State Univ. Press, 1978.

———. "Tales and Politics: *The Corsair, Lara*, and *The White Doe of Rylstone*." *Byron: Poetry and Politics: Seventh International Byron Symposium, Salzburg 1980*. Ed. Erwin A. Stürzl and James Hogg. Salzburg: Univ. of Salzburg, 1981. Pp. 204–30.

Marchand, Leslie A. *Byron: A Biography*. 3 vols. New York: Knopf, 1957.

———. *Byron's Poetry: A Critical Introduction*. Boston: Houghton Mifflin, 1965.

———. "John Hunt as Byron's Publisher." *Keats-Shelley Journal*, 8 (1959), 119–32.

Marjarum, Edward W. *Byron as Skeptic and Believer*. Princeton Studies in English, No. 16. Princeton: Princeton Univ. Press, 1938.

Marshall, William H. *Byron, Shelley, Hunt, and "The Liberal."* Philadelphia: Univ. of Pennsylvania Press, 1960.

———. "The Catalogue for the Sale of Byron's Books." *Library Chronicle*, 34 (1968), 24–50.

————. *The Structure of Byron's Major Poems*. Philadelphia: Univ. of Pennsylvania Press, 1962.

Medwin, Thomas. *Conversations of Lord Byron*. Ed. Ernest J. Lovell, Jr. Princeton, N.J.: Princeton Univ. Press, 1966.

Mellor, Anne K. *English Romantic Irony*. Cambridge, Mass.: Harvard Univ. Press, 1980.

Moore, Thomas. *Letters and Journals of Lord Byron: With Notices of His Life*. 2 vols. London: John Murray, 1830.

Paulson, Ronald, ed. *Satire: Modern Essays in Criticism*. Englewood Cliffs, N.J.: Prentice-Hall, 1971.

Peterfreund, Stuart. "The Politics of 'Neutral Space' in Byron's *Vision of Judgment*." *Modern Language Quarterly*, 40 (1979), 275–91.

Ramage, Edwin S., David L. Sigsbee, and Sigmund C. Fredericks. *Roman Satirists and Their Satire: The Fine Art of Criticism in Ancient Rome*. Park Ridge, N.J.: Noyes Press, 1974.

Reiman, Donald H. "*Don Juan* in Epic Context." *Studies in Romanticism*, 16 (1977), 587–94.

————, ed. *The Romantics Reviewed: Contemporary Reviews of British Romantic Writers*. Part B: *Byron and Regency Society Poets*. 5 vols. New York: Garland, 1972.

Ridenour, George M. "The Mode of Byron's *Don Juan*." *PMLA*, 79 (1964), 442–46.

————. *The Style of "Don Juan."* Yale Studies in English, No. 144. New Haven, Conn.: Yale Univ. Press, 1960.

Ruddick, William. "Don Juan in Search of Freedom: Byron's Emergence as a Satirist." *Byron: A Symposium*. Ed. John D. Jump. London: Macmillan, 1975. Pp. 113–37.

Rutherford, Andrew. *Byron: A Critical Study*. Edinburgh: Oliver and Boyd, 1961.

St. Clair, William. *Lord Elgin and the Marbles*. London: Oxford Univ. Press, 1967.

Scott [Ryberg], Inez G. *The Grand Style in the Satires of Juvenal*. Smith College Classical Studies, No. 8. Northampton, Mass.: Banta, 1927.

Sheraw, C. Darrell. "*Don Juan*: Byron as Un-Augustan Satirist." *Satire Newsletter*, 10 (1972–73), ii, 25–33.

Shilstone, Frederick W. "Byron's *The Giaour*: Narrative Tradition and Romantic Cognitive Theory." *Research Studies*, 48 (1980), 94–104.

Smiles, Samuel. *A Publisher and His Friends: Memoir and Correspondence of the Late John Murray*. 2 vols. London: John Murray, 1891.

Sperry, Stuart M. "Toward a Definition of Romantic Irony in English Literature." *Romantic and Modern: Revaluations of Literary Tradition*. Ed. George Bornstein. Pittsburgh, Pa.: Univ. of Pittsburgh Press, 1977. Pp. 3–28.

Stavrou, C. N. "Religion in Byron's *Don Juan.*" *Studies in English Literature,* 3 (1963), 567–94.

Sutherland, James R. *English Satire.* Cambridge: Cambridge Univ. Press, 1958.

Trueblood, Paul G. *The Flowering of Byron's Genius: Studies in Byron's "Don Juan."* Palo Alto, Calif.: Stanford Univ. Press, 1945.

———. *Lord Byron.* Twayne's English Authors Series. 2d ed. Boston: Twayne, 1977.

Vassallo, Peter. *Byron: The Italian Literary Influence.* New York: St. Martin's Press, 1984.

Wilkie, Brian. *Romantic Poets and Epic Tradition.* Madison: Univ. of Wisconsin Press, 1965.

Wise, Thomas J. *A Bibliography of the Writings in Verse and Prose of George Gordon Noel, Baron Byron. . . .* 2 vols. London: Privately printed, 1932–33.

Woodring, Carl. *Politics in English Romantic Poetry.* Cambridge, Mass.: Harvard Univ. Press, 1970.

Yarker, P. M. "Byron and the Satiric Temper." *Byron: A Symposium.* Ed. John D. Jump. London: Macmillan, 1975. Pp. 76–93.

INDEX

tive satiric goal, 4, 6, 8, 19, 131, 198, 199
Socrates, 46, 64
Socratic irony, 128
Sotheby, William: as Botherby (*Beppo*), 88–90; as Botherbý (*The Blues*), 179; Byron's grievances against, 87–88, 89; as obnoxious literary type, 5. Works: *Ivan*, 87, 90; *Saul*, 88; *Tragedies*, 90; translation of Tasso, 88; translation of Wieland's *Oberon*, 88
Southcott, Joanna, 155, 159
Southey, Robert: attacked in *The Blues*, 179; in Byron's letters, 79, 105–6; in *Critical Review*, 31; in *Don Juan*, 5, 105, 107, 109, 110, 113, 122, 123, 124, 153, 159; in *Edinburgh Review*, 30, 41; in *English Bards*, 41; in *Hints from Horace*, 55–56; in *Poetry of the Anti-Jacobin*, 10, 24, 31; in *The Simpliciad*, 41; in *The Vision of Judgment*, 5, 180–95, 198. Works: "The Battle of Blenheim," 180; biography of Henry K. White, 180; biography of John Wesley, 181; *Joan of Arc*, 41; *Madoc*, 31, 42; "The Old Man's Comforts," 21; *The Poet's Pilgrimage to Waterloo*, 181; *Thalaba*, 30, 39, 41, 56; *A Vision of Judgement*, 181, 182, 183, 184, 186, 189, 191, 194; *Wat Tyler*, 180, 181
Souvarow, Alexander, 157, 158
Spencer, William R., 87
Spenser, Edmund, 53
Spenserian tradition, 46–47, 48
Staël, Madame Germaine de, 132; *Corinne*, 84
Steffan, Truman Guy, 114, 163

Stendhal (pseudonym of Henri Beyle), 83
Stoicism, 133, 140–43
Styles, in *Don Juan*, 124–26
Sutherland, James R., 135
Swift, Jonathan, 6, 12, 92; lampooning ballads, 6

Thompson, James R., 138
Thomson, James, 47
Times, The (London), 167, 169
Tragic satire, 14, 143, 148
Travesty, 10, 100, 182, 186, 194
Trelawny, Edward J., 122
Truth (reality), 65, 104, 123, 128, 129, 132, 133, 155, 197; in Juvenal, 146; as the satirist's guide, 19, 22, 32, 37, 132; as the satirist's objective, 5, 19, 46, 64, 149, 198
Tyranny (oppression), 143, 177; intellectual, 32, 119, 155, 156, 196; military, 49, 157, 168–69, 173–74, 196; political, 5, 14, 75, 125, 155, 156, 168–69, 173–74, 175, 189, 196; religious, 154, 189

Verona, Congress of, 171–72, 173
Verres, 60
Villiers, George, 2d Duke of Buckingham, 12
Virgil, 144; *Aeneid*, 173; *Eclogues*, 179
Voltaire (François Marie Arouet), 149

Walpole, Robert, 142
Washington, George, 157, 174, 191
Webster, James Wedderburn, 83
Wellesley, Richard Colley Wellesley, Marquis of, 48, 72